John Lukacs

THE HITLER OF HISTORY

John Lukacs was born in Hungary and came to the United
States in 1946. Now emeritus, he has been a visiting pro-
fessor at various universities. The recipient of the 1991
Ingersoll Prize, he is the author of nineteen other books.
He and his wife live in Chester County, Pennsylvania.

ALSO BY JOHN LUKACS

The Great Powers and Eastern Europe

*Tocqueville: The European Revolution and
Correspondence with Gobineau* (editor)

A History of the Cold War

Decline and Rise of Europe

Historical Consciousness

The Passing of the Modern Age

The Last European War, 1939–1941

1945: Year Zero

Philadelphia: Patricians and Philistines, 1900–1950

*Outgrowing Democracy: A History of the
United States in the Twentieth Century*

Budapest 1900: A Historical Portrait of a City and Its Culture

Confessions of an Original Sinner

*The Duel: 10 May–31 July 1940: The Eighty-Day
Struggle Between Churchill and Hitler*

The End of the Twentieth Century and the End of the Modern Age

Destinations Past

*George F. Kennan and the Origins of Containment 1944–1946:
The Kennan-Lukacs Correspondence*

A Thread of Years

The Hitler of History

THE
HITLER
OF
HISTORY

John Lukacs

VINTAGE BOOKS

A Division of Random House, Inc.

New York

FIRST VINTAGE BOOKS EDITION, NOVEMBER 1998

Copyright ©1997 by John Lukacs

All rights reserved under International and Pan-American Copyright
Conventions. Published in the United States by Vintage Books,
a division of Random House, Inc., New York, and simultaneously
in Canada by Random House of Canada Limited, Toronto.
Originally published in hardcover in the United States
by Random House, Inc., New York, in 1997.

Permissions acknowledgments may be found on page 281.

Library of Congress Cataloging-in-Publication Data
Lukacs, John, 1924–
The Hitler of history / John Lukacs.
p.   cm.
Includes bibliographical references and index.
ISBN 0-375-70113-3
1. Hitler, Adolf, 1889–1945.
2. Germany—History—
1933–1945—Historiography.
3. National socialism—Historiography.
4. Heads of state—Germany—Biography. I. Title.
DD247.H5L84   1998
943.086'092—dc21   98-26451
[B]   CIP

Book design by Misha Beletsky

www.randomhouse.com

Printed in the United States of America
10 9 8 7 6 5 4 3 2 1

This book is dedicated to
Jim McBride

CONTENTS

8

ADMIRERS AND DEFENDERS, OPEN AND HIDDEN
Main arguments for Hitler's rehabilitation—The relative
hierarchy of its proponents—Their argumentation
223

9

THE HISTORICAL PROBLEM
Pieter Geyl's question in 1944—The comparison with Napoleon
—The semantic question of "greatness"—Catastrophic results
of Hitler—Enduring consequences—His place in the history of
the twentieth century and at the end of the Modern Age
240

PREFACE
AND
ACKNOWLEDGMENTS

ADOLF HITLER was the most extraordinary figure in the history of the twentieth century, for more than one reason; the Second World War, for instance, was inconceivable and remains incomprehensible without him. The portrait of Hitler that emerges from this book will contain elements—more precisely, questions—about his character and his career that are more complex than what seems to be generally assumed. This is not simply the result of an evolving perspective more than half a century after his disappearance; it is largely the result of a half century of assiduous researches, of which many of the most valuable contributions have been made by German historians. This book is a history of a history: the history of the evolution of our knowledge of Hitler, apparent as that is in the writings of a great variety of his many biographers. It will be evident that there are significant varieties in their interpretations; and to the consequently principal—and some still outstanding—questions this work is directed.

Recent evidence of a—relatively new—interpretation of the "Hitler problem" was implicit in Joachim Fest's new introduction to a reissue of his great biography of Hitler (1973). In chapter 1 of this book I state my opinion that Fest's is probably the best of the large-scale biographies of Hitler. Yet in this new introduction (reprinted in the *Frankfurter Allgemeine*, 7 October 1995), some of his statements are debatable. (The style of his writing, too, is not comparable to the clarity of the 1973 book.) To be sure, this new introduction does not imply a rehabilitation of Hitler. It is, moreover, natural and permissible for an author to rethink and revise what he wrote almost twenty-five years earlier. But in this 1995 introduction Fest writes that the portrait of Hitler has become more and more "unclear"; that he is still "our contemporary"; that "the shadows of his contemporariness are becoming deeper and deeper"; that much of Hitler's rise must be understood as a reaction against the dangers of communism (a questionable thesis with which Fest associated himself as early as 1986 and about which there is further discussion at several points in the present text); that there are questions and topics about Hitler that remain "taboos"; and that he has "not at all become historical." Fest says that Hitler has been unduly "demonized" and that a "historicization" of Hitler is missing. That the demonization of Hitler begs many questions, that it sweeps the entire problem of Hitler under the rug, is all too true. But the "historicization" of Hitler has been well advanced, is going on, which is what prompted my writing of this book, whose very title should be telling: *The Hitler of History*.

It is not a biography of Hitler, but a history of his history, and a history of his biographies. That is an unending story, because our historical perspective is always liable to change. There is no reason to doubt that within the next fifty years more biographies of Hitler will appear, and that some of their perspectives may be relatively new and even valuable, and not necessarily only because of some newly discovered fund of documents. That is, by and large, inevitable; but it does not mean that earlier works are necessarily less "historical" than newer ones. It simply means that, contrary to the "scientific" illusion, in the research and the writing of history there are no final results. And the purpose of history is often not so much the definite accounting of the events of a period as it is the historical description and understanding of problems: description, rather than definition; understanding, rather than completeness—because while a perfect completion of our knowledge of the past is not possible, a reasonable and proper understanding of it is within our powers.

Such are the conditions of history: a general statement that is particularly applicable to the problem of Hitler. The mass of biographies of Hitler, let alone other historical studies concerning him, is so enormous that a pretense of completeness would be both mistaken and improper. This book attempts to treat the important and significant biographies and biographical studies of Hitler, and it also includes many other books, studies, and articles that contain significant details or other contributions to the understanding of certain problems. It draws on a few new archival sources; but, at the risk of presumption, I feel compelled to state that it is also the result of many decades of reading and of contemplation of those problems. That this book deals with problems should appear from its table of contents even before its text. As a result, I must admit that, together with my treatment of the variations and evolutions of Hitler's biographies, it necessarily, and inevitably, includes my own consideration and treatment of these problems. And in this respect many of its pages represent what I think are proper applications of the principles of historical understanding set forth in my earlier books: *Historical Consciousness* (1968, 1984, 1994), *The Last European War, 1939–1941* (1976), and *The Duel* (1991). These principles involve such questions as the difference between motives and purposes, between racism and nationalism, between nationalism and patriotism, between public opinion and popular sentiment, between National Socialism and Fascism (including—contra such different writers as, say, Ernst Nolte and Hannah Arendt and, lately, Joachim Fest—the unreasonable parallels drawn between National Socialism and communism, including between Stalin and Hitler, under the category of "totalitarianism").

I am pleased to express my gratitude to those who helped me: The Earhart Foundation facilitated my work in Germany. There my thanks are principally directed to the Institut für Zeitgeschichte in Munich and to its most excellent and amiable archivist, Herr Hermann Weiss (and also to my temporary assistant, Frau Katja Klee). Also to my great and good friend the English historian Philip Bell; the Old Master of American diplomatic history Robert Ferrell, who encouraged me to write *this* particular kind of book; an American historian of modern Germany, Donald Detwiler, who (together with Mrs. Ilse Detwiler) read the entire manuscript and made most precise and detailed suggestions, with the great majority of which I instantly agreed. Such, too, was the reading of my wife, Stephanie—who also said when I first mentioned the plan of this book to her, "You will be walking through a minefield." (Well I know: plenty of delayed mines yet to burst.) I prefer to think of it rather as the clearing and planting of a grove in a jungle, while aware of the presence of a beautiful and serious horticulturist, the toil and sweat alleviated by the prospect of delicious dinners prepared by the same horticulturist. Still: a picnic it wasn't.

1994–1996
Pickering Close
(near Phoenixville, Pennsylvania)

The Hitler of History

I

Historiographical Problems

---

*The purpose of historical knowledge—The extraordinary popular
interest in Hitler—Its development and continuation—His treatment
by historians—Its evolution—The relationship of history and
biography—Principal problems—The documentary problems—
The limits of our knowledge*

W E ARE NOT YET FINISHED with Hitler ("[wir sind] mit
Hitler noch lange nicht fertig"), wrote two members of
a younger generation of German historians, independently of each other, in the 1980s*—and this is so in both the
broader and the narrower sense of "finished." The first of these
should be evident. History means the endless rethinking—and
reviewing and revisiting—of the past. History, in the broad sense of
the word, is revisionist. History involves multiple jeopardy that the
law eschews: People and events are retried and retried again. There
is nothing profound in this observation, since this is what all
thinking is about. The past is the only thing we know. All human
knowledge springs from past knowledge. All human thinking involves a rethinking of the past.

---

*Gerhard Schreiber (1940–), the principal bibliographer of Hitler, in the concluding sentence of his *Hitler: Interpretationen 1923–1983* (2nd, expanded ed., Darmstadt, 1988 (hereafter: SCHRB), p. 335. Rainer Zitelmann (1957–): "in many fields . . . The research is only in its beginnings," in *Adolf Hitler: Eine politische Biographie*, Göttingen, 1989 (hereafter: ZIT/B), p. 10.

This is true in the narrower sense, too, involving the historical profession. The notion that once the scientific method has been applied accurately, with all extant documents exhausted, the work will be finished and the result will be final ("the final and definitive history of the Third Reich, certified by German, American, British, Russian, liberal and conservative, nationalist and Jewish historians") is a nineteenth-century illusion. There are now probably more than one hundred biographies of Hitler, while there is no certainty that the 101st may not furnish something new and valid. What may matter even more than the accumulated *quantity* of the research (note the word "re-search") is the *quality* of the revision. What is its purpose? In the broader sense, the purpose of historical knowledge is more than accuracy; it is understanding. In the narrower sense, the purpose of a revisionist historian may be exposé, scandal, sensation—or the more or less unselfish wish to demolish untruths. It may be his desire for academic or financial success, to further his advancement in the eyes of his colleagues, or, in the greater world, to gain publicity; or to further the cause of a political or national ideology—on which the treatment of his subject sometimes depends. There will be evidence in this book that this applies—on occasion— to the historical treatment of Hitler too.

BEFORE I TURN to professional historians and biographers of Hitler, I must pay some attention to the extraordinary, and continuing, interest in Hitler during the last fifty years. The quantity of books, articles, films, and television programs dealing with Hitler surpasses that addressed to other main figures of the now-ending twentieth century: Stalin, Roosevelt, Churchill, de Gaulle, Mussolini, Mao. Fifty years after Hitler's death, popular interest in him continues. I must essay at least a sketchy account of its course.

During Hitler's lifetime, his *Mein Kampf** was, of course, a publishing success—in England and the United States especially before the war—though few people (including Germans) took the trouble to read it in its entirety. Unlike Mussolini and other dictators,

---

*Hereafter: MK.

Hitler did not wish to see an adulatory biography of himself published during his lifetime in Germany; in fact, except for a few odd earlier biographies, photographic albums, and collections of his speeches, there were none. (Hitler himself deemphasized, if not altogether dismissed, *Mein Kampf* after 1936, in private conversations at least—even though it was written in the first person, and even though the first part amounted to his intellectual autobiography.) From his various remarks, it also seems that—unlike Churchill or De Gaulle, or even Napoleon at St. Helena—in the event of his retirement, Hitler would have had little inclination to write or dictate his memoirs.*

The news of his death left the world numb. That was not the numbness of a stunning shock; it was, rather, the news of something that had been somehow expected and perhaps even discounted in advance. Of course there was a difference between the reactions of the German people and those of other peoples of the world, understandably so—but there was, perhaps, one overwhelming (or was it an underwhelming?) condition: people did not want to think much about Hitler when there were so many other immediate and pressing things for them to think about. That condition prevailed for some years. Among some of his German contemporaries, there was—and still is—a tendency to blame Hitler for all the evils that he had visited on the world and for what also had befallen themselves†: an understandable tendency that somehow *separated* him from them, distinguishing his life and his doings from their lives and their doings during the war. Examples of this were the memoirs of many German generals (most of them published in the early 1950s), who blamed Hitler, not themselves, for blunders in the war, for great battles lost—often exaggeratedly, and sometimes incorrectly. Around 1960, there developed a change—outside Germany at first

---

*He made one half-joking remark late in the war to one of his secretaries that during his retirement, in Linz, he might even dictate his memoirs. Interview with Trudl Junge, typescript in the Institut für Zeitgeschichte (hereafter: IFZ), June 1968.

†Among many other "average" Germans, the opposite tendency prevailed long after the war: Hitler was less to blame than many others: "If only the Führer knew." See below, chapter 7.

and then in Germany too. Interest in Hitler, in the Third Reich, in World War II, including the "Holocaust" (a word that was not then current), arose anew, especially in the United States. Books such as William Shirer's superficial *The Rise and Fall of the Third Reich* (1960) became best-sellers, or near-best-sellers. The capture and trial of Adolf Eichmann, as well as other events, revived first the American, then the German and worldwide, interest in the history of the mass murder of Jews during World War II—to which American Jews and their organizations had not devoted extensive interest before the 1960s.

There were, I think, three main reasons for this revival of fascination with World War II and Hitler. The first was the emergence of a new generation of people who were too young to have lived through the war, whence their interest in its dramatic figures and events. The second, more evident reason was the publication and the availability of more and more sources and documents. The third was the gradual abatement of the so-called cold war with Russia: It was now obvious that World War II was not only more dramatic than the cold war but that Hitler was more interesting than Stalin (and Nazis than Communists). All of these conditions still prevail nearly forty years later, at the time of this writing. In the 1960s and 1970s, biographies of Hitler began to multiply; so did other books, articles, plays, television programs, films, including so-called documentaries, and so forth. By the early 1970s, German commentators had begun to speak of a "Hitler-Welle," a "Hitler-wave"—a phenomenon applicable to some extent to the United States and perhaps Britain too. However, a wave has a crest and a trough, and that trough has not yet appeared. During the last twenty-five years the price of Hitler memorabilia has risen steadily, outpacing not only inflation but the price of almost all other objects or works of art or of manuscripts and autograph letters achieved at world auctions. In 1981, a German forger went to much trouble to manufacture pages of a diary that was supposedly handwritten by Hitler. The result was a worldwide sensation (lamentably, at least two celebrated— non-German—historians declared the "documents" to be plausibly genuine) until the forgery became evident. Sixteen years later it is fair to say that popular interest (which, to be sure, is not and will never be accurately measurable) in Hitler is as prevalent as before, in many places of the world, and on many levels.

These levels vary, of course: from the honest curiosity of amateurs of history to the kind of prurient or near-prurient curiosity evinced by people who are attracted to manifestations and incarnations of evil. To these, alas, a new kind of curiosity may be added, especially now after the collapse and virtual disappearance of communism: the interest of those who are beginning to wonder whether Hitler and National Socialism did not represent, *mutatis mutandis*, an alternative not only healthier than communism but healthier than the decaying liberal democracy of the West.

In any event: the evolution, and the endurance, of the popular interest in Hitler did not altogether differ from the evolution of studies of Hitler among reputable and professional historians. In 1985, the German historian Martin Broszat stated that historians must proceed from the "demonization" to the "historicization" of National Socialism and, consequently, of Hitler—a desideratum as well as a statement of something that, for some time, had been obvious.* The view that Hitler was not a "demonic"—that is, at least by inference, an ahuman and ahistorical—phenomenon but a historical figure, incarnating various human characteristics and endowed with recognizable talents, is shared not only by some historians but by more and more people. All of this eventually leads to the question—question, if not problem—of his place in the history of the twentieth century or, indeed, in the history of the world. I shall have to come to this in the last chapter of this book, even though its principal topic is not Hitler's life but his treatment by historians. I know that the two topics are not altogether separable, since the history of history is history too. But the two themes are not identical: This work is not a biography of Hitler. It is a treatment of a historical problem—more precisely, of a number of problems.

---

*M. Broszat, "Plädoyer für eine Historisierung des Nationalsozialismus," in *Merkur* 39 (1985). But already Karl-Dietrich Bracher, "Probleme und Perspektiven der Hitler-Interpretation," in *Zeitgeschichtliche Kontroversen*, M, 1976, pp. 79–100.

THE FIRST PROBLEM, OR, RATHER, condition—in order, though not necessarily in importance—is the tremendous accumulation of materials about Hitler. The canon of professional historiography, established in the nineteenth century (and mostly in Germany), calls for the professional historian to exhaust all of the sources (above all, the primary sources) relating to his topic. For more than a century now, the volume of printed materials alone has become such that for most topics—especially, but not exclusively, twentieth-century topics—the complete fulfillment of this requirement is no longer possible. Obviously this includes the topic of Hitler. An annotated and judiciously commentated bibliographical study by Gerhard Schreiber was published in 1984, with a subsequent expanded edition in 1988; yet, because of the very nature of its subject, this excellent guide to research could not be complete, either.*

This does not mean that the serious historian should throw up his hands in despair. Every historian necessarily proceeds on the basis of incomplete evidence. At the same time the extent of his admissible evidence is potentially limitless—another difference between history and the law. As the great Jacob Burckhardt once said: There is, strictly speaking, no definite historical method; what the historian must be good at is *bisogna saper leggere* (Burckhardt put it in Italian): He must know how to read (another suggestion of quality as well as of quantity). This leads us to the second condition. Among those who "know how to read," among serious historians dealing with Hitler, does "serious" mean "professional"? Yes, and no. Or, more precisely: no, rather than yes. The notion that serious—meaning not only readable but reliable—history can be written only by professional historians, holders of a Ph.D. degree, was another nineteenth-century idea: an idea not without considerable merit and substance, with many enduring and positive results, but an illusion

---

*SCHRB mentions the inevitable incompleteness of bibliographies, p.15; in any case, see his list of bibliographies, p.341ff.—to which should be added the excellent seriatim bibliographies of the *Vierteljahrshefte für Zeitgeschichte* (hereafter: VFZ).

nonetheless. This, too, is especially evident in the twentieth century. Among the best and most reliable historians of Hitler we find professional and nonacademic writers alike. We will see that, perhaps especially in Hitler's case, the possession of a professional degree, or even of a prestigious university chair, has been no guarantee against some rather serious errors, while for other writers the absence of such academic qualifications has not compromised, circumscribed, or otherwise limited their valuable achievement.

Such are two elementary conditions of a survey of Hitler historians; and again, because of the tremendous mass of books about Hitler a survey is all this can be. It will be limited to some of the main works, and to the general evolution of Hitler study: for an evolution there has been, with a few recognizable milestones (and—as late as 1996—an evolution without a perceptible end).

More than sixty years ago, the first substantial study of Hitler was written by Konrad Heiden (1901–1966) and published in Zurich in 1936.* Heiden was a German émigré, a journalist—a condition that, in his case, was an advantage rather than a handicap because of the readable and crisp style of his writing, much of which was in the historical present tense. At the same time the work was a serious one. Heiden had evidently followed Hitler for many years, with acute interest. His account of Hitler's life and career (the book ended with June–July 1934) was dense with details and often remarkably accurate. Nearly forty years later, Joachim Fest paid his tribute to Heiden's book, which had obviously stood the test of time.† This was in spite of the obvious condition that Heiden could not have read materials that had appeared since. Some of his errors were picked up by other historians, nota-

---

*Konrad Heiden, *Adolf Hitler: Das Zeitalter der Verantwortlosigkeit*, vol. 1 (hereafter: HD); U. S. ed.: *Adolf Hitler: The Age of Irresponsibility*, Boston, 1944.

†". . . in many ways [I am] indebted to [Heiden]; this first historical attempt . . . remains exemplary to this day because of the boldness of its questions and its free judgment." This is the first footnote in Joachim Fest, *Adolf Hitler: Eine Biographie.* B, 1973 (hereafter: F). Also SCHRB, p. 23, eleven years later: "[Heiden's] biography of Hitler still has a definite impact on contemporary historical research."

bly Maser,* decades later. But the value of Heiden's biography was enhanced by his often insightful and personal commentaries about political figures and the political atmosphere of the period—while he was honest enough to dismiss legends and anecdotes about Hitler after having scrutinized them. Heiden's main thesis is as valid now as it was more than sixty years ago: Hitler was underestimated, dangerously so, by his opponents as well as by his temporary allies. All in all, this is a creditable achievement, better than both Heiden's subsequent volume about Hitler's foreign policy (1937) and a Hitler biography by another German émigré journalist, Rudolf Olden.†

And then, despite the unchartable flood of books about Germany and Nazism before, during, and after World War II,‡ no considerable study or biography appeared until more than fifteen years after Heiden's work, and more than five years after Hitler's suicide. There was one exception worthy of mention—exception, because, strictly speaking, Hugh Trevor-Roper's *The Last Days of Hitler* (1947) was neither a biography nor a study of Hitler; it dealt with only the last ten days of Hitler's life in the bunker underneath the New Reich Chancellery (a dramatic enough topic that has since

---

*Maser (M/A [below], pp. 14, 17) emphasized that Heiden's mother was Jewish; another malicious comment appeared on p. 75. Irving, in I/w, dismissed Heiden as "worthless." I noted at least two questionable assertions in HD: that Hitler was not secretive, p. 30, and that Goebbels was not the creative master of National Socialist propaganda, p. 94. Heiden also accepted a few erroneous assertions about Hitler's ancestry.

†Heiden, *Ein Mann gegen Europa*, z, 1937; Olden, *Hitler the Pawn*, L, 1936. More estimable: James Murphy, *Adolf Hitler: The Drama of His Career*, L, 1939.

‡An important exception—though not a biography—was the "conversations" with Hitler described by Herman Rauschning, *The Revolution of Nihilism*, NY, 1939. Several German editions, including criticism of the authenticity of some of the statements attributed to Hitler, were published in the 1960s and 1970s. (Theodor Schieder, *Hermann Rauschnings 'Gespräche mit Hitler' als Geschichtsquelle*, Opladen, 1972; and Wolfgang Hänel, *Hermann Rauschnings 'Gespräche mit Hitler': Eine Geschichtsfälschung*, Ingolstadt, 1984. The latter is critical of the former: Hänel thinks that Schieder was not critical enough of Rauschning.) While open and covert apologists for Hitler dismiss Rauschning altogether, Jäckel and Fest give him his due: F, p. 695: "[Rauschning's books], meritorious though they were at their time, are not . . . primary sources, but [important] memoirs of the kind of a 'creative dialogue.' "

attracted at least a dozen other writers, memoirists, amateur historians, and novelists). Trevor-Roper's book was inspired by his participation in a British intelligence group that attempted to ascertain the actual circumstances of Hitler's death. The result was fairly comprehensive and accurate; well written, too, with perhaps one shortcoming: The description of the then physically broken, hobbling, fanatic, cornered dictator, irrational in some of his expectations and directives, did not consider or admit Hitler's remaining rational considerations in his capacity as a statesman (to which we shall turn in chapter 5)—"rational," that is, as some of these were from his own viewpoint. This relatively small book proved to be an important element in Trevor-Roper's (later Lord Dacre) career: this late-Tudor and Stuart historian became a respectable and judicious commentator on the historiography of Hitler and the Third Reich.

In 1952, Alan Bullock (1914– ; later Lord Bullock) produced the first substantial biography of Hitler by an English historian.* Composed in the British tradition, without academic jargon, it was, commercially speaking, perhaps the most successful of all Hitler biographies. It was an important achievement, also, because its author could profit from the unusually rapid availability of captured German documents produced at Nuremberg and published soon after the war. Its direct and straightforward narrative style was, and still remains, an important element in its reputation and success. At the same time, Bullock's interpretation—or, rather, description—of Hitler's character was one-dimensional: that of "an entirely unprincipled opportunist."† We ought not to attribute to Hitler high principles or great moral virtues; but Bullock's portrait was much too simple. (His short descriptions of others—to wit, Hess and Göring—were very good.) Of course this was an early biography: Bullock could not yet profit from the subsequent outpouring of

---

*Hitler: A Study in Tyranny, L, 1952; rev. ed., 1962; later editions, as well (hereafter: BU).

†"The only principles of Nazism were power . . . for their own sake." He contrasted Hitler with Robespierre and Lenin, for whom "the will to power . . . coincided with the triumph of principle."

documents, papers, memoirs, and at least partial revelations over the next forty years. Still, even in the later editions many of Bullock's original errors—errors of judgment as well as fact—remained.*

Meanwhile, in the very year of Bullock's publication, a significant development occurred within Germany (more precisely, West Germany) itself. This was the establishment of serious historical studies to be devoted to recent German history, including that of the Third Reich and thus, at least indirectly, of Hitler. "Zeitgeschichte" in German signifies something slightly different from the English term "contemporary history," where, in accord with both the traditions and the practice of the language, the meaning of "contemporary" rolls on largely undefined (and even more different from France, where, for a long time, "histoire contemporaine" has meant history after 1815, an increasingly senseless definition). Eventually (this was not made clear before 1951), "Zeitgeschichte" in Germany came to denote history after 1914, a fairly sensible categorization (which, however, will gradually lose its point as the twenty-first century proceeds). Thus in 1951 and after, "Zeitgeschichte" (and, of course, mainly German contemporary history) was accepted as a respectable academic discipline, to be researched, studied, and taught in German universities. There was a moral purpose underlying this proposition. It was the wish to establish for Germans a reputable and solid fundament for a proper perspective on their recent past. The result was the founding of the Institut für Zeitgeschichte and of its scholarly historical quarterly, the *Vierteljahrshefte für Zeitgeschichte* (vFz), which remains to this day the best journal of con-

---

*bu, p. 121: "*Mein Kampf* contains very little autobiography." Not so. p. 40: "Hitler belonged, by right, he felt, to the *Herrenmenschen*"—not as simple as that. Bullock was wrong about Hitler's relationships with women (pp. 392–93); about the number of Hitler's public speeches after Stalingrad (p. 722); about the Reichstag fire in 1933—a version shared by Shirer. bu, p. 313: "For an excellent summary of the most important facts [about the Nazi system] the reader should turn to Chapter 8 of *The Rise and Fall of the Third Reich*, by William R. Shirer." This will not do. See Jäckel on bu in *Geschichte in Wissenschaft und Unterricht* (hereafter: gwu), 1977, p. 708: ". . . a standard work, but surpassed by [later] research; besides, its treatment of Hitler's place in history was highly unsatisfactory." Kershaw, *Hitler: Profile in Power*, ny, 1991 (hereafter: ker), p. 149: "Bullock's was a masterpiece when written in 1952, but is now showing signs of age."

temporary history in the world. Its principal founders were Hans Rothfels, a German conservative historian, who had returned from his exile in the United States, and Theodor Eschenburg, a German political thinker with unsullied credentials. Thus it may be said that the "historicization" of the Third Reich had begun more than thirty years before Professor Broszat pronounced its desirability. Yet there was—and still is—an appreciable difference between the "historicization"—that is, the de-demonization—of the Third Reich and that of Hitler.

Around that time, the first serious German postwar biography of Hitler appeared, by Walter Görlitz (1913–1991) and Herbert A. Quint (1922–   ).* They were amateur historians (Görlitz went on to a respectable career in journalism), Pomeranian conservatives who were particularly interested in military history. They concentrated on the political Hitler. Written from a German conservative perspective, in a readable and rapidly flowing style (though perhaps with an excess of exclamation points), the book contained some inaccuracies but also some insightful observations that would later be made independently by other historians.† The best part of their work dealt with the political ascent of Hitler, and with the fatal—moral as well as political—shortcomings of his potential opponents and actual allies in the 1930–34 period. The book's weakness lay in its authors' very brief treatment of the last six years of Hitler's life and the war (only 92 out of 633 pages). The Görlitz-Quint portrait of Hitler was unexceptionally condemnatory: that of a fanatic

---

*Görlitz and Quint, *Adolf Hitler: Eine Biographie*, s, 1952 (hereafter: GQ). Both authors used pseudonyms: The former's original name was Otto Julius Frauendorf; the latter's was Richard Freiherr v. Frankenberg.

†One inaccuracy: an exaggeration of the role of Princess Stephanie Hohenlohe, GQ, pp. 376, 506. Valuable: an early observation, contrary to still-accepted ideas, that Hitler was *not* an avid watcher of the trials and the executions of the July 1944 conspirators, and that he was critical of the awful presiding judge, Roland Freisler: "He did not want . . . theatrics," GQ, p. 612. Also about Hitler's dismissal of some things he had written in MK, p. 239 (written more than a decade before Maser's study of *Mein Kampf*). Also: "[Hitler] never let himself go, he never talked about problems of mercy-killing or about the final solution of the Jewish question, these belonged to the most carefully protected secrets," p. 575: a very early, then still undocumentable, but accurate observation.

radical who destroyed much that was valuable in Germany, including the unity of the German state. In depicting Hitler as such, they did not entirely differ from Bullock's "unprincipled opportunist," but their perspective was, of course, different.

There was, during the 1950s, a certain duality with regard to the Hitler era. Because of the existence—more important, the perception—of Russian and Communist aggressiveness, there was a popular (and, in many instances, public) tendency to regard communism and Russia as more dangerous and perhaps even more evil than were Hitler and the Third Reich—a tendency then evident in the United States, though not in Britain. Within West Germany, this corresponded to the popular inclination to regard World War II as consisting of two different wars: the war of the Third Reich against the Western democracies which was regrettable and should have been avoided; and the war against Soviet Russia, in which Germany had been a defender of Western civilization, something the Western democracies should have understood. Essentially, this tendency amounted (and still amounts) to at least a partial exoneration of the German people and of their armies during World War II, though not of Hitler. Except for a few pamphlets and fragments of Nazi memoirists, no serious attempt at an apology for Hitler was then made. On the other hand, among younger historians the scholarly study of aspects of the Third Reich had begun, as was evident in many studies and articles not only in the VFZ but in many other political and cultural periodicals. During the 1950s the first significant works of later Hitler-specialists such as Andreas Hillgruber first appeared—even though it was not until the 1960s that "Zeitgeschichte" began to be included in the curriculum of upper-level German schools (and that the trials of Germans accused of war crimes were put on the docket of German courts).

We have seen that interest in Hitler revived around 1960, and this had visible effects on historiography too. The 1960 publication of *The Origins of the Second World War* by the self-confident maverick among English historians, A. J. P. Taylor (1906–1990), must be mentioned here, even though Taylor was not a biographer of Hitler. (Nor was his book—as has sometimes been wrongly stated—a stunning attempt to rehabilitate him.) What Taylor attempted to assert was that Hitler was not so different (if different at all) from other ambitious German statesmen of the past; that during the 1930s he knew how to take advantage of the weakness of his opponents and of the opportunities they made possible for him; that, in short, Hitler was more of a short-term opportunist and less of a long-range ideologue than it was assumed. On occasion, Taylor presented his evidence on the sudden development of some of Hitler's decisions convincingly; at other times, with considerable legerdemain.* His book had an effect on the diplomatic history of the period, but practically none on the evolving historical portrait of Hitler.

In the early 1960s, there appeared three biographical studies of Hitler, by Heiber, Gisevius, and Schramm—in ascending order of their importance.† Of these, Helmut Heiber's (1924–) portrait was the most conventional, though not devoid of insightful passages. Hans Bernd Gisevius (1904–1974) had been connected to the 1944 conspirators against Hitler; he worked for a while for Allen Dulles and the OSS in Switzerland. Valuable elements in his biography were his analysis of the Hitler-Papen and Hitler-Hindenburg relationships, and his treatment generally of Hitler in the early 1930s; noteworthy, too, was his shrewd recognition of Hitler's duality, suggesting that Hitler often incarnated diverse personalities, even in his photographs.‡ At the same time, his presentation of Hitler's world of ideas was somewhat superficial: While Gisevius (as did many others) tended to rely heavily on *Mein Kampf,* he also wrote that Hitler's ideas were not at all original.

Percy Ernst Schramm (1894–1970) was a truly exceptional—and first-rate—German historian, whose relatively short study of Hitler reflected the personal qualities of its author. The son of an old Hamburg patrician family (his father was once the city's mayor), Schramm

---

*See especially pp. 18–20, 31, and 44 in my *The Last European War, 1939–1941,* NY, 1976 (hereafter: LEW).

†Helmut Heiber, *Adolf Hitler: Eine Biographie,* B, 1960 (hereafter: HB); Hans Bernd Gisevius, *Adolf Hitler: Versuch einer Deutung* (*Adolf Hitler: Attempt at an Explanation*), M, 1963 (hereafter: GI); Percy Ernst Schramm, *Hitler: The Man and Military Leader* (Donald Detwiler, ed.), Chicago, 1971 (hereafter: SCH), an appropriate combination of two Schramm essays, 1961 and 1962.

‡See especially the introduction of GI, p. 6.

was a historian of unusually varied interests—a medievalist of world-wide reputation, an expert in iconography and muniments, a historian of Hamburg patriciandom, of German overseas commerce, and of his own family. He became the editor of the War Diary of the High Command of the Wehrmacht in 1943, leading to one or two occasions when he was able to observe Hitler in person. Schramm's two studies of Hitler, written as introductions to volume 4 of the *War Diary* and to the Picker edition of Hitler's *Table Conversations* (about which see page 47), were put together by the American historian Donald Detwiler. Their value is twofold. The first, and most obvious, asset was Schramm's emphasis on Hitler the military leader and the statesman (*not* a word used by Schramm); here we must keep in mind that with few exceptions (Hillgruber; Irving), most Hitler-scholars and Hitler-biographers have written much more about Hitler's rise than about the last six years of his life and the war. Schramm's second, and more important, contribution lay in the sophisticated refinement and moral quality of his judgment, issuing from the perspective of a traditionalist patrician and embodied in the prose of a master historian.*

---

*From Detwiler's introduction: "Through long years of pioneering in his medieval detective work, Schramm refined his ability to interpret scanty original sources, both verbal and visual. This often enabled him to cut through spurious encrustations of popular myth and historiographical tradition," SCH, p. 8. Also pp. 6–7: "The picture of Hitler which flows from Schramm's skillful pen is worlds removed from the widely known caricature of . . . an agitator with a Charlie Chaplin moustache. . . . No reader can reflect on Schramm's pages without realizing the folly of the common trivialization. . . ." Schramm himself on the psychological force of Hitler's impact on people, p. 35: ". . . like a magnetic field. It could be so intense as to be almost physically tangible. As widely attested as this strange power of Hitler's was, there were nevertheless many people upon whom it had absolutely no effect." Also p. 69: "Although there is much to say about Hitler's appreciation of art and music, he had remarkably little interest in literature . . . [he] had no appreciation for poems, particularly lyric poetry." This is entirely opposite to Maser in M/A, pp. 85–86, according to whom "before 1913 Hitler attempted to perfect his literary learning, read the German classics, and occupied himself with German lyric poetry." Another—chronological—inconsistency in Maser M/F, p. 88: "Before the summer of 1921 (and again especially between December 1923 and December 1924) [Hitler] undoubtedly read more than most professional intellectuals of his age." In M/A, pp. 229 and 231, Maser criticized Schramm for the latter's critique of Hitler's historical views—in my opinion, wrongly so.

His insights into Hitler's personality and character were not only remarkable; they are enduring. They were the perceptions and recognitions of a rich and wise maturity. (After all, Schramm was nearly seventy when he composed them.)

A very different historian was Werner Maser (1922–   ). His provenance, life, and career were quite unlike Schramm's: almost thirty years younger, Maser was born in East Prussia in simpler circumstances; he served as a common soldier, became an American and then a Russian prisoner of war, studied in East Berlin, and passed over to the West only at the age of thirty. After earning his degree, he worked as a journalist; and though he later received respectable teaching assignments, he secured neither a full professorship nor a university chair, and he failed to be admitted to the higher circle of German academic historians. Again, unlike Schramm's, Maser's entire scholarly and literary production, manifest in an extensive list of books and other publications, was almost without exception devoted to Hitler and National Socialism. His contributions were considerable. Four massive volumes within eight years—between 1965 and 1973—dealt with the early history of the National Socialist Party and Hitler's early career; a study of *Mein Kampf*, a Hitler biography, and a study of Hitler's papers and documents followed.* Maser's main achievement was the unearthing of large quantities of data through his tireless research, particularly in the following and important spheres: Hitler's provenance, especially involving the heredity of his father, other family members, his early life, his financial and material circumstances; and later—with perhaps excessive emphasis—entire chapters devoted to women, to Hitler's medications, to graphological studies and tabulations, including a comparison with Napoleon. The efforts of Maser the researcher were more impressive than were his talents as biographer. In his principal Hitler biography (M/A) there was a frequent interlacing (and therefore a thematic interruption) of the events of

---

*Die Frühgeschichte der NSDAP: Hitlers Weg bis 1924, Frankfurt, 1965; Hitlers Mein Kampf, M, 1966; Adolf Hitler: Legende, Mythos, Wirklichkeit, M, 1971 (hereafter: M/A), whose first four chapters are, however, elaborations of M/F; Hitler: Briefe und Notizen, D, 1973 (hereafter: M/HB).

the war, with paragraphs dealing with Hitler's health and emotional state; and Maser was inclined, if not to overrate, at least to over-emphasize, the importance of his "finds."* Quarrelsome and inde-fatigable, Maser criticized and, in turn, was criticized by some of the principal historians and biographers of Hitler, perhaps unfairly on some occasions, though understandably on others; but Maser's cate-gorical statement in the introduction (p. 8) of M/A that "gaps in the picture of Adolf Hitler's life may now [presumably owing to Maser's achievements] be seen as completely filled" ["lückenlos nachzei-chenbar"] was an exaggeration.

In 1965, there appeared a massive book about Hitler the strate-gist and war leader† by the aforementioned Andreas Hillgruber (1925–1989). Like Maser, Hillgruber was born in East Prussia. The terrible destiny of his homeland at the end of the war left a perma-nent impression on his young mind, inspiring him to become a prominent—perhaps the most prominent—German specialist in the history of World War II *and* of Hitler. A specialist: because, of his astonishingly numerous publications, amazingly few (only five among a list of fifty-seven books and articles) were devoted to subjects other than the period of World War II. Hillgruber and Schramm were per-haps the first professional historians whose work concentrated on Hitler as a statesman and a military leader: but if Schramm's work—while fulfilling all of the desiderata of scholarly method—could be considered a superb historical essay, Hillgruber's large volume was crammed with the equipment of traditional academic scholarship (which also led to his appointment to a university chair). And here the question arises whether the nineteenth-century customs and methods

---

*Thus, for example, in his introduction to M/A, p. 7: After the publication of his first two books dealing with Hitler, "important witnesses presented themselves: Hitler's schoolmates, friends from his youth, war comrades . . . enemies and friends, relations and descendants, putting documents and papers at my disposal . . . for which historians and biographers had been looking in vain over fifty years. Numerous handwritten Hitler letters and notes could now be evaluated, as well as the hitherto unavailable papers and statements of physicians who had treated Hitler." In M/HB, p. 7: ". . . the documents and my work on this book presented me with surprises I had not counted upon."

†Andreas Hillgruber, *Hitlers Strategie: Politik und Kriegsführung 1940–1941.* Frankfurt, 1965 (hereafter: HST).

of academic historiography, including the ideal—though, alas, often the pretense—of professional "objectivity" were, and are, entirely sufficient guarantees when dealing with topics such as Hitler. This is, of course, a very large philosophical (more precisely, an epistemological) problem, which I cannot discuss here.* Let me only say that the still-accepted usage of the categorical "objective" and "subjective" adjectives, part and parcel of the Cartesian division of the universe into Object and Subject, have proved to be less than absolute or leakproof, even in the physical sciences—even though some historians continue to employ them for their own purposes.†

Hillgruber was not a fine writer (I found sentences of his running to more than two hundred words), especially when compared with someone like Schramm; but more important was the condition, inevitably intruding into the problem of "objectivity," of Hillgruber's nationalist-conservative (again, unlike Schramm's patrician-conservative) political and ideological inclinations. These would appear, increasingly, during his involvement in the historians' controversy in the 1980s (which will be discussed on pages 32–36). But they—generally unmentioned by most other historians‡—were, or should have been, apparent in his otherwise very valuable HST. The "dual war" theory, which he then assiduously propagated in the 1980s, was already implicit in HST, where Hillgruber referred, more

---

*See my *Historical Consciousness*, NY, 1968; extended ed., 1994 (hereafter: HC). Or Henri-Irénée Marrou (the French classical historian), *De la connaissance historique*, P, 1956: "The massive intrusion of the historian's personality—his thoughts, intentions, inclinations—shapes his historical knowledge, and gives it form and countenance." That is, the historian's knowledge is personal—personal, rather than "subjective"—and participatory.

†See page 224. Or Bullock (a very different historian from Hillgruber) in his introduction to BU, p. 16: ". . . I wrote this book without any particular axe to grind or case to argue. . . . Nor has it been my purpose either to rehabilitate or to indict Adolf Hitler. . . . However disputable some of my interpretations may be, there is a solid substratum of fact—and the facts are eloquent enough." No: facts are never eloquent by themselves—for many reasons, one of which is that no "fact" is separable from its statement. The historian's task is not to define but to describe; his instruments are words (words of the everyday language); and his selection of every word is not merely a scientific or stylistic problem but also a moral one.

‡One exception: LEW, pp. 240, 343.

than once, to World War II before June 1941 as an "europäisches Normalkrieg"—that is, a traditional war conducted with traditional methods of warfare: a doubtful thesis, to say the least.

A very different work was Eberhard Jäckel's (1929–) short and weighty study of Hitler's ideology.* Here Jäckel summed up the evidence according to which Hitler's decisions—first of all his liquidation of the "Jewish problem" and his attempted conquest of European Russia—were the direct consequences of his earlier crystallized ideology in which he remained consistent throughout his life and career and the war. Other commentators had argued thus earlier, but Jäckel's achievement was much more than a restatement of the obvious, justifying his chair at the university of Stuttgart and his reputation as one of the best Hitler-scholars. Implicitly, therefore, Jäckel disagreed with both the "opportunist" and the "dual war" arguments—though perhaps (we shall see about this in chapter 5) he may not have put sufficient emphasis on the dualities in Hitler's mind. It may be proper to mention, too, that Jäckel may have been the first of the German postwar Hitler-scholars of a nonconservative political persuasion (he joined the German Social Democratic Party in 1967). In the 1980s, he and Hillgruber were opponents during the German historians' controversy about World War II, but well before that, Jäckel's various publications and commentaries about Hitler,† as well as his judicious statement of still-outstanding problems,‡ contributed to a deserved recognition.

In 1969, an excellent biography of Hitler by Ernst Deuerlein (1918–1971) appeared—the best short Hitler biography, in my estimation.** (The best *long* biography may be Fest's, to which I shall

---

*Hitlers Weltanschauung: Entwurf einer Herrschaft, Tübingen, 1969; new and extended ed., s, 1981 (hereafter: JHW). Later: Hitlers Herrschaft, s, 1988 (hereafter: JHH). Also: Hitler in History, Hanover, N.H., 1984 (hereafter: JH).

†Foremost among them (for our purposes): a collection of early Hitler papers and documents, Hitler: Sämtliche Aufzeichnungen 1905–1924 (with Axel Kuhn), s, 1980, and JH.

‡"Everything, including and perhaps especially what is wholly repellent and vexatious ["das ganz Widerwärtige"], must be soberly analyzed and understood. That is still the first task of historical research."

**Ernst Deuerlein, Hitler: Eine politische Biographie, M, 1969 (hereafter: D).

soon come.) If I had to choose but one book about Hitler for students or intelligent readers, this would be it. Very well written, with short and tellingly phrased sentences, reflecting a masterful economy of style—in spite of long quotations occasionally buttressing Deuerlein's argumentation—D was a biography that not only comprised many significant details but that remains a pleasure to read. This excellence of style was but one of its author's virtues. Deuerlein's text suggested his astonishingly wide and compendious reading as well as his careful handling of his factual materials. In many instances, Deuerlein pointed at still-unresolved problems about Hitler, giving credit to various historians and to their varieties of interpretations. This Catholic historian had already produced studies of distinction, including a 1962 work on the Hitler putsch of 1923. The emphasis in D was how Hitler had been possible—that is, his relationship with the German people—especially in Deuerlein's long last chapter ("Hitler's Ermöglichung"). In sum, it was an almost-perfect short biography, replete with very considerable psychological insights. Its only relative shortcoming (as in the case of most Hitler biographies) is a very short treatment of Hitler during the war.

At the beginning of a new decade the "Hitler-Welle" arrived: In the 1970s, the mass of publications (and films, including documentaries) involving Hitler was on the increase. The appearance of massive Hitler biographies was around the corner. But before that, mention must be made of two extraordinary, and related, works by the Austrian Catholic historian Friedrich Heer (1916–1983).* This cultural historian of an extraordinary range of reading and with a nervous and direct prose style—very different from standard or near-standard academic prose, which may have been one reason that Hitler scholars seldom paid more than marginal interest to Heer and that, despite his great reputation, he did not have a university chair. Heer expressed his ardent convictions, according to which Hitler's ideology—indeed, his view of the world (including his anti-Judaism)—could not be understood apart from the Judeophobic, at

---

*Friedrich Heer, *Gottes erste Liebe: 2000 Jahre Judentum und Christentum: Genesis des österreichischen Katholiken Adolf Hitler*, M, 1967; and *Der Glaube des Adolf Hitler: Anatomie einer politischen Religiosität*, M, 1968 (hereafter: HR).

times conservative, other times folkish ideology, background, and intellectual atmosphere of the Austria in which Hitler had grown up (and which to some extent persists even now). The motive force in Heer's work, therefore, was the intense concern of this deeply religious scholar with what he saw were the moral shortcomings of Austrian (and not only Austrian) Catholicism. We shall see in chapter 2 that Heer's attribution of the direct effect of these influences may have been exaggerated; yet at the same time, much credit remained due to Heer for the truly extraordinary range of his illustrative documentation—and, even more, for his sudden and sometimes startling insights into the character and personality of Hitler,* which accorded (perhaps even unbeknownst to Heer) with the solitary and incisive insights of such thinkers and writers as the French Georges Bernanos ("a deeply humiliated child") and George Orwell.

In 1973 (preceded by a volume that had already demonstrated his biographical talents), Joachim Fest's great biography of Hitler was published. Like Maser, Hillgruber, Jäckel, and Heer, Fest (1926–) was born in the mid-1920s—thus too young to have served in the war, save for a very short period at its end. After completing his university studies (he had a particular interest in art history), Fest made his career as a journalist, working also in television. He was a member of the Christian Democratic Party (for some years he served as an elected deputy in Berlin-Neukölln). The success and the appreciation of his Hitler biography led to Fest's invitation to an important and influential editorship of the *Frankfurter Allgemeine Zeitung* (hereafter: FAZ), an appointment reflecting a commendable practice of German cultural life (similar opportunities were tendered to Görlitz and Zitelmann, too). In his now influential position, Fest went on to play a significant role in contributing to and commenting on evolving studies of the Third Reich and Hitler (including the controversies of the 1980s) until his recent retirement. The excellence of his big volume (1,184 pages in the German edition) was mainly due to his biographical insights. Fest's background as a journalist did not com-

---

*One debatable assertion in HR, p. 343: "We know today that Hitler's [temporary] blindness [suffered after a gas attack on the front in October 1918] was the consequence of hysteria."

promise but, to the contrary, enhanced the quality of his work—which was the result, too, of his wide reading (as he often cited and quoted such thinkers as Burckhardt, Proudhon, Nietzsche, Constant, etc.). Fest had done little archival research, for which he was, unfairly, criticized by Maser; but some of the best German historians praised him without qualification.*

Especially good about the Vienna years and the 1919–33 period in Hitler's life (though again somewhat short on the war years), Fest's psychic portrait of Hitler was further enriched by his five "Zwischenbetrachtungen" ("Interim Considerations") of the meaning of a particular question (two of these, at the beginning and the end of the volume, about Hitler's place in history).† Another, at that time unusual, feature of this biography was Fest's assertion that had Hitler been assassinated at the end of 1938, "few [Germans] would hesitate to name him as one of the greatest statesmen of Germany, perhaps even the fulfiller ["der Vollender"] of her destiny."‡ This argument was not exculpatory; it was an argument that other historians have come to share (this author, Haffner, and Zitelmann, for example). Fest showed no inclination to rehabilitate Hitler. Here and there, he was criticized for his considerable reliance on the memoirs

---

*Three examples: Jäckel in GWU, p. 706: "No one has written about Hitler in such good German since Thomas Mann." Karl-Dietrich Bracher in *Die Zeit*, 12 October 1973: ". . . on the one hand, a historical reconstruction and a biography, while on the other hand intensive and frequent intellectual considerations form new viewpoints . . . because of the ability of this author to [arrive at] profound as well as wide-ranging interpretations." SCHRB (1983): the best biography of Hitler.

See, however, my comment about Fest's somewhat curious introduction to the 1995 reprinting of his book in the preface (pages xi–xii). Also see the critical review by Hermann Graml, "Probleme einer Hitler-Biographie: Kritische Bemerkungen zu Joachim C. Fest," VFZ, January 1974, p. 91: "It is surely debatable whether an adequate representation and interpretation of National Socialism and of National Socialist rule can be achieved in a biography of Hitler. There are good arguments pro and con."

†Examples of Fest's judiciousness: his previously cited consideration of Rauschning; his willingness to admit that the question of Hitler's relationship to his niece Geli Raubal (who committed suicide in 1931) remains unresolved (pp. 446–67). The subsequently published multivolume Goebbels diaries revealed almost nothing that proved to be a necessary corrective to Fest's portrait of Hitler.

‡F, p. 25.

of Albert Speer,* published during Fest's writing of his book, a reliance supplemented by his many conversations with Speer. Such criticism was largely unwarranted, in my opinion, since I regard Speer, in spite of a few lapses, as a very important source on Hitler, with whom Speer was especially close, particularly during the war.†

In the 1970s, the "Hitler wave" was rolling ahead, turning up not only a mass of printed matter‡ but also documentaries and feature films. The latter included a film whose scenario was written by Fest (1977), for which—mostly because of a frequency of scenes showing Hitler's popularity in the 1930s—he was criticized by some historians. And in 1977, the first big biography of Hitler by an American, John Toland (1912–   ), appeared.** Toland was an

---

*Albert Speer, *Erinnerungen*, B, 1969 (hereafter: SP). See also Gitta Sereny, *Albert Speer: His Battle with Truth*, NY, 1995. Critical of Speer: Adelbert Reif, ed., *Albert Speer: Kontroversen um ein deutsches Phänomen*, M, 1978; and Mathias Schmidt, *Albert Speer: Das Ende Eines Mythos*, Bern, 1982; also Giesler and Breker, see chapter 8.

†There was much good writing in SP, whose psychological insights were also remarkable; they also reflected a certain independence of mind; altogether, a very human document. SP, p. 292: "Hitler may have become the object of sober studies for the historian. But for me he possesses to this day a substantiality and physical presence, as if he still existed in the flesh." About the "physical" Hitler, see also Hans Frank, *In Angesicht des Galgens*, M, 1953 (hereafter: FR), for example, p. 17: "I saw Hitler in ways in which millions of our people have not." But the qualities of FR (as well as those of its executed author) do not compare with those of SP.

‡For example, Jäckel's excellent survey: "Literaturbericht: Rückblick auf die sogenannte Hitler-Welle" ("A Look at the So-Called Hitler Wave"), GWU, 1977, pp. 695–711; also Hillgruber in *Historische Zeitschrift* (hereafter: HZ), 1978, pp. 600–21: "Tendenzen, Ergebnisse und Perspektiven der gegenwartigen Hitler-Forschung" ("Tendencies, Results and Perspectives of Contemporary Hitler Research"). A very important survey: Gregor Schöllgen, "Das Problem einer Hitler-Biographie" ("The Problem of a Hitler Biography"), in *Neue Politische Literatur* (hereafter: NPL), 1978, pp. 421–34, especially good about Toland, Fest, Irving, Binion, and Haffner. One of his valuable contributions was his observation that the German translation of Toland's *Hitler* altered and abbreviated important portions of Toland's U.S. text. (This applies to some German editions of Irving, too.)

**John Toland, *Adolf Hitler*, NY, 1977 (hereafter: TO). Other American authors of Hitler biographies included Robert Payne, *The Life and Death of Adolf Hitler*, NY, 1973, the well-read amateur historian Eugene Davidson, *The Making of Adolf Hitler*, NY, 1977, and his *The Unmaking of Adolf Hitler*, Columbia, Mo., 1996 (only *one-eighth* of which deals with the second half of Hitler's rule, the war—and wasn't the war *the* unmaking of Adolf Hitler?).

American journalist, much interested in World War II, about which he produced a number of successful popular histories. He was, rather evidently, fascinated by Hitler. The novel feature of his book was his collection and employment of materials that most historians had until then eschewed. This involved Toland's extensive travels, personal contacts, interviews, and, on occasion, his acquisition of papers from Hitler's secretaries, cooks, chauffeurs, servants, and bodyguards.* He said that he had interviewed 159 people. Such endeavors do belong within the biographer's craft, since, at least potentially, all is grist to his mill: even gossip, when illustrative and properly handled, may fit into it on occasion. At the same time Toland made no effort (and no pretension) to conform to the methods of professional historians; his archival research seems almost nonexistent; he paid little attention to the writings of other Hitler biographers; his employment of both primary and secondary sources was very selective. In many instances, too, Toland found it useful to incorporate information from the works of other historians without much referential evidence; nor did he present documentation for some of his, often surprising, statements.† In sum,

---

*In his foreword (TO, p. xii): "I conducted more than two hundred and fifty interviews with his adjutants (Puttkamer, Below, Engel, Günsche, Wünsche and Schulze); his secretaries (Traudl Junge and Gerda Christian); his chauffeur (Kempka), his pilot (Baur); his doctors (Giesing and Hasselbach); his favorite warriors (Skorzeny and Rudel); his favorite architects (Speer and Giesler); his first foreign press secretary (Hanfstaengl); his military leaders (Manstein, Milch, Dönitz, Manteuffel and Warlimont); the women he most admired (Leni Riefenstahl, Frau Professor Troost and Helen Hanfstaengl). All but a dozen of these interviews were recorded on tapes which presently are stored in the Library of Congress for safekeeping." This is an impressive—though selective—list. Earlier in this paragraph, Toland stated that he "interviewed as many as possible of those who knew Hitler intimately—both worshipers and deriders. Many agreed to talk freely and at length about the unhappy past"—but a scrutiny of this list will show few "deriders"; rather, men and women whose memory of the Hitler years was not at all that of an "unhappy past."

†Examples: "Fear that his father may have been partly Jewish"—possible; but then, "which could be a substantial part of why he wanted no children"—an insubstantial speculation—p. 232. In the trenches during World War I: "He made a portentous prophecy to his comrades: 'You will hear much about me. Just wait until my time comes,'" p. 64—there is no evidence for this. "His analysis of crowd psychology indicated he had read Freud's *Group Psychology and the Analysis of the Ego*

the portrait of Hitler that emerged from Toland's composition was a curiously (and perhaps worrisomely) inconsistent one. On the one hand, Toland, in his breezy and metallic-staccato style (with a Broadway tinge), made his summary statements condemning Hitler, paying verbal obeisance to the customary clichés; on the other hand, indications of his admiration for Hitler were detectable throughout the book—unnoticed by most of his reviewers but largely in accord with Toland's general view of World War II.* (I shall return to some of these in chapter 8: "Admirers and Defenders, Open and Hidden.")

During the 1970s, three American academics (two of them historians) published psychoanalytic biographical works about Hitler. Their books were different and had been written independently of each other; what they had in common was their acceptance—indeed, their exemplification—of a prevalent intellectual and academic fashion of their time. This was the fad (I am loath to give it another name) of psychohistory, meaning not merely the application of psychology to historical figures (something that every serious historian or biographer has done ever since Polybius or Plutarch) but of psychoanalytic "technique," predominantly Freudian, to their subject. This is not the place to argue against, or even to sum up, the essential and, yes, shortsighted faults of Freudianism, save to say that if their application to the diagnosis and the therapy

---

published a few years earlier in Germany" (pp. 220–21)—no evidence whatsoever. Add to this Toland's assertions about Hitler's womanizing; repeated statements about the influence of the astrologer Hanussen; and his reference to Hitler's "uncontrollable flatulence," p. 275—as early as 1932, *before* Hitler's stomach troubles began.

There were, however, a few small nuggets of interest: Toland may have been the first to note a Hitler habit of some small significance: the—somewhat vulgar—habit of slapping his thigh in moments of satisfaction (pp. 85, 251; also noted by Irving). The significance of that connects with Toland's research: He was among the first to record that the famous film sequence (reproduced hundreds of times even in history textbooks) showing Hitler jumping up and down in a jiglike dance upon receiving the news of the French surrender in June 1940 was faked by a Canadian filmmaker by speeding up the film. What had happened was another thigh-slapping.

*Example: Toland, *Infamy*, NY, 1981—attributing Pearl Harbor to the conspiratorial machinations of Franklin Roosevelt.

of living human beings is often questionable, this must be even more so when it comes to the application of psychoanalysis to the dead. I cannot avoid at least a passing observation about the intellectual climate of the 1960s, when there arose a swelling of neo-Marxist and neo-Freudian interpretations across the academic landscape. In the American historical profession, this swelling rose after December 1958, when the respected senior diplomatic historian William L. Langer of Harvard entitled his presidential address to the American Historical Association "The Next Assignment," exhorting his fellow historians to follow "the speculative audacity of the natural scientists" and proceed "to the urgently needed deepening of our historical understanding through expositions of the concepts" of modern Freudian psychoanalysis. And while it is not legitimate for historians, including myself, to attribute motives to their colleagues, a proper indication of their purposes is valid. Whether they had been inspired by William Langer or not, whether they had been influenced by the intellectual climate of the 1960s or not, the purposes of Walter Langer (William's brother), R. L. Waite, and Rudolph Binion* were evident—indeed, asserted by themselves: the application of psychoanalysis to Hitler. Of these three books, Langer's was the least, and Binion's the most, worthy of attention. The first was a rehash of a psychological projection of Hitler that Langer had constructed in 1943 in behalf of the OSS (much of his material culled from an interview with the then interned Stephanie Hohenlohe in Texas). The second amounted to an assertion of Hitler as a psychopath ("a borderline personality"). In the third, Binion, a very learned scholar in the intellectual history of modern Europe, made a substantial study of Hitler; but his thesis, according to which Hitler's hatred for Jews was, among other things, the result of his suppressed but searing memory of Dr. Eduard Bloch, the Jewish physician in Linz who had inflicted a painful treatment on Hitler's mother in the last months of her life, was not

---

*Walter C. Langer, *The Mind of Adolf Hitler: The Secret Wartime Report*, NY, 1972; Robert C. L. Waite, *The Psychopathic God: Adolf Hitler*, NY, 1977; Rudolph Binion, *Hitler and the Germans*, NY, 1976.

convincing—and Binion's subsequent hypothesis was even less so.*

Then, in 1977, there appeared the first commercially successful and substantial partial rehabilitation of Hitler, by the English journalist David Irving (1938–   ). That a historian's life cannot be separated from the history he writes has been especially evident in Irving's case. Early in his youth, he evinced an acute interest in Germany; he spent a year as a factory worker there to perfect his knowledge of German. Since then, his interest and his ambitions have been largely devoted to World War II, and especially to the Third Reich and Hitler. At the age of twenty-one, he began writing articles in German periodicals; in 1963, he published his first, and generally unexceptionable, work, *The Destruction of Dresden*. There followed many books, of which the foremost was *Hitler's War*, published in 1977,† which revealed for the first time (that is, to careful readers) his admiration of Hitler: a gradual progression from partial exoneration, through rehabilitation, to the virtual elevation of Hitler to a level of historical and moral greatness. This evolution of Irving's histories reflected a corresponding evolution in his personal history: through many public quarrels and court cases involving libel (and his successive appearances as speaker at neo-Nazi rallies in Germany), this erstwhile amateur revisionist has revealed himself to be an unrepentant admirer of Hitler.

Other recalcitrant, apologetic, and—at least implicitly—admiring books about Hitler already existed, of course, but their range, circulation, and effects had been small enough to omit them from this admittedly incomplete survey of Hitler historiography (though I

---

*That is: that Hitler suppressed or transmuted this personal trauma of his (and later substituted Germany as his mother-symbol), even as Dr. Bloch was one of the very few Jews whom Hitler praised (and whom he treated with consideration) later in his life. See pages 195–196. Allow me to contrast this with a—in my opinion, proper and penetrating—use of psychological statements by Heer, HR, p. 344, about some of Hitler's expressions: "Some of Hitler's own words we may consider as expressions that were not only the results of deliberate speaking but that in moments of fatigue or high stress break out, carrying his wishes, hopes, anxieties as they surge up to the surface of his consciousness." (About "the primacy of the conscious mind," see HC, 1994 ed., pp. 344ff.)

†Hereafter: 1/H. This was quickly followed by *The War Path: Hitler's Germany 1933–1939* (1978); hereafter: 1/W.

shall have to refer to some of them occasionally in later chapters, especially in chapter 8). But—perhaps unfortunately—Irving's contributions to the study of Hitler cannot be ignored, and not only because of the—again, regrettably—widespread readership of his books.* Irving, much more than Toland, was able to gather a daunting quantity of papers and to meet many survivors of the Third Reich's hierarchy, especially men and women of Hitler's close circle,† particularly those who were sympathetic to Irving's views. Probably the most significant of his documentary collections were the diaries of Walter Hewel, Ribbentrop's confidant at Hitler's headquarters during the war (Hewel, an early partisan of Hitler, followed Hitler by killing himself at the end), along with the scattered pages of a secret Göring-established German intelligence organization collecting information from foreign sources, the so-called Forschungsamt. "These are used here for the first time," Irving wrote. But where did he get them? "Tragically, the entire Forschungsamt archives were destroyed in 1945."‡ In the 1970s, Irving deposited these papers in the archives of the Institut für Zeitgeschichte (whose archivists soon found it necessary to distance themselves from him). Again, like Toland, Irving paid almost no attention to the works of professional historians, dismissing and

---

*At least two of his books, including his biography of Rommel, were on bestseller lists in Germany; they were advertised on posters affixed to kiosks in the streets; in Dresden in 1990, he was hailed as "the master historian of the Third Reich"; and so on. Oddly—or perhaps not so oddly—the New York publisher (Viking) of I/H found it proper to print on the cover: "By no means exculpated, but assuredly de-demonized, David Irving's Hitler will stand athwart the annals of Nazi Germany and World War II from this time forward." In 1996 (!), the celebrated military historian John Keegan: "Certainly among the half-dozen most important books on 1939–45." A questionable assertion.

†In his foreword to I/H, Irving emphasized his ability to gather important and previously unknown materials from the diaries and papers of Hitler's employees (secretaries, adjutants, servants) who, Irving insisted, were without exception forthcoming and extraordinarily willing to assist him. However, Jost Dülffer in GWU, 1979, p. 11: "One can draw no appropriate picture of Hitler from the perspective of his domestic personnel. What kind of importance has a questioning of Hitler's valet or of other [such persons]?"

‡I/H, pp. xv, 25. Like almost all of Irving's references, they must be considered with caution.

deriding them often—in his case, not merely because of his self-satisfaction with his own research but also because of his pride in his own achievement as an amateur.* He attacked professional historians not only for being unduly narrow in their methods but also for being compromised by their politic calculations—that is, for their unwillingness to give any credit to Hitler where credit was due. But then—apart from moral questions of judgment—questions should have been raised (and, alas, they were seldom so raised)† about the very methods of this tirelessly ambitious amateur historian. Like so many amateurs (as well as professionals on occasion), Irving proceeded from what the great Spanish historian Altamira once stated as "the idolatry of the document"—meaning that a single document, or fragment of a document, was enough for Irving to build a very questionable thesis on its contents or on the lack of such. Worse than this were many of the archival references in Irving's footnotes (unlike Toland, the indefatigable Irving had pored through reels of microfilms in a variety of archives), many of which were inaccurate and did *not* prove or even refer to the pertinent statements in Irving's text. Thus, Irving, who often accused other people (including Churchill) of "falsifications" of documents, indulged in his own manipulations, attributing at least false meanings to some documents or, in other instances, printing references to irrelevant ones.‡ Finally, even in this necessarily sketchy summation of his work, mention must be made of the condition that Irving's

---

*1/w, p. ix: "As in the writing of *Hitler's War*, I have avoided as far as possible the use of all published literature in favour of the available primary sources of the day." 1/H, p. xxii: "As for autobiographical works, I preferred to rely on the original manuscripts rather than the published texts, as in the early postwar years apprehensive publishers (especially the 'licensed' ones in Germany) made changes in them," etc. A serious charge, though not always implausible.

†It is at least remarkable that certain professional historians—for example, Hillgruber, Zitelmann, and the British John Charmley (Charmley: Irving "has been unjustly ignored")—not only found it useful to cite some of Irving's materials but also paid at least half-respectful reference to him in their footnotes, thus treating him with more consideration then they treated others among their fellow historians with whom they quarreled or disagreed.

‡See pages 230–232. One example: Irving's consistent, repeated—and doctored—"evidence" that Russia was ready to attack Germany in June 1941.

ideological commitment was not devoid of considerable hypocrisy, since his admiration for Hitler was frequently disguised by his persistent efforts to blacken all of Hitler's opponents, both foreign and German.*

But then history, including the history of history, is never of a piece. A few months after Irving's blockbuster, one of the finest studies of Hitler appeared, by Sebastian Haffner (1907–).† Haffner, a liberal-conservative (these adjectives are used in the best sense of their original meanings) journalist, publicist, and amateur historian, was a man of great honesty. He emigrated from Germany in 1938, then worked as a serious journalist in London, writing mostly about Germany and Europe. He returned to Berlin with his wife around 1960 and achieved, in his mature age, a reputation of almost-universal respect among German readers for his probity and judgment. The reserved modesty of his study of Hitler accorded with the character of its writer. Haffner—not because of insufficient study and certainly not because of any want of energy—did not aspire to the authorship of a full biography of Hitler. Instead, in this very well written book—essentially a long historical essay—he wished to draw attention to certain often-unemphasized or even unnoticed features of what may be called Hitler's place in history. The great strength of this work is Haffner's excellent description— and his brief but cogent analysis—of Hitler's indubitable political

---

*See my *The Duel*, NY, 1991 (hereafter: DL), p. 244: ". . . any serious historian dealing with [Irving's] subjects must not refrain from looking at . . . the small nuggets of materials that Irving may have unearthed; but two serious caveats are in order here. One is that Irving's extensive gathering of documents must be treated with special caution; I have found archival numbers in some of his notes erroneous or even nonexistent; in sum, references to his sources must be carefully verified. The more important caveat involves the purposes of Irving's writing. He is an admirer of Hitler's; yet, with all of his drive to be a daringly unconventional historical writer, he does not quite have the courage of his convictions. His method of rehabilitating Hitler is by denigrating Hitler's opponents—in this case, the blackening of Churchill in every possible way."

†*Anmerkungen zu Hitler*, B, 1978 (hereafter: HF/AN); U.S. ed. *The Meaning of Hitler*, NY, 1979 (unfortunately, this book attracted little notice, not even a review in the *New York Times Book Review*); also *Von Bismarck zu Hitler*, B, 1987; U.S. ed.: *The Ailing Empire: Germany from Bismarck to Hitler*, NY, 1991 (hereafter: HF/AI).

talents;* but also his summary description (and implicit analysis) of the political and cultural condition of Germany in the 1930s—a description of the national climate, with great insight and yet without undue philosophizing—that was perhaps unique. By and large, Haffner's view accorded with Deuerlein's and Fest's, asserting the undoubtable unity of Hitler and the German people in the 1930s (if "unity"—my word—is too strong, the word "popularity" may be too weak). My only questions relate to Haffner's bafflement at Hitler's declaration of war on the United States in December 1941, which, in my opinion, Haffner wrongly interpreted as wholly irrational and avoidable; and—perhaps—to Haffner's assertions about Hitler's rejection of the German people at the end of the war.†

In the five years that followed the publication of Haffner's work (1978–1983), there was no relaxation of the scholarly (or of the popular) interest in Hitler. Some of the most valuable monographic studies about the Third Reich, articles about both the Third Reich and Hitler, and papers presented at conferences addressed to Hitler studies were published during these years, but in this brief survey of the evolution of Hitler historiography, I must forgo a listing, let alone a description, of them. Still, it must be noted that it was around 1980 that the first new generation of scholars—meaning men and women born after 1945, for whom the Hitler period had no personal memories—began to appear on the academic scene and in the pages of respectable journals. At the same time a debate (a debate, rather than a controversy) between so-called Functionalists and Intentionalists developed. The functionalists, first among whom

---

*HF/AI, p. 171: "Hitler was underestimated. The biggest mistake his enemies made was to treat him with disdain, to ridicule him. Hitler was a truly evil man, not an insignificant, ridiculous one. Great men are often evil. And Hitler, despite all of his horrifying attributes [I would say: not despite, but with] was a great man, as he demonstrated over and over again by the boldness of his vision and the cunning of his instincts. Hitler had a magic touch, and none of his adversaries could compete with him." On the problem of "greatness," see chapter 9.

†For a discussion of these questions, see chapters 5 and 7. In HF/AN, pp. 20–21, Haffner wrote of Hitler's inclination toward suicide; this is debatable. On p. 4, Haffner accepted the notion that Hitler had fathered an illegitimate son in France in 1917; however, his statement that "The experience of fatherhood is lacking in Hitler's life" was correct.

was Hans Mommsen, grandson of the great classical historian, were attempting to prove that Hitler's decisions (especially during the war) were often hesitating, and that, largely because of the increasingly complicated and even byzantine conditions within the Nazi hierarchy, Hitler may have been, at least often, a "weak" dictator.* The intentionalists were those who argued that, to the contrary, Hitler's intentions and decisions were the evident applications of his ideological convictions.† Jäckel's argument is also worth considering: that the Third Reich was both a monocracy and a polycracy. The importance of this debate should not, I think, be overrated (even as echoes of it remain). In some (though not in every) sense, the functionalist-intentionalist debate‡ was but a continuation of the previously mentioned and diverse interpretations of Hitler the Opportunist versus Hitler the Ideologue. This does not mean that the debate was nugatory, as indeed the aforementioned Broszat exhortation (1985) to proceed, finally, from the demonization to the historicization of Hitler and of the Third Reich was not.

During these years, two important contributions to Hitler studies were made by young English historians. William Carr's (1921–1991)

---

*But already Speer had stated in SP, p. 349: "Unfortunately the Fuehrer was all too frequently not a man of firm decisions" ("festen Entschlüssen"). Mommsen: Had there not been advantageous political conditions, Hitler's political career would have ended in 1923. See also his earlier argument in Michael Bosch, ed., *Persönlichkeit und Struktur in der Geschichte: Historische Bestandsaufnahme in didaktische Interpretationen*, D, 1977. In different ways, similar arguments were made by Maser, *Adolf Hitler: Das Ende der Führer-legende*, M, 1982; and Zitelmann, *Adolf Hitler: Selbstverständnis eines Revolutionärs*, S, 1991 (hereafter: ZIT/A), p. 253: Hitler was "not omnipotent; he was not a Führer of decisive [strong] decisions" (der entscheidungsstarke Führer). The term "functionalist" may have been first employed by the British historian Tim Mason in 1981.

†Very well put by Albrecht Tyrell (the best student of the early Nazi period) in *1933*, p. 99: yes, the National Socialists were a mass movement with its own dynamics, but Hitler was the central figure in every stage of the development of the Nazi party from 1921 to 1945 ". . . both within the party and after 1933 also in matters of state [he] exercised the power of decision in all questions."

‡Perhaps by coincidence, the debate took place around the same time as the Structuralist-Deconstructionist "debate" in literary theory. But the latter was an ungainly application of vocabulary, often at the expense of thought (in reality, it concerned the older, respectable questions of hermeneutics and epistemology), which the functionalist-intentionalist debate was not.

*Hitler: A Study of Personality and Politics** was in some ways exemplary. Carr achieved a remarkable synthesis in dealing with Hitler's personality together with his career, and in describing and collating significant observations on the relationship of the private and the public Hitler, of his political practices and his personal inclinations. Ian Kershaw (1943–   ), who began his scholarly career as a medievalist historian, devoted his principal interest to the study of Hitler's influence on the German people—a complex and inexhaustible subject. Kershaw's first book was published in Germany even before it came out in England. He relied on the still-accumulating materials recording evidence of German public opinion and popular sentiment during the Third Reich. His biography of Hitler followed:† a short and succinct volume that will be succeeded by a large biography, scheduled for publication in 1998.

Ten years earlier, in 1986, a controversy erupted among German historians and intellectuals—a controversy whose reverberations, suggesting rather profound divisions about the assessment of the Third Reich (and at least indirectly of Hitler), have still not disappeared. I write "controversy," not "debate" (the latter term is used by British and American accounts of it).‡ The German word was "Historikerstreit," meaning "The Historians' Quarrel": a proper term, except for its suggestion of a quarrel among specialist scholars. Yet a tempest in a teapot, even *pace* Jane Austen ("If you live in a teapot, a tempest may be a very uncomfortable thing"), the Historikerstreit was not. Its bitterness was such that it did not contribute to the furthering of historical understanding—in many ways it was a dialogue, or even a diatribe, among the deaf. Again, I cannot avoid suggesting at least a minimal reference to the larger scene of its

---

*L, 1978 (hereafter: c). U.S. ed.: *Face of a Dictator*, NY, 1979.

†Ian Kershaw (KER) began modestly and properly: "This is not a biography of Hitler." Critical of the "demonization" of Hitler, Kershaw leaned toward the functionalist side, p. 6: ". . . even the best biographies have seemed at times in danger of elevating Hitler's personal power to a level where the history of Germany between 1933 and 1945 becomes reduced to little more than an expression of the dictator's will."

‡The best German anthology of the "Historikerstreit" is the Piper edition, M, 1987 (hereafter: HS).

time. As in many other places of the Western world (Reagan's America, Thatcher's Britain), the West Germany of Chancellor Kohl was marked by a powerful neoconservative tendency—in many ways an expectable reaction to many of the leftist and radical tendencies of the late 1960s. I write "neoconservative" because of significant differences between the more traditional and the newer versions of conservatism, in Germany as well as elsewhere; but this is not the place to discuss these further, except perhaps to note that many of the neoconservative historians who took part in the Historians' Quarrel belonged to a younger, postwar German generation. They were impatient and irritated with what seemed to be a leftist consensus largely governing intellectual life and the commerce of ideas in Germany, and the rapid burgeoning of the Historians' Controversy reflected this.*

The controversy erupted because of two different publications about the Third Reich, by Ernst Nolte and Andreas Hillgruber. Nolte (1922–), who was the older of the two, had established his academic standing in 1964 with a large study, *Three Faces of Fascism*, a book whose research material was voluminous but whose main thesis was debatable for two reasons.† One was Nolte's application of the term "Fascism" to German National Socialism (the impropriety and the inaccuracy of which are discussed in chapter 4); the other was the consequent lumping together of the histories of the French Action Française, Mussolini's Italian Fascism, and German National Socialism under the same title, when in reality the Action Française was a pre-Fascist, whereas the Third Reich (especially the SS state) was a post-Fascist, phenomenon. At that time, Nolte showed no indication of his later ideological inclinations. Though he was involved in politics, he published relatively little in the 1970s. But by the early 1980s he had begun to work on another large volume,

---

*For further discussion, see pp. 232–236 in chapter 8. As far as historiography went, some (though only some) roots of this controversy may be traced back to the debate occasioned by Fritz Fischer's *Griff nach der Weltmacht* ("The Attempt at World Power," 1961), where this young German historian presented evidence of the German government's aggressive designs before and during World War I in an eloquently argued book.

†See my review in *The Catholic Historical Review*, October 1968.

Der europäische Bürgerkrieg, 1917–1945 (The European Civil War, 1917–1945), the thesis of which he summarized in a public lecture in early 1986; this was then published by Fest in FAZ in June. Nolte's main thesis—obstinately held and further developed since—was that German Nazism must be understood as a reaction to Russian Bolshevism; that the horrors of the Soviet camp system (the Gulag) both preceded and led to those of Auschwitz; and—a minor but particularly sensitive point—that Hitler's declaration of war against the Jews was, if not unconnected with, at least paralleled by, a declaration of Chaim Weizmann, who in an open letter in September 1939 offered the support of the World Jewish Congress to the British government in the war against Germany. In any event, Nolte's article and his subsequent book suggested at least a partial exoneration—though surely not a rehabilitation—of Hitler. At the same time as the publication of Nolte's article there appeared a book by Andreas Hillgruber (a small volume by a historian not noted for the brevity of his prose) that amounted to a rehabilitation of some of the efforts of the German armed forces, including some National Socialist officials of the Third Reich, though not of Hitler. In *Zweierlei Untergang. Die Zerschlagung des Dritten Reiches und das Ende des europäischen Judentums* (The Destruction* of the Third Reich and the End of European Jewry), for the first time a reputable German historian (indeed, the more or less accepted leader of German specialists of the history of the Second World War) declared that the time had come to appreciate the desperate struggle of many Germans (including even SS and National Socialist functionaries) against the frightful onslaught of the Soviet Russian armies in 1944–45. The much smaller second part of the volume consisted of Hillgruber's fair summary of the Holocaust.†

---

*"Zerschlagung" suggests not only destruction but a deliberate smashing—in line with Hillgruber's often expressed condemnation of British policy regarding Germany during World War II.

†It must be said in Hillgruber's favor that this historian, who in his earlier works paid little or no attention to the history of Jews during the Third Reich, devoted more attention to that topic in the later stages of his career; also, that Hillgruber, who in the 1950s showed some inclination to suggest that Hitler's invasion of Russia in 1941 may have been, at least to some extent, a preventive response to some of Stalin's moves, at the end of his career rejected the argument in then-multiplying (and generally shoddy) works to the effect that the Soviet Union had made ready to attack Germany in 1941.

Immediately after these publications, the German social philosopher Jürgen Habermas attacked Nolte and Hillgruber in *Die Zeit*. The stylistic quality of Habermas's arguments was considerable, but his sharpness of tone led to the eruption of a polemic in which many German historians now took part. Significant, too, was the sudden public appearance of defenders of Nolte and Hillgruber—including Fest—and of younger, reputable German historians such as Michael Stürmer (an adviser to Chancellor Kohl) and the somewhat less effective Klaus Hildebrand. Against them were arrayed a few older German historians (Christian Müller), but also Eberhard Jäckel and Hans-Ulrich Wehler (whose argumentation I found cogent, even though markedly partisan).*

In their partial defense it must be noted that in the early 1970s both Nolte and Hillgruber were victims of unreasonable attacks from the Left. At least one of Hillgruber's lectures was interrupted violently by some students, while Nolte's courses were rudely boycotted for a while. (The documentary film that Fest produced in 1977 also received sharp and sometimes improper criticism.) However, what the entire "Historikerstreit" revealed was the growing presence of a deep ideological and political division among historians in their perspectives on the Third Reich, or at least on some of its aspects—a division that has threatened the acceptance of a general consensus for which many respected German historians and intellectuals had been aiming for at least forty years.† This division

---

*In Hans-Ulrich Wehler, *Entsorgung der deutschen Vergangenheit? Ein polemischer Essay zum "Historikerstreit,"* M, 1988 (hereafter: H S/W). (Exoneration of the German past? A polemical essay about the 'Historikerstreit.') Two valuable summary arguments: "This survey is directed—among other matters—against the apologetic effect of the tendency of interpretations that once more blame Hitler alone for the 'Holocaust'— thereby exonerating the older power elites and the army, the executive bureaucracy and the justiciary . . . and the silent majority of those who knew." "The 'Historikerstreit' is, in sum, more than a strictly scholarly controversy within scholarly limits."

†See chapter 8, pp. 230–236, and, especially, 238–239. Also SCHRB, p. 332: ". . . the opposing fronts have become rigid. In the opposing camps of historians there is no concrete sign for the possibility of a movement away from confrontation, toward cooperation." Fest in HS, p. 112: "Hitler and National Socialism remain still, despite years of consideration, more myth than history; and their public discussions still aim to adjure rather than to understand." Hillgruber, cited in HS/W, p. 162, wrote of the superseded "cliché-like picture" of the Third Reich.

survived the sudden unification of Germany in 1989. (Incidentally, that was something that none of the historians of the *Historikerstreit* had foreseen; indeed, they had deemed it to be impossible in any foreseeable future.)

What remained constant was the tendency to separate the history of the Third Reich (and, indirectly, the German people) from Hitler. Then, in 1987, there appeared an important study of Hitler by Rainer Zitelmann (1957–   ):* a significant contribution to and at least a partial revision of the portrait of Hitler after many years. As early as 1982, at the age of twenty-four, this brilliant young historian had already published a most competent bibliographical essay about Hitler studies: *Hitlers Erfolg: Erklärungsversuche in der Hitler-Forschung* (Hitler's Success: Explanatory Attempts in Hitler Research),† the very title of which suggested the thrust of Zitelmann's forthcoming works: Why—and how—was Hitler successful? In ZIT/A, Zitelmann made at least two, if not three, undeniable contributions.‡ First, that Hitler was truly a revolutionary, and that, consequently, his aspirations and visions were *modern* (no matter how deeply rooted in some traditional German attitudes); and so were his ideas and plans about the remaking of German society (an argument seldom proposed cogently before Zitelmann, except by the American historian David Schoenbaum). This also meant that, contrary to accepted opinion, Hitler was neither ignorant of nor indifferent to economics. All of this was illustrated and buttressed by Zitelmann's extensive reading of papers and other documents, many of them of the 1928–32 period, during which—again contrary to generally accepted views—Hitler not only spoke but wrote and dictated much. Perhaps the only shortcoming of ZIT/A was the brevity of the space that Zitelmann devoted to Hitler's statesmanship. There again, he emphasized Hitler's revolutionary character, but

---

*ZIT/A, unfortunately, was not translated and published in Britain or the United States.

†In NPL (1982), pp. 47–69, citing, among others, Jäckel: "the confusing multiplicity of serious explanations." Zitelmann: "One could easily fill a book with their list."

‡An excellent and praiseworthy summary of Zitelmann's theses was made by Jost Dülffer in FAZ, 7 July 1987.

perhaps without sufficiently recognizing Hitler's conscious duality (his different and sometimes entirely contradictory views and expressions concerning foreign statesmen and political forces).

Two years after the publication of ZIT/A, this young historian published a no less remarkable shorter book about Hitler.* No less remarkable for our purposes, because while ZIT/A was principally an analytical study of Hitler's ideas, ZIT/B was a biography. In his preface, Zitelmann posed the question: Why yet another biography, when Bullock, Fest, and Toland exist? "Some of these biographies," he wrote, "were excellent for their time, but today they must be seen as superseded in many ways."† In his research, Zitelmann depended much on the finally completed edition of the Goebbels diaries as well as on a few until then largely unexplored sources, including a new series of notes of Hitler's wartime table conversations. But the significance of Zitelmann's Hitler biography lay not so much in its author's research as in his determined convictions. Here is his own summation of his achievement: "The picture drawn here of Hitler differs from [others] very substantially. He appears here as a politician, whose thinking and actions were essentially much more rational than hitherto accepted." Also: ". . . in some fields research about National Socialism is still in its beginnings. . . . In the end the picture of Hitler appears as essentially more complex, differentiated, and uncertain." A strong, perhaps exaggerated, statement by a young historian, but not without substance. "Soberness is also needed in the language. That is far from the truth in all of the biographies of Hitler [including Fest's]."‡

---

*Rainer Zitelmann, *Adolf Hitler: Eine politische Biographie*, Göttingen, 1989 (hereafter: ZIT/B).

†ZIT/B, p. 7. Also p. 8: "Biographies such as Joachim Fest's, whose study was undoubtedly a milestone in the understanding of a dictator, have used questionable or falsified sources *uncritically*."

‡ZIT/B, pp. 9–11. His repeated and nervous exhortation for "soberness": "Perhaps 15 years ago, when Fest's pioneering work was published, it was not yet possible to write a Hitler biography differently." (Why not?) At the conclusion of his preface, Zitelmann voices a renewed insistence on "soberness of language" in order "to understand, rather than to evaluate." (Fair enough; but can "understanding" be separated from "evaluation"? Allow me to repeat: The choice of every word is not only a technical or stylistic but a moral choice.)

Such a sober, well-written, and concise work was achieved by Wolfgang Wippermann, *Der konsequente Wahn: Ideologie und Politik Adolf Hitlers*, D, 1989, p. 9: "The present book," Wippermann modestly stated, "does deal with Hitler's life and his ideology, and also with the history of National Socialism; but it is neither a biography of Hitler nor a summary presentation of the history of National Socialism. Its purpose is to stimulate a confrontation with [Hitler] and with a time that only seems to be past and gone" [die nur scheinbar Vergangenheit ist].*

We are now nearing the end of this survey. In 1991, there appeared a commendable, and largely faultless, Hitler biography (the first substantial one in French) by Marlis Steinert (1922–   ), a lady of German origin and a professor (now emerita) at the Institute of Higher International Studies in Geneva.† Besides her unexceptionable scholarship, Mme. Steinert's important contribution was her implicit argument against the two-war theory, contrary to Hillgruber and others (whom she did not openly debate): Hitler's war before 1941 was no "traditional European war"; consider the orders given for the treatment of Poles, and, of course, Jews, already in September 1939.‡ The only shortcoming (and it is a debatable one) may have been Mme. Steinert's liberal employment of the term

---

*Also, p. 9: "This book is not a contribution to the 'Historikerstreit.' It is not an argument for a biographical or for an institutionalist approach."

†Marlis Steinert, *Hitler*, P, 1991 (hereafter: ST). Twenty years earlier, Professor Steinert published a significant scholarly study of the important and complex problem of the mentality of the German people during World War II: *Hitlers Krieg und die Deutschen: Stimmung und Haltung der Deutschen Bevölkerung im II. Weltkrieg*, D, 1970 (hereafter: ST/HKD).

‡I cannot refrain from mentioning Mme. Steinert's perceptive remark about Hitler's physiognomy as "vulpine" (to my knowledge, not thus seen or expressed by other biographers)—a perspicacious observation, not to speak of the fact that Hitler himself liked it when his friends referred to him as "Wolf." (When the British occupation authorities in 1948 permitted the reopening of the Volkswagen works in their zone, in the town of Wolfsburg, they did not know that the town had been given this name in 1938–39 in honor of Hitler, promoter of the "People's Car.")

"megalomania,"* not altogether untrue when applied to Hitler but perhaps not true enough.

And now, before concluding, I feel compelled to direct some attention to the persistence of a regrettable source of acrimony among German historians—including Zitelmann, who has found it necessary to range himself more and more on the rightist (or neo-conservative, or, perhaps more precisely, neonationalist) side,† ascribing all kinds of dishonesties to its opponents. Among the latter, he included not only the "1968" generation (the year of leftist university riots) but men and women who have insisted on a German consensus, on an acceptance of the responsibility of Germans for the war and for its atrocities. (Zitelmann attacked Richard von Weizsäcker, the much-respected former president of the West German Republic, and Golo Mann, as well as Max Domarus, the commendable collector and compiler of Hitler's public statements.) In Zitelmann's frequently repeated arguments for the historicization of Hitler—which remains a proper endeavor—there exist latent elements of at least a partial rehabilitation.‡

ALLOW ME TO REMIND my readers again that my treatment (and list) of Hitler biographies is not— and cannot be—complete. It does not include valuable works dealing with some particular portion or chapter of Hitler's life—for instance, with the crucial event of his 1923 putsch attempt in Munich.** Among other limitations, this

---

*ST, p. 336: "1936 seems the year when Hitler begins to fall into megalomania." Questionable. Also p. 391: Did Hitler want to be "greater" than Frederick or Bismarck or Napoleon? Arguable.

†This had already been suggested by Zitelmann two years after the original publication of ZIT/A, when its new edition carried his new preface, "Research After the Historikerstreit," written in October 1988, much of it a sharp polemical attack against Nolte's and Hillgruber's critics.

‡For further discussion of this, see chapter 8.

**Two exemplary American works: Harold J. Gordon, Jr., *Hitler and the Beer Hall Putsch*, Princeton, 1972; also Bradley F. Smith, *Adolf Hitler: His Family, Childhood and Youth*, Stanford, 1967, in addition to the already mentioned Albrecht Tyrell, *Vom Trommler zum Führer*, M, 1975; and D, mentioned on p. 19.

chapter includes few articles (later chapters will, when needed), even though many significant additions, interpretations, and revisions of our knowledge of Hitler's life and career may be found in some of them. But now I must essay some generalizations. One applies to the national level. During the last fifty years many Germans did not want to think much about Hitler. But many of their historians did. It was in Germany that historians and other writers have made strenuous, earnest, and honest efforts to come to terms with this chapter of their national history—and that is to their credit. Such attempts among Germany's wartime allies have been few—not many in Italy and even fewer in Japan.

Almost all of the principal, and serious, biographies of Hitler have been written by German, British, and American historians. Nothing comparable has been attempted in other languages—curiously enough, not even in France, even though signs of acute interest in Germany and World War II have existed in France for many years now. (One exception is the work of the Finnish historian Vappu Tallgren.) The contributions of Russian and Eastern European writers have been either nonexistent or nugatory. (This includes—perhaps especially—writers in Slovakia, Croatia, and Romania: wartime allies of Hitler.) The contributions of East German historians during the forty years' existence of the German Democractic Republic were, with very few exceptions, useless. But the same is largely true of Marxist interpretations of Hitler written by intellectuals and academics in the Western world. There are many reasons for this, foremost being the myopic and cramped categories of the Marxist view of the world, and of human nature; but then, the life and career of Hitler, as well as much of the history of the Third Reich, are living refutations of the economic interpretation of history—indeed, of the whole notion of Economic Man.

This brings me to a brief discussion of the question of the relationship of history and biography. History is, of course, more than biography, since its topics involve not one person but many; yet it is not as simple as that. It is "the essence of innumerable biographies," as Carlyle once put it; but that striking phrase, as so often with Carlyle, is imprecise: not innumerable biographies but innumerable lives. It was in the nineteenth century, too, that the

English historian John Seeley wrote: "History is past politics, and politics present history"—a phrase that, surely without knowing of Seeley, Hitler repeated when once (in 1936, I think) he said, "Politik ist werdende Geschichte" (politics is history in the making). But during the twentieth century many historians recognized that history, after all, must go beyond politics; that it cannot be restricted to political history and that it must deal with great numbers of people. Thereby social history became an accepted, and lately even dominant, theme and topic of their works. At one (and unfortunately frequent) extreme, this led to a degeneration of history research and history writing into a kind of retrospective sociology—while, on the other hand, it produced some excellent works of historical socio*graphy*.* Because of the acceptance of the social-scientific idea, some people (for example, the superb biographer Harold Nicolson) once feared that the traditions of biography would wither away; but this has not happened. Indeed—perhaps as an instinctive reaction on the part of readers thirsting for representations of reality, for a narrative description of real people and their real lives—biography and history have grown closer together, beyond their unavoidable overlapping. And the widely accepted idea (propagated not only by Marxist historians), according to which history was—and continues to be—made not by individual persons but by great underlying social conditions and economic forces, has been obviously disproved and is especially inapplicable to Hitler—indeed, to the entire history of the Second World War. That that war would not have come in 1939 except for Hitler, and that the course of that entire war would have been entirely different but for Churchill, Stalin, and Roosevelt, needs no further explanation.

That not every historian is a biographer, and not every biographer a historian, is obvious; but so is the condition that every serious historian must have biographical interests and talents, while every serious biographer must know a great deal of history (and not only

---

*-*Ology* is a science, producing and dependent on *definitions*, while the purpose of -*graphy* is reconstructive *description*.

the history of his subject or even of its times).* To these obvious
desiderata we must add one advantage that *some* (most certainly
not all) nonprofessional historical biographers *may* have over such
professionals whose work and whose lives are restricted within academic circles: The former may know more of the world, including
a great variety of people. That *may* enable them to have certain
insights into their biographical subjects that, again, *some* (but of
course not all) professional historians lack.† It is thus that the psychic portrait of Hitler was better drawn by Schramm or Deuerlein
or Fest or Haffner than by, say, Bullock or Maser or Hillgruber (not
to speak of Toland or Irving). But enough of these lucubrations:
suffice it to say that the biographical problem of Hitler *is* a historical one—and also the reverse.

OR, RATHER: PROBLEMS. Contrary to popular belief, the historian's
work involves the descriptive analysis of problems as much as of
periods. This surely includes Hitler. We have now seen that there
are significant variations in the way he is interpreted by different
historians. And when problems are wrongly (or inadequately) stated,
the results of the analysis are affected, just as an inadequate diagnosis affects the results of the consequent therapy. But before I
revert to historians and their—our—problems, I must devote a few
lines to a grave misunderstanding that has affected historians less
than it has people at large. This is the popular view that Hitler was
mad. By asserting—and thinking—that he was mad, we have failed
twice. We have brushed the problem of Hitler under the rug. If he

---

*A discussion of this can be found in SCHRB, p. 306: Among other things, "the
biographer must attempt—in retrospect—to be an integrator of [his subject's]
times. This means that he has to evaluate, to judge, and to organize an extraordinary and by no means harmonious ["keineswegs einheitliche"] body of researches—
among them those of ancillary disciplines and marginal studies. Beyond all [of
these] implications of methodology there exists the question in the background:
whether a single author may be capable of that."

†One (randomly picked) example: Fest's description of Hitler's erstwhile ally
Hugenberg in F, p. 369: "Small and corpulent, with a stiff moustache and bristly
crew-cut, he presented the militarily stylized appearance of a pensioned janitor, but
not of a proud man of strong and hard principles that he wished to appear."

was mad, then the entire Hitler period was nothing but an episode of madness; it is irrelevant to us, and we need not think about it further. At the same time, this defining of Hitler as "mad" relieves him of all responsibility—especially in this century, where a certification of mental illness voids a conviction by law. But Hitler was not mad; he was responsible for what he did and said and thought. And apart from the moral argument, there is sufficient proof (accumulated by researchers, historians, and biographers, including medical records) that with all due consideration to the imprecise and fluctuating frontiers between mental illness and sanity, he was a normal human being.

This brings me to the adjective (and argument) of "evil." (Again, there are people who are interested in Hitler because they are interested in evil: the Jack the Ripper syndrome, if not worse.) Yes, there was plenty of evil in Hitler's expressed wishes, thoughts, statements, and decisions. (I emphasize *expressed*, since that is what evidence properly allows us to consider.) But keep in mind that evil as well as good is part of human nature. Our inclinations to evil (whether they mature into acts or not) are reprehensible but also normal. To deny that human condition leads to the assertion that Hitler was abnormal; and the simplistic affixing of the "abnormal" label to Hitler relieves him, again, of responsibility—indeed, categorically so.*

It is not only that he had very considerable intellectual talents. He was also courageous, self-assured, on many occasions steadfast, loyal to his friends and to those working for him, self-disciplined, and

---

*More complicated is the category of "criminal," since crime—unlike evil—is a category established by society, whereby it is also restricted to acts, whereas evil may be recognizable from the expression of its inclinations alone. In this respect, consider Haffner in HF/AN, p. 125: "There is no doubt that Hitler is a figure of world political history; there is equally no doubt he belongs to the annals of crime. . . . [But unlike other conquerors] Hitler is not a criminal merely because he followed in their footsteps. He is a criminal for a totally different reason. Hitler had countless harmless people put to death, for no military or political purpose, but merely for his personal gratification." (Also, p. 126: ". . . his lust for murder was even stronger than his by no means slight ability for political calculation.") Here I must depart from this excellent writer. "Personal gratification" may be too much. Hitler was not a sadist, not even when it came to his hatred of Jews. (See chapter 6.) This, again, makes him *more* responsible, not *less so*. For sadism is a form of lust—that is, of a weakness of the flesh. Hitler's evil inclinations were spiritual, not physical.

modest in his physical wants. What this suggests ought not to be misconstrued, mistaken, or misread. It does not mean: lo and behold! Hitler was only 50 percent bad. Human nature is not like that. A half-truth is worse than a lie, because a half-truth is *not* a 50 percent truth; it is a 100 percent truth and a 100 percent untruth mixed together. In mathematics, with its rigidly fixed and immobile numbers, 100 plus 100 makes 200; in human life 100 plus 100 makes *another kind* of 100. Life is not constant; it is full of black 100s and white 100s, warm 100s and cold 100s, 100s that are growing and 100s that are shrinking. This is true not only of the cells of our bodies but of all human attributes, including mental ones.* In sum, God gave Hitler many talents and strengths; and that is exactly why he was responsible for misusing them.

Such is the main moral problem in our consideration of Hitler. I know that this may be the most arguable of my arguments in this work, this moral one, but isn't every argument really moral to some extent? So let me now descend to a more mundane level—from *how* we see or ought to see him to what we know or do not know about him. One last remark that may touch on the question of mental illness. One of Hitler's weaknesses was something akin to (though not quite identical with) hypochondria. Latest by 1938, he had convinced himself that he did not have long to live.† This led not only to certain changes in his personal habits but to his very decision to speed up his preparations for a possible war. (On the fatality of this,

---

*Zitelmann in an interview with the Swedish historian Alf W. Johansson (Berlin, November 1992) about "historicization": "We must see things [less simply] and scientifically. The black-and-white pictures are no longer convincing." (See also his previously mentioned dismissal of "subjective factors.") Does this mean that—especially from a distance—the proper image of Hitler must be gray? That is not what Zitelmann seems to mean. He would, I think, agree that because of the coexistence of good and evil, the composition of human nature may be likened to the coat of a zebra, with black and white stripes in its makeup. But what matters is *not* the ratio of the black stripes, not their quantity, but the quality—and intensity—of their blackness. And in this respect no quantitative (*pace* Zitelmann: "scientific") analysis or a meticulous pointillism will do. What kind of blackness—a question that transcends scientific or even artistic analysis.

†In M/A, p. 327, Maser writes "latest by 1935." Arguable.

see chapter 5.) We have extensive records of his medical examinations and his extraordinary ingestion of medications.* There is no doubt that at least during the last nine months of his life Hitler was ill, afflicted with—among other things—Parkinson's disease, which affected his physical and mental condition.† The two conditions are not separable, but there is absolutely no convincing evidence to the effect that his physical ailments affected or even obscured his thinking and his judgments to the point of irrationality. We may as well dispose of this question (and therefore, again, not relieve him of any kind of responsibility).

There is no disagreement about this among most historians. What we may detect among them—especially among the German ones—is a slight difference of emphasis. What they ask from the record—and from themselves—are two questions: How could Hitler have come to such power? And: What kind of man was he? It is understandable that the interest and concern of Germans may be directed to the first rather than to the second of these two questions, though, of course, not exclusively so. After all, the first question involves their own history, their people. Among all of the German studies and writings of the Hitler era, the most unexceptionable, the most detailed, and, in many ways, the least contested are the massive works dealing with the end of the Weimar Republic, with the question of how Hitler gained his power (though in these, too, there is

---

*See especially Ernst Günter Schenck, *Patient Hitler: Eine medizinische Biographie*, D, 1989 (hereafter: PH). Earlier, Schenck published his memoirs of the fantastic last weeks in Hitler's bunker in 1945: *Ich sah Berlin sterben. Als Arzt in der Reichskanzlei*, Herford, 1970—indicating his then, more than considerable, respect for Hitler.

†Yet Maser's assertion in M/HB, p. 205, that already in 1943 Hitler was a broken man is not reflected in contemporary photographs. Arguable, too, in M/A, pp. 378, 379, 389, is the suggestion of a near-total change: "Not the events of the war had changed Hitler but the development of his illnesses that affected the development of the war, which he himself knew." Haffner (HF/AN, p. 51) is more convincing: "Accounts presenting Hitler during the final years of the war as a mere shadow of himself, a pitiable human wreck, are all hopelessly overdrawn. Hitler's disastrous failures from 1941 to 1945, following the preceding twelve years of successes, cannot be explained by physical or mental decline."

perhaps more about the weakness of Hitler's opponents and the mistakes of his conservative allies than about Hitler himself).* Assuredly, the second question is the more difficult one, since being is inseparable from becoming. His very vision of himself—of his destiny in the world as well as his physical condition—underwent a change several times: in 1919, in 1924, and in 1937–38, for example. That is not unusual; it happens in the lives of many people. But in Hitler's case, of course, it affected the history of the world. There was also a duality in his character—another common human condition—that manifested itself, among other matters, in his conscious intention to obscure (obscure rather than suppress) certain elements of his past and—equally important—of his present thinking.†

There are, consequently, major questions still outstanding about his life, problems to whose consideration the greatest part of this book is devoted. They include the question whether Hitler's ideology really crystallized in Vienna (as he himself said) or in the thirtieth year of his life, in Munich; the question (which is not merely a semantic one) whether he was a revolutionary or not; the

---

*See their detailed discussion in SCHRB, pp. 160–222. A fine, balanced summary statement in D, p. 162 (the italics are Deuerlein's): *"He did not make it himself.* . . . A historical situation did not push him to the fore but it made [his coming to power] possible. The doubtful provability of this statement nevertheless does not relieve us of the necessity of searching for the man Adolf Hitler."

†Dualities in his behavior were remarked by a few foreign observers, e.g., the French ambassadors André François-Poncet and Robert Coulondre. For a more profound analysis, see F, p. 664: ". . . the element of duality belonged to the innermost character of Hitler . . . with an impact on all [forms of] his behavior, of his tactical, political, and ideological conceptions."

The person most perceptive—and aware—of Hitler's dualities was Speer. For a crucial example of this, note the difference between Hitler's reactions to Speer on 23 March and 29 March 1945, when Hitler issued orders to have all installations behind the retreating army destroyed. Speer, SP, p. 480: "I have often asked myself since whether he had not always known instinctively that I had been working against him during these past months and whether he had not deduced this from my memoranda; also whether . . . he had not provided a fresh example of the multiple strata in his mysterious personality. [die Vielschichtigkeit seiner rätselhaften Natur]. I shall never know." See also the discussion of the secretiveness and the dualities of his statesmanship in chapter 5.

question whether his nationalism was part of his racism, or the reverse; the question of his statesmanship—was it entirely dominated by his ideology?; the question whether his obsession with Jews had any limits at all; the question of the purposes of his partial defenders; the question of his place in the history of Germany, of the twentieth century, of the world.

These are the successive chapters of the present book. Despite the ocean of materials and the continuing flood of historical interpretations, many of these questions are still open—meaning that they are worth recognition and discussion, even though, like everything in life, they will not lead to a final solution. Moreover, Hitler was a very secretive man—much more secretive than Napoleon or Churchill, though perhaps not less secretive than Stalin (who was secretive in a very different way). Hitler's secretiveness* was of course obscured by his public outpourings, by the volubility of his speeches as well as his monologues, as recorded by different conversants, table companions, and stenographers.† That mass of his sayings is extensive; they have been analyzed carefully, and they

---

*In HR, p. 376, Heer cites Hitler's statement to Admiral Raeder on 23 May 1939: Hitler said that he possesses three kinds of secrecy, "the first, when we talk among ourselves; the second, I keep for myself; the third, those are problems about the future about which I must keep thinking" [die ich nicht zu Ende denke]. Also see HR, p. 265, about Hitler's gradually developing and self-enforced loneliness.

†His speeches: Max Domarus, ed., *Hitler, Reden und Proklamationen 1932–1945*, M, 1965, two volumes (divided in half volumes). Very valuable (on occasion unfairly criticized by Irving, also by Zitelmann). There are various editions of his "Table Conversations." The first is by the stenographer Henry Picker (first ed. Bonn, 1951; English translation L, 1953). This edition was arranged thematically; a later edition, carefully annotated, and introduced by Schramm (1963), is more extensive and chronological. Picker took down many of Hitler's after-dinner talks in his headquarters from 21 March to 2 August 1942. More extensive are the records of Heinrich Heim in *Adolf Hitler: Monologe im Führerhauptquartier 1941–1944*, ed. Werner Jochmann, Hamburg, 1980 (hereafter: HM), mostly from 21 July 1941 to March 1942. There are also at least two other manuscript records of such "Table Conversations," one by Werner Koeppen (Alfred Rosenberg's personal aide), from June to November 1941 in the IFZ archives utilized by Zitelmann; and the previously mentioned Hewel notes, used by Irving. Finally, the so-called Bormann Notes (stenographer not known), seemingly authentic (though that has been questioned)

furnish us with important clues to his thinking.* At the same time, his very secretiveness is a matter of record. Often he told his secretaries, "Don't write that down."† I noted this habit in *The Duel* (pp. 46–47), contrasting it to Churchill, who was much less secretive (p. 112). Another contrast between the latter: a man of the written word, and Hitler, a man of the spoken word (who once said that *Mein Kampf* was a book that must be spoken, not read).‡ He was extraordinarily aware of the purposes—both hortatory and educational—of his utterances; in other words, of his ability—and the necessity—to impress and influence people.** (Necessity: for he

---

and very interesting because they focus on the last months of Hitler's life: The Dictator's Last Thoughts. They were carried by Bormann's wife first to Italy, then transmitted by an Italian to Hitler's respectful admirer, the Swiss François Genoud; published as *Libres Propos sur la Guerre et la Paix*, P, 1952; and *The Testament of Adolf Hitler*, L, 1959. (About the peculiarities [and the absence] of the *original* manuscript, see the discussion, including the elusive Genoud, in a colloquium of the IFZ, also published in Munich-Vienna, 1978, pp. 44–53.) The introduction to HM shows something of Hitler's duality and his secretiveness, p. 22: "[Heim's] transcripts prove the great self-assuredness but also the suspicious reservedness of Hitler." P. 24: ". . . even in his talking to his closest circle he never failed to consider the psychological effect of his words. . . . Certain of his statements were aimed in the first place to fortify the confidence of his circle." (All in all, these transcripts are *not* clues to the *private* Hitler.)

*Already Heiden, in HD, pp. 332–33, produced a very interesting analysis of Hitler's methods and habits of speech. For a discussion of Hitler's speaking style (and his prosody), see Cornelius Schnauber, *Wie Hitler Sprach und Schrieb*, Frankfurt, 1972. It does not deal with *Mein Kampf* but with such matters as Hitler's rhythm (p. 104): "Most unusual is the melodic range of Hitler's pronunciation."

†See the often quarrelsome but interesting autobiography of his secretary Christa Schroeder, *Er war mein Chef*, M, 1987. Yet no one wrote more incisively about Hitler's work habits than Speer, especially in SP, chapter 9, where he relates the changes and oddities in Hitler's work habits to the dualities of his character. Also see Philipp W. Fabry, *Mutmassungen über Hitler*, Urteile von Zeitgenossen, D, 1969.

‡In SP, pp. 511 and 219, Hitler declared MK to be "superseded." Also Sereny, *Speer* (see p. 22, above), p. 361, citing Bormann (reminiscences of the latter's son): "I do not have to read it, it has been surpassed by events. (As Speer told me [Sereny] Hitler told him the very same thing.")

**Including pictorial representations. Hitler was very close to his photographer, Heinrich Hoffmann; he had the habit of poring over photographs, including his own, allowing Hoffmann to retouch many of them for propaganda purposes. On the subject of Hoffmann's many Hitler albums, see SCHRB, p. 5 (retouchings which Hitler "propagandistisch aufschminkte"). This from a man who, as was previously noted, did *not* want to have an adulatory biography of himself published during his lifetime.

often *felt* the need to speak.) That is, for example, why his table conversations show the "public" rather than the "private" Hitler. In their private table talk, Churchill, Napoleon, and even Stalin often appear to be more human and varied than in their public and recordable utterances. This was not so with Hitler, who, relatively late—at the age of thirty—suddenly discovered his ability to influence people through his speaking. The year 1919 was a decisive milestone, indeed a turning point in his life; but no human being changes entirely; with all his speaking talent,* Hitler remained a secretive man in many ways, keeping many of his most important thoughts to himself.†

One of the problems of the historiography of Hitler is the scarcity of written documents he left behind—among them, the absence of any written instructions that connect him to the awful decision to carry out the mass liquidation of Jews—though the decision was made. (See chapter 6.) At the same time, there is more and more evidence that he read much (his retention capacity was phenomenal): books and all kinds of papers (including speeches by Goebbels); even during the war, he wrote in the margins and made corrections in these books.‡

---

*Before his crucial political campaigns in 1932, he took voice lessons from the tenor Paul Devrient in Munich.

†Bullock interview in the FAZ Magazin *Woche*, 6 December 1991: "Hitler was always quite open, by and large he said what he wanted to do." Not so. Speer, SP, p. 107: "I remember . . . in 1938 . . . sitting in the Deutscher Hof in Nuremberg. Hitler spoke of the need to keep to oneself things not meant for the ears of the public." Fest cites Hitler in F, p. 710: For a Führer, "it is exceptionally important that nothing that one may discuss should be written down, never!" And: "Too much is being written down. . . some of that can always become troublesome." Fest's concluding remark: "He was constantly observing himself. . . never spoke an unconsidered word. . . the widespread image of the emotionally uncontrolled, wildly gesticulating Hitler [was seldom correct]; his was a most concentrated existence, self-disciplined to the extent of rigidity."

‡Schroeder (see above, p. 48), p. 225: "He himself corrected very often." SP, p. 179, quotes Hitler in the summer of 1939: ". . . the drafts of the Foreign Ministry are, again, useless. I better draft them myself." Many other instances in SP, e.g., p. 569: "I heard from Below that Hitler read this and also other memoranda of mine very carefully, even making marginal remarks and other corrections." Maser in M/HB, p. 153, noted this and claimed that after 1933 Hitler's style improved. In M/A, p. 178, Maser wrote that Schramm had underestimated the young Hitler's book-buying habit.

He also wrote or dictated many weekly articles (especially between 1928 and 1931) for his party newspaper (the *Illustrierte Beobachter*); their importance was first noted and evaluated by Deuerlein and then by Zitelmann.

But his secretiveness is only one element within the larger issue. We shall never know everything (and perhaps we shall never know enough) about him. That is not a reason for despair. It is not given to human beings to know everything—as Kierkegaard said, the pure truth is for God alone; what is given to us is the pursuit of truth.* As a matter of fact—or, rather, condition—the understanding of the limits of our knowledge, instead of impoverishing us, may actually enrich us. Or, as Pascal said, we understand more than we know, which is not a paradox; it suggests that it is not necessarily the amassing of knowledge that eventually leads to understanding but that understanding may actually precede the accumulation of knowledge. On the first page of this book I wrote that the purpose of historical knowledge may be understanding, even more than accuracy—though of course not deliberately at the expense of the latter—and a recognition of this condition may be even more applicable to the analysis and description of historical "problems" than of "periods."

And Hitler Was, Is and Remains a Problem. Everything has its history, including memory: fluctuating and fallible human memory that may be obscured or clarified by distance, strengthened or weakened by perspective. It is not only the tremendous accumulation of materials, research, and writings about Hitler but a certain perspective that allows me to make a shocking statement: He may have been the most popular revolutionary leader in the history of the modern world. The emphasis is on the word *popular*, because Hitler belongs to the democratic, not the aristocratic, age of history. He is not properly comparable to a Caesar, a Cromwell, a Napoleon. Utterly different from them, he was, more than any of them, able to ener-

---

*Here again is the profound Heer in HR, p. 11: "In the heart of every human person there remains something that no human being—not even that person himself—may entirely grasp, discover, or unravel. That untouchableness of his deepest kernel Adolf Hitler shares with every other human being."

gize the majority of a great people, in his lifetime the most educated people of the world, convincing them to follow his leadership to astonishing achievements and extraordinary efforts and making them believe that what they (and he) stood for was an antithesis of evil. He led them to prosperity and pride, inspiring in them a confidence with which they conquered almost all of Europe, achieving a German hegemony soon lost because he overreached himself. His Reich, which was to have lasted a thousand years, ended after twelve; yet he had an enormous impact and left a more indelible mark upon this century than any other dictator, a Lenin or a Stalin or a Mao. That is why his place in the history of the world—which is not the main subject of this book—will be pondered by people for a long time to come. We are not yet finished with Hitler. . . .

2

The Crystallization.
Vienna and/or Munich?

B IOGRAPHY IS A PRODUCT of the Modern Age, and autobiography even more so. From the beginning of recorded history people have been writing about other people, but their works were not biographies, certainly not in the modern sense of the word. Plutarch, Suetonius, and Eusebius were not biographers, since the portraits of their subjects were *static*; they did not deal with the development—that is, with the history—of their subjects' lives and minds. It seems that the Greek word *biography* (βιογραφια) does not appear until an obscure Byzantine uses it in the sixth century A.D. A minor point: what is more important is the condition that the present sense of biography—that is, the history of a person's life—appears in England and Western Europe only at the time of—or after—the Renaissance; and the first autobiography worthy of record is Benvenuto Cellini's picaresque account of his own life, around the same time. It was a very successful work, but not only by virtue of its entertaining contents. This is not the place to discourse on the reasons and the relative lateness of this development, save to say that they are inseparable from the contemporary rise of historical consciousness, which, in turn, was inseparable from the then also contemporary rise of the human consciousness of self. And a few pages earlier, we saw what I consider to be one of the very few promising literary developments now, at the end of the Modern Age, which is the increasing historicization of biography, together with the continuing appetite of readership for it: meaning, for instance, that biography and autobiography have gradually ceased to be "purely" literary forms; they have become inseparable from history.

In *Mein Kampf*, Hitler felt compelled to begin this large book of his political credo with an autobiographical portion: an autobiography sui generis, but an autobiography nonetheless. His purpose was to tell us—more accurately, not "us," since he declared that *Mein Kampf* was written for his followers rather than for an audience at large—how and where and why his political ideas and his worldview congealed, this being the best way to explain their plausibility and to impress his readers with their authenticity. *Mein Kampf* ("My Struggle")—the very title is telling—is a large, formless volume containing (1) autobiography, (2) statements of a political and ideological creed, and (3) elements of a political program. Written in the first-person singular, it is not precisely determinable where the autobiographical part ends and the political programming and propaganda begin, since they, especially because of the constant use of the first-person singular, overlap; but it can be safely stated that the first, the autobiographical portion, ends with Hitler's arrival in Munich in early 1919, a point that he himself hammered down in a sentence: "I resolved to become a politician." We may as well take his word for that, but we shall return to it, since it is germane to the main question raised in this chapter.

Hitler's account of the first thirty years of his life is sufficiently well known for us to summarize it only briefly. He was born in a town on the very frontier of the Austrian and the German empires, which to him was most significant; very early in his life he saw himself as belonging to the community of Germans, rejecting sentiments of loyalty to the multinational Habsburg empire. He described his parents, both of whom he lost before the age of nineteen; and then his life in Vienna, where he told how he lived in great poverty, struggling for his daily bread, and where his eyes opened and his entire worldview crystallized. After six years in Vienna he moved to Munich, where he immediately felt at home. A year later came the war in 1914, where he served bravely, almost from the first day to the last. Then came his second wounding at the front, a stay in a military hospital, together with the shock of Germany's defeat, after which he returned to Munich and "resolved to become a politician."

It is of course in the nature of most autobiographies that they—in spite of the best will of an honest author—are seldom meticulously accurate, and that they—consciously or not—conceal certain matters as well as they reveal others. In the case of *Mein Kampf*, there are at least four matters about which Hitler consciously misled his readers. (I write "consciously," and "his readers," because—unlike what happens in many autobiographies, indeed, in the very memories of a *persona*—there is evidence that in these retouchings of his past Hitler was not deceiving himself.) These matters involve his father; the material circumstances of his life in Vienna; the formation of his mind in that city at that time; and the time of his move from Vienna to Munich. Of these four topics, the latter three are the subjects of this chapter; I shall return, albeit briefly, to the unsolved and almost certainly unsolvable question of his deeper relationship to his father in chapter 6. But first I must say something about the distorted picture of that relationship that is remarkable in *Mein Kampf*.

There he drew a pleasant, if not altogether idyllic, picture of his early youth. On the very first page, he overemphasized the importance of his birthplace—significant, of course, since Braunau am Inn stood on the frontier between Austria and Germany (even though his family moved away from Braunau soon after his birth).* More significant is the extent of his account including his father. He wrote more about his father than about his mother. Yet we know that he was much closer to his mother than to his father—indeed, extraordinarily so. As Dr. Bloch, the Jewish physician who cared for

---

*There *was* another symbolic significance, unnoticed by his later biographers: His bride Eva Braun, of a simple Bavarian family, lived and attended school for some years in Simbach, the Bavarian village across the Inn River from Braunau.

Hitler's mother, wrote both before and after his emigration from Austria, in nearly forty years of his career as a doctor he had never seen a young man as broken with grief as Adolf Hitler at the death of his mother. He was an exemplary son during his mother's final illness. Of course, he was the male head of the family then, his father having died three years earlier; but there was more to it than that. He loved his mother; and he feared (and possibly hated) his father. This is not a mere psychoanalytic speculation; there is enough evidence of it. He mentioned the matter, often late at night, to some of his closest circle—for instance, to General Edmund von Glaise-Horstenau (by coincidence, also born in Braunau), who found this significant enough to record it in his posthumously published memoirs; and also to Speer.* Hitler's father was domineering and crude: he drank; he mistreated his wife; he beat his young son. Yet in *Mein Kampf* Hitler wrote about his father in reverent and respectful phrases, emphasizing only one, rather natural, disagreement between father and son: His father wanted him to choose the career of an Austrian civil servant (which had been the father's special achievement, against many difficulties), when his young son wished to become an artist. Of that disagreement, too, Hitler wrote in a wistful and pleasant tone. Yet to a few insightful observers, throughout his adult life he gave the impression that he had been a deeply humiliated child.†

Hitler lived in Vienna for six years after his mother's death, from the eighteenth to the twenty-fourth year of his life. Those are formative years in any man's life, and they were undoubtedly so for Hitler, too—except that, according to *Mein Kampf*, they were formative not only partially or largely but categorically and definitively. We know much about these years, from many sources, but first among them is *Mein Kampf*, in which Hitler described them at length. Yet we now know that his account of his years in Vienna

---

*To Glaise-Horstenau (in April 1939): "I feared my father, but I loved him not at all." sp, p. 139: "My father often beat me severely. . . ."

†See above, p. 20 (George Bernanos). GQ, p. 29: "His childhood reminiscences must have left a deep [and lasting] impression on his soul, but it is also characteristic of him that he conceals that impression from others very carefully."

was, at least in one important respect, incorrect; and, in another, questionable. According to *Mein Kampf*, these were years of constant and abject poverty. But the researches of historians have shown that he had some money,* and that he was seldom beset by hunger. We may speculate on why he kept underlining his penniless existence in Vienna (perhaps to prove his understanding of and empathy for the working classes?). At any rate, there is little left to further research about the material conditions of the Viennese period of his life. What remains open to question is the extent and depth of the formation of his convictions then and there.† Of that he wrote categorically in *Mein Kampf*: "Vienna" was "the most fundamental schooling" of his life, "the most difficult school," where "I gained the fundament of my world-view." He repeated that phrase often: "The granite-hard fundament of my later actions." He left Vienna for Munich in 1913, where he found himself very much at home.‡

Most, though not all historians, have, by and large, accepted Hitler's statement about the decisive (and categorical and final) impact of Vienna on his mind. There is, after all, a frightening directness connecting the autobiographical with the programmatic part of *Mein Kampf*; Hitler's strident and polemical account of the crystallization of his ideology in Vienna convinces because of what we know of its actual and evident consequences. There is also considerable evidence about the influence on his mind of anti-Semitic and radically nationalist catchphrases and literature of that time; of his memories of unseemly riots in the parliament, and of great street demonstrations; and of one of his idols, the charismatic Mayor Karl Lueger. Much has been written about Vienna and the young Hitler (including the weird extremist publications and the "atmosphere" of

---

*A summary statement in M/A, p. 81: "The hard [bitter] fate in Vienna of which Hitler liked to speak had with financial matters nothing to do." An exaggeration, but not without some substance.

†The valuable and impressively detailed work by Brigitte Hamann, *Hitlers Wien. Lehrjahre eines Diktators*, M, 1996, was published after the completion of my manuscript. Her conclusions accord with mine.

‡Probably not only or principally, as some of his biographers wrote (HF/AN, p. 10), "in order to avoid service in the Austrian Army," though it was a factor.

"decadent" Vienna before 1914). It is unquestionable that for the formation of Hitler's mind the Vienna chapter of his life was important, perhaps even decisive. But was it definitive? In other words, did his ideas finally crystallize in Vienna? We know that the most important turning point in Hitler's life occurred in Munich, in 1919. Of course, crystallization and turning point are not identical (save perhaps chemically speaking), but they are not separable either. So, with all of the reservations due to such a metaphor, was it, then, in Vienna or Munich that the crystallization—if not of his personal destiny, then at least of his worldview—occurred? There are contradictory evidences of this, to which I must now turn.*

IT IS AT LEAST POSSIBLE—and I am inclined in that direction—that this crystallization occurred not in Vienna but in Munich, and surprisingly late, during the thirty-first year of Hitler's life—perhaps exactly around his thirtieth birthday, which fell on 20 April 1919.

Ten days after Hitler's thirtieth birthday, the Munich Soviet Republic collapsed. Regiments of the German army, along with volunteer corps, were marching into Munich, where what was to be called the White Terror began. The president of the Soviet Republic was beaten to death by the soldiers; in the following days and weeks, more people were executed than during the months of the Munich Soviet rule. Yet the White Terror was popular, whereas the Red Terror had not been. I write "the Munich Soviet Republic" because the authority of that "government" had hardly extended beyond the city of Munich. Of the few episodic Communist regimes in Europe after World War I, it was the most incompetent. In Munich a revolution in November 1918 preceded the proclamation of the German Republic in Berlin; during the following months the regime slid more and more to the Left. In late February its head, Kurt Eisner, was assassinated by a counterrevolutionary; thereafter the Munich Soviet regime ensued. Its members were Communists,

*The important work on this is A. Joachimsthaler, *Adolf Hitler 1908–1920: Korrektur einer Biographie*, M, 1989 (hereafter: JO), and now Hamann (see footnote, p. 56). Joachimsthaler is very critical of Maser, but very respectful of Deuerlein.

intellectuals, bohemians, many of them Jewish, and here and there men who had been certified insane. (Its composition and its ideas were not dissimilar to those of some of the American crazies of the 1960s, except, of course, that the latter never had the slightest chance of even coming close to the exercise of power.) Thereafter the city of Munich, traditionally Catholic and more easygoing than many other German cities of the north, became the principal seat of radical rightists (members of the National Socialist Party among them).

We do not know where Hitler celebrated his thirtieth birthday, if he celebrated it at all. Of his entire life, the spring months in Munich in 1919 are the most obscure. In October 1918, the soldier Hitler was gassed at the front. At the time of the German collapse he was in a hospital in the town of Pasewalk, in Pomerania. In December he made his way back to Bavaria and rejoined an army unit there. We know very little about his activities from February to May 1 of 1919, when the Red Terror, though not omnipresent, was murderous and stalked the streets of Munich. In *Mein Kampf*, he wrote that he returned to Munich in March. Yet Joachimsthaler proves that he was already there in late January.* There is some evidence that Hitler wore the red armband required of soldiers at that time; in any event, he lay low. What is undoubtable is that his political activities began immediately after the collapse of the Reds: he volunteered as a propaganda speaker for the army; he attended the university lectures of a noted nationalist professor; and he began to speak up in public, perhaps as early as June 1919 (the first direct documentary evidence of his public speaking dates from August of that year). Thereafter the evidence multiplies rapidly, and the story is well known. Even before he joined the party from which his own National Socialist German Workers' Party would grow, his speeches contained all the recognizable features of extreme nationalism, Judeophobia, fanaticism; the very ideas that would make him famous were there, to be repeated over and over again.

The question of *when* the crystallization of Hitler's ideas occurred is not merely a question of chronological curiosity. According to him,

---

*JO, p. 191. Also p. 189: "What did Hitler do [in the spring of 1919 in Munich]? Nothing!"

not only did his first realization of the Jewish "menace" take place in Vienna, but it was there that he thought the Jewish "problem" through: "I left Vienna as an absolute Anti-Semite, as a mortal enemy of the entire Marxist world view." Yet he had Jewish acquaintances, perhaps even friends, in the youth hostel where he lived; some of them helped to sell his watercolors, others framed them. In at least one instance he enjoyed the hospitality of a cultured Jewish family for an evening of chamber music in their home. He also admired the musical ability of (the Jewish) Gustav Mahler.* We have no evidence of anti-Semitic utterances (private or public) by Hitler before his thirty-first year. That he was struggling with the Jewish problem, is probable. But it seems that he felt no need to express these sentiments while they were still inchoate, before they had crystallized into a categorical idea or a powerful obsession. It is at least possible (in my opinion, probable) that what crystallized these ideas—crystallized them rather than produced them out of the void—were his experiences during the winter and the spring of 1918–19: the German collapse, but, even more, his witnessing of the ridiculous and sordid episode of the Munich Soviet Republic, with its Jewish and lumpen intellectuals, et al.

Sustaining this thesis is a massive volume, *Hitler: Sämtliche Aufzeichnungen 1905–1924*, a documentary collection of all of Hitler's surviving writings and speeches from 1905 to 1924, published in 1980 by Eberhard Jäckel and Axel Kuhn. It contains every letter, every postcard, every note, every poem that could be found, every draft for a speech from Hitler's pen, from his sixteenth year onward. This collection of primary sources is substantial (more than 1,300 pages); the items before 1919 amount to more than seventy (items, not pages—they do not include Hitler's drawings and watercolors). There is a drastic change in both the content and the tone of these personal documents in 1919, but not before. The impression one receives of the younger Hitler is that of a loner, a dreamer, a German idealist—an impression that accords with the reminiscences of those who knew him during the war. In Hitler's extant notes, letters, and postcards to his friends, whether sent from the front or while on leave, the expressions are often childlike, showing

---

*Fest's statement (F, p. 56) that he knew nothing of Mahler is incorrect.

a doglike loyalty and deference to his officers and his country. With one exception—a letter to an older Munich acquaintance in February 1915, to which I shall return—they are also apolitical. Typical is a postcard to a friend, in October 1917, from Berlin, where he was on a short leave: "Arrived here only Tuesday. The A. family is very kind. I could not have wanted anything better. The city is magnificent. A real cosmopolitan capital (Weltstadt). The traffic even now is enormous. I am walking around all day. At last I have the chance to study the museums even more. In sum, everything is fine" ["Es fehlt mir nichts"]. Then there are poems. (Except for a poem in a guest book dated 1906, there are none before 1915 or after 1919.) So this is the young Hitler: drawing sketches, painting watercolors, writing poetry in the trenches. The poems are inspirational; their principal theme is patriotic loyalty. Of course, Hitler was no Rupert Brooke, but the poems are not laughable. They express the fervent sentiments of a German idealist. They are nationalistic, youthful, lonely, and sad. They are not exactly doggerel because of the pathetic touch they carry; they are expressions of devotion to the fatherland. In spite of the masculine gender of that word, it is as if the fatherland were a feminine entity; these are expressions of devotion to a great, adored, and now endangered mother.

After the publication of the above-mentioned volume, its editors were alerted by two letters that drew attention to the questionable authenticity of some of the documents. After a thorough examination, the editors concluded that these doubts were justified; they published a short notice accordingly in the vfz (April 1981, p. 304). Jäckel and Kuhn were not to blame—a fair number of the documents had come to them from a private owner who did not wish to have his name published. The questionable items are a very small portion of the entire documentary collection: sixteen or seventeen out of a total of nearly seven hundred documents. What they have in common is that most are accompanied by a note from the Reichsleitung, the high directorate of the National Socialist Party, and these notes are typed on Reichsleitung stationery. What is interesting is that the questionable documents include some of Hitler's poems during the war and poems and jottings from the early months of the year 1919 in Munich. In the introduction to the Jäckel-Kuhn volume, the scholars indicated that some of these poems may not have been Hitler's but were instead copied out by Hitler. Until 1980, we did not know that Hitler wrote, or that he copied out, poems. (There is at least one additional falsification: A short poem is included that was written and published well after the war; Hitler could not have copied it.) Six of these questionable items are dated January and February of 1919.

It is unlikely that these insertions in the Party archives were made without Hitler's knowledge. As in *Mein Kampf*, his intention may well have been to show that the crystallization of his ideology occurred earlier than the collapse of the Munich Soviet Republic. He concluded the autobiographical part of *Mein Kampf* with the statement that it was in November 1918, in that hospital in Pomerania, that he experienced the defeat and the collapse of the German empire, and where his gas-injured eyes opened: "I now resolved to become a politician."* It is at least possible that he did not resolve his doubts, that he did not resolve to become a politician, until six months later, after the bloody collapse of the ridiculous Munich Soviet Republic.

But my main question is not whether it was Pasewalk or Munich but whether it was Vienna or Munich. And this is not an either/or question but, rather, an and/or one. There is evidence on both sides—evidence to be considered seriously—as long as one does not exclude the other, and as long as we accept what "crystallization" may mean.

---

*One man who understood the searing experiences of Hitler in that hospital, and saw in it a turning point of his interior life, was Churchill. In the first volume of his memoirs of the Second World War, Churchill began a chapter with the description of Hitler in that hospital. Written in 1948, it is still a most penetrating summary description. I wrote in DL, p. 41: "On the first page of that short chapter, which he dictated walking up and down in his room in Chartwell, Churchill described Hitler's career and his personality astonishingly well. The remarkable quality of those passages was not only the result of Churchill's rhetorical and literary mastery. It was the result of his insight. He recognized, for example, how the decisive element in the formation of Hitler's mind—and not only in his career—came in 1918–19, and not before the war; in Munich, not in Vienna. Yet Hitler in *Mein Kampf* had insisted—and most historians even now accept the thesis—that while his life took a sudden turn in late 1918 and then in Munich, his political ideology had already crystallized in Vienna. Many professional historians, bombinating in their airless circles, tend to ignore or dismiss Churchill the historian. Yet in these pages Churchill's understanding of Hitler is phenomenal."

At any rate, the Vienna/Munich question has not been raised to the point where it became a matter of argument among historians. Most (though not all) of them have—properly—dismissed assertions connecting Hitler with some of the bizarre and extreme racialist and anti-Semitic groups and pamphleteers during his Vienna period— for example with Jörg Lanz-Liebenfels, set forth in a 1958 book (H. Daim, *Der Mann der Hitler die Ideen gab* ("The Man Who Gave Hitler His Ideas"). At the same time, serious consideration is due to Heer, who in HR produced the richest mass of material about Hitler's "Austrianness." Heer went so far as to claim that Hitler's character had been fully formed between 1905 and 1908 in Linz; that is, before his move to Vienna. This is debatable, but what is not debatable is the mass of Heer's kaleidoscopic and encyclopedic evidence of the Austrian—and Austrian-Catholic—elements in Hitler's thinking. Besides Hitler's "Austrian" mannerisms, gestures, and habits, remarked by many people (very much including his secretaries), this evidence accumulated again during the war, when, in that last chapter of his life, Hitler talked more and more about his memories of Vienna, often in a mood of nostalgia, praising (this was quite unlike his mood in *Mein Kampf*) many things about Vienna's atmosphere, culture, theaters, actors, and so forth. However, we must keep in mind that Heer's main interest was not the "Viennese" but the Austrian Hitler. In Heer's view it was the Austrianness, not the Viennese years, that had been formative. His most telling statements and quotes include startling, and at times shocking, proof of how certain conservative Austrian Catholics and their institutions not only welcomed Hitler in 1938 but expressed themselves both before and after 1938 in truly Hitlerian terms.* Heer's tremendous

---

*One example: Carl Freiherr v. Bardolff, a conservative and before 1914 the Archduke Franz Ferdinand's close adviser, greeted (as had also other high officers of the old Austrian army) Hitler enthusiastically in March 1938. In his subsequent book Bardolff described World War I as "the great war of the world against Germanness." The archduke and his close advisers never allowed "the representatives of the Jewish press to enter the Belvedere" (the archduke's palace). "It was Franz Ferdinand's absolute conviction that Freemasonry, Materialism, Liberalism, Marxism and Jewish world capitalism" were enemies. He ended his book (*Soldat im alten Österreich*) "with a full homage to Adolf Hitler, springing from my heart."

knowledge of Austrian history, culture, and literature, together with his own religious and psychological beliefs, gives us deep insights into Hitler's career and character,* rather than relating directly to the Vienna/Munich question. There *is* at least one document that seems to suggest that the crystallization of Hitler's ideas had occurred before Munich: his (above-mentioned) letter to a Munich acquaintance, written from the front in February 1915. In this letter Hitler speaks of the "inevitable" struggle against the enemy within Germany.† There is also some evidence that he talked about politics with his comrades in the dugouts.

Together with such contradictory evidence, contradictory statements among Hitler's principal biographers remain. "One of the most decisive questions of Hitler's life [remains] the effects of the years in Vienna on his development," wrote his earliest postwar German historians more than forty-four years ago. Yet these same authors wrote in the same book: "His world-view and his ideology ["Weltbild" and "Weltanschauung"] undoubtedly formed themselves very early in Vienna."‡ Or consider Fest on Vienna and *Mein*

---

*In another book by Heer (*Land im Strom der Zeit*, Vienna, 1958, p. 266): "Adolf Hitler, highly talented with many gifts, possessed an outstanding talent, springing from his Austrian background: his knowledge of human nature. But there are two kinds of that knowledge, and Hitler's came from the bottom, not the top: his genius lay in his understanding of human weaknesses."

Interesting, too, is Heer's argument in HR: that Hitler was influenced by the Austrian emperor Joseph II as much as, if not more than, by the Prussian Frederick the Great. Also telling: Hitler's decision on the last day of his life, naming the Austrian Catholic and Nazi Seyss-Inquart as foreign minister of the next, and last, Reich government: "That, too, was one—the last—return of the prodigal son Adolf Hitler to Austria."

†Letter to Ernst Hepp, cited in M/HB, p. 100; also printed in the Jäckel-Kuhn volume: "Those of us who will be blessed by fortune to see our homeland again, a homeland cleansed of aliens . . . by the sacrifices and the suffering of hundreds of thousands, their blood spilled every day against an international world of enemies, not only of [foreign] but domestic ones, against the dangers of our domestic internationalism, to be destroyed. That would be worth more than all of the gain of new territory." These sentiments accord entirely with Hitler's beliefs in 1919 and after.

‡GQ, pp. 43 and 61: "Weltbild" and "Weltanschauung": In JHW, Jäckel stated that these two words are not necessarily identical, though they do overlap. A similar argument was made by GQ. Jäckel did not pursue this distinction further. For our purposes it is unnecessary.

Kampf: "Wearisome and difficult as its reading is, it nonetheless gives a remarkably accurate picture of its author. . . . In effect Hitler's world-view, as he had insisted, had not changed." Yet in the same biography we find: "In Vienna he was not inclined to be a revolutionary; he was only lonely."* Jäckel gave a convincing statement in JHW: "Historical research of his youth . . . has proved in many instances that the autobiographical passages of *Mein Kampf* gave a very free and also overly simplified and false picture of the circumstances of the period of his youth." Also: "The only evidence about his Vienna years are almost exclusively his own statements, thus resting on uncertain source material." And: "The definite finalization [i.e., crystallization?] of his ideology occurred only after his writing of the autobiography in *Mein Kampf.*"† According to Jäckel, the development of Hitler's ideology was gradual (p. 158): "It is an important fact that the final completion [Ausbildung], contrary to Hitler's own statements, in 1919 had only begun." Perhaps significant but of uncertain validity: "Hitler had apparently earlier discussed with one of his comrades at the front whether after the war he would become an architect or a politician."‡ Zitelmann in ZIT/A, p. 15, admitted that Hitler's own Viennese account "certainly includes particulars that were not proven or cannot be proven," while they remain important; but Zitelmann did not deal with either the Vienna/Munich question or the problem of the origins and development of Hitler's Judeophobia. Görlitz and Quint wrote that Hitler's thudding sentence about his decision to become a politician was more of a rhetorical device than the memory of the lightning conversion when Hitler the fledgling artist turned to become a politician. During that cold, dreary, and dreadful winter, he was still

---

*F, p. 292, but also p. 58. It is very questionable (F, p. 60) that Hitler had met the previously mentioned Lanz-Liebenfels in Vienna (cf. F, pp. 60–61; also p. 1051), or that he had joined an "Antisemitenbund."

†JHW, pp. 18, 147, 154. In my opinion he puts the date of "crystallization" too late.

‡KER, p. 21, note 147: Here Kershaw quoted M/A, p. 194, where the reference comes from a statement made to Maser by a wartime comrade of Hitler more than fifty years after that event.

dependent on external circumstances that were "much more mean-
ingful than his private daily life in those months"*—a plausible for-
mulation of a phase in the life of a man who thereafter showed
himself to be capable of affecting circumstances by the expression of his own ideas. Speer recorded how Hitler often stated in
conversation that while "his political, artistic, and military ideas
formed a unity," they were formed "in detail between the ages
of twenty and thirty,"† which includes both the Vienna and the
Munich years.

It is significant that Hitler himself misdated the time
of his move from Vienna to Munich in *Mein Kampf*. He wrote
that it occurred in 1912, whereas it was in 1913. It is unlikely that
the error was unintentional, because Hitler possessed an extraordinary memory. In that sentence he also wrote of his "final"
(endgültig) move to Munich, when, in reality, that was his first visit
to that city. There he found himself largely at home. His desire to
identify himself with Germany and not with Austria was obvious
from the beginning of his life, and remains indisputable. That this
desire led to a non-native's becoming a great national leader is also
obvious (as was the case with the Corsican Napoleon and the Geor-
gian Stalin), while perhaps one unanswerable and intriguing question remains: could he ever have become a successful *Austrian*
politician?

In any event, in the life of this deeply unhappy young man the
setting and his settling in Munich in 1919 turned out to be fortunate—for a variety of reasons and on different levels. We have
already seen that public opinion as well as popular sentiment in
Bavaria turned out to be overwhelmingly radical, nationalist, populist, anticosmopolitan, anticapitalist, anti-Marxist, and anti-Jewish
by May 1919, and that thereafter Munich and Bavaria, even more

---

*GQ, pp. 65, 103; also 174: ". . . his decision to become a politician . . . was not
really made in Pasewalk but only with his stepping forth as a speaker in the fall of
1919." (In my opinion, this puts it a little too late.)

†SP, p. 120.

than other cities in Germany, were centers of such political activities and organizations. There was the proximity—geographic, racial, and linguistic—of Lower Bavaria with Austria. Elsewhere in Germany Hitler's Austrianness (including his diction) may have been a political handicap, but in Munich it was not a disadvantage. These circumstances were important and helpful, but what was really decisive was Hitler's self-discovery: his ability as a speaker. That may have occurred as early as late April 1919,* and thereafter developed quickly. It was not entirely independent of its circumstances: The extreme and hyperbolical character of his oratory echoed better in the raucous atmosphere of Munich than in the tighter-lipped north: the rough and beery, jocular South German virility summed up in the untranslatable Bavarian-German word "Gaudi."†

Consequent to his ability to impress people with his speaking came the discovery of his ability (and the exercise of his will) to influence them: a less ephemeral and more enduring task, amounting to the truly political portion of his genius. His confidence in that ability grew gradually. Where Demosthenes failed, this modern demagogue succeeded: he became the leader of a party, then the leader of *his* party, and finally the leader of a national movement. That does not concern us in this chapter; what should concern us here is the change or development in Hitler's public and private *persona*. It was in Munich that this odd (and odd-looking) young man

---

*Possibly the first consequential event: Hitler haranguing (and convincing) his fellow soldiers in the barracks not to follow the Red leader Egelhofer into the streets. (This happened on 29 or 30 April 1919, the day of his suicide twenty-six years later.)

†Closest English suggestion: a rough feasting—in our case, rejoicing in hearing something brutally exclaimed. The Old English word "gaudy" (OED) also meant rejoicing, but without the element of brutality; at most, a prank (Oxford Oriel College gaudies: annual college dinner events).

Fest is very good about this in F, p. 212: ". . . . Hitler's party could profit, too, from the specific Bavarian crudeness ["Grobianismus"], in accord with its political rules of the game. The beer-hall battles with their crashing chairs and flying beer steins, the songs calling for 'murder,' the big thrashings; it was all a tremendous Gaudi." He adds that it was then that the word "Nazi" first appeared: "to Bavarian ears an abbreviation of the name 'Ignaz' [but] thereby a familiar sound, evidently a help in the widely spreading awareness of the Party."

became not only a political figure but an attractive personage—at least to some people, and in his case especially to women: older, respectable women. In Munich—with some help from friends—he was eventually introduced to respectable upper-middle-class and even patrician families, acquiring a few necessary manners, becoming, as the Germans say, "salonfähig," that is, introducible and admissible, an assistance in the necessary acquisition of his respectability. As some of Hitler's friends (Dietrich Eckart and Otto Strasser) said at the time, the very fact that this young man was a bachelor made him appealing—by which I mean nothing directly sexual: The ladies Bechstein, Reventlow, Wagner, Dirksen, Bruckmann, Hanfstaengl,* saw him with near-motherly eyes, a once poor young man in need of affection and assistance (perhaps, again, the once humiliated child?).† None of this means, of course, that in Munich there occurred a *complete* transformation of his character. Many of his personal habits did not change. His disdain for finances, for economics, continued; it stood him in good stead. But throughout his career many of his closest and stubbornest followers were Bavarians and Austrians, ex-Catholics such as himself. The happiest (or, at least, the most satisfactory) years of his life were those of the mid-1930s: the national leader surrounded by his friends in this or that small restaurant or café in Munich, in a simple and convivial circle. It was not by accident that he built his favorite mountain house (which was more than a retreat) in the Bavarian Alps. He remained grateful to Munich throughout his life. On one occasion, he mentioned to the architect Giesler that his tomb should be in Munich. (Later, he changed that to Linz.)

---

*Helene Bechstein: "I wished he'd been my son." Hitler's note on a gift to a Frau Carola Hoffman, Christmas 1925 (note the relative lateness of this date): "To my beloved true little mother [*Mütterchen*], Christmas 1925, with my homage" (HD, p. 112).

†The adoration that so many German women had for Hitler did have some sexual characteristics. (So had the frenzied adulation of Viennese women for the unmarried Mayor Karl Lueger, who was both an example and an inspiration for Hitler.) That Hitler was unmarried was a factor. Yet there remained an element of motherliness in the trust and hope with which they would say, when hearing of shocking or unpleasant events: "If only the Führer knew!"

HITLER MADE OCCASIONAL STATEMENTS to the effect that a man should not engage in politics or, indeed, in anything important, before his thirtieth year.* We have seen that maturity came to Hitler relatively late—a condition that led Heer to write that throughout his life there remained something incomplete in his personality. It might be said that in Munich, at thirty, the earnest and taciturn youth Hitler became a man; it might even be argued that this astonishing man, with all of his talents and self-discipline, never really reached maturity—by which I mean the existence of that deep-seated private judgment whereby a person comes to terms with the relationship of himself and his circumstances (a recognition that is not necessarily identical with his view of his destiny, or with a sense of that resignation which comes with age).

Because of the inevitable relationship of body and mind, there are marks (or, rather, signs) of a man's development in his physiognomy. To begin with, such signs are apparent in the pictures of Hitler before and after 1919. A few mundane items: the mustache cut shorter, the hair over his forehead longer.† The extraordinarily powerful effect of his eyes now became apparent: it had less to do with their attractive and suggestive blueness than with his conscious act of directing them, looking fixedly at his interlocutors as if stabbing them with his gaze. Heiden wrote two interesting and penetrating pages about Hitler's looks and appearance (in HD, pp. 336–37), asserting that no photographs did justice to the duality of Hitler's character. (He also concluded that, once in Munich, Hitler not only began to pay more and more attention to his appearance but that he now found it necessary to appear "normal" and

---

*"The way of men who were called upon to achieve something great in their lives was indeed a strange one. Only in the case of Mozart was such a person recognized as having special talents when still a child. Somewhere along their way through life, fate suddenly struck at these men and their special strengths were revealed." (Table Conversations, 10 May 1942)

†It is not certain that the famous enlarged picture of a man in a crowd cheering the declaration of war in a Munich square on 2 August 1914 is that of Adolf Hitler.

respectable.) That complexity was noticed by others. Peter Kleist, one of Ribbentrop's satellites, wrote in his memoirs: "I had the opportunity to study his face carefully. It has always amazed me because of the multiplicity of expressions it contained. . . . Photography, by selecting only a single moment out of context, could show only one aspect, thereby giving a false impression of the duplicity or multiplicity of being which lay behind this image." He added: "I tried to find some explanation for the hypnotic effect of those eyes without arriving at any explanation."*

Hitler was extraordinarily aware of his pictorial image. We have already noted his assiduous interest in his photographic portraits. When at the age of forty-eight (a normal time) he found it necessary to use glasses, he ordered that no picture should be taken showing him wearing spectacles. To Speer he once said that his disciplined eating habits were also the result of his decision to keep his weight down: "Imagine me going around with a potbelly. It would mean political ruin."† One (if not the best) physical description extant was written by the patrician Schramm: "The man's head seemed to dominate his entire body; torso, arms, legs—all seemed to hang down from it." He also noted Hitler's extreme mania for cleanliness. "Yet he never achieved elegance. His jacket hung about him like a sack; his trousers did not sit well. . . ."‡ More important than these doubtless accurate observations by a Hamburg patrician are Schramm's remarks about the ambivalence of Hitler's expressions:

---

*Peter Kleist, *Die europäische Tragödie,* Göttingen, 1951, p. 199. About Hitler's physical appearance see Günther Scholdt, *Autoren über Hitler,* Bonn, 1993 (hereafter: SCHO), pp. 199–209.

†SP, p. 301. One exception to his ascetic habits: his extraordinary fondness for creamy Viennese cakes.

‡SCH, pp. 17–18. One important item of Hitler's physiognomy that is rarely noted—and is obscured by the trademarks of his famous mustache and the strand of hair over his forehead—was his nose. It was a very large, almost brutal, perfectly triangular, pyramidlike nose, but this impression of its size was somewhat reduced by the mustache. Whether that mustache was cultivated because of Hitler's consciousness of his nose is questionable; what is not questionable is the existence of this consciousness. In Irving (1/w, p. 71), there is one of Hitler's sketches of himself in the 1920s: The emphasis is on that large triangular nose, and not on the determined chin ("from an original in the author's [i.e., Irving's] possession").

"The friend of women, children and animals—this was one face of Hitler neither acted nor feigned, but entirely genuine. There was, however, a second face which he did not show to his table companions, though it was no less genuine."*

One element in his character was that of the artist. He was a talented draftsman and painter, and a potential architect. These talents were often unjustly dismissed or inaccurately categorized (Fest, as also others, overemphasized the late-nineteenth-century influences); yet they were recognized by others (for example, the Scottish stage designer Edward Gordon Craig, who collected nearly one hundred of Hitler's sketches and watercolors). Maser cited Cézanne, who said that painting in the studio amounts to nothing compared to plein-air painting: "Hitler knew that, too; and his few nature pictures suggest an extraordinary talent; but that did not matter to him, because by that time he wanted to be not a painter but an architect."†

When it came to architecture, Hitler was a dilettante (Speer: "one of his characteristics"), but he was talented. Speer kept all the sketches that Hitler drew in his presence, more than one hundred of them. When it came to the discussions of Speer's building plans— Hitler's favorite pastime, if not occupation—Hitler kept drawing sketches "incessantly. They were thrown off easily, accurate in their perspectives . . . an architect could not have done it better. [Sometimes] he showed me a well-developed sketch that he had completed during the night; in most cases however these sketches were done rapidly during our discussions."‡ Hitler's addiction to drawing was known to his secretaries: he required sketch pads on his desks; he also drew sketches while telephoning, or on pieces of paper in restaurants. Speer also conceded that Hitler's approach to architecture was not rigid or "doctrinaire"; he understood the need for different styles for different buildings, and he was not impervious to criticism. (Nevile Henderson, Mussolini, and Stalin, among others, were interested in his building plans for Berlin.) My purpose here is

---

*sch, p. 24.
†m/a, p. 96.
‡sp, p. 157.

not a summation of Hitler's artistic talents for the sake of a complete Hitler portrait; it is, rather, a recognition of the artistic element in his character. A bohemian Hitler was, as Speer often remarked, very evident in his working habits—until about 1942 he rose late, ate late, and frittered away many hours. Speer commented, "When, I would often ask myself, did he really work?"* (This when he was the most powerful dictator in the world.)

At any rate, in Munich in 1919 the aspirations of a national leader rose above the aspirations of the artist (the opposite of a Nero), but one did not exclude the other: The duality remained. And (as with Nero), it would be utterly wrong to think that the artistic element in Hitler amounted to a soft or dreamy side of his character. Yes: "He wanted to make his German Reich more powerful, prestigious, vital and healthy than ever; after the war (as he often said to his circle), he would retire to peaceful occupations. He was interested in building, not razing; but if building required razing, razing it must be—with no exceptions and no mercy."† And here we arrive at a prime and powerful element in his developed character: his hate, and his consciousness of those hatreds. Maser was probably right: Hitler "recognized in Vienna that life is but a continuous bitter struggle between the weak and the strong, that in that struggle the stronger and abler will always win, and that life is not ruled by the principles of humanity but by victory and defeat." But in Hitler's case this brutal, and by no means rare, view of the world was fortified (if that is the word) further by his consciousness of hate. As early as 1921, he said in one of his speeches: "There is only defiance and hate [Trotz und Hass], hate and again hate!" He had now learned that always two things matter: "to hate and to be hard . . . a lesson devoid of love."‡

This impressed Goebbels when he met Hitler in 1926. Hitler kept telling him that he, Hitler, "had learned to hate." "His most beautiful phrase [sein schönstes Wort] yesterday: 'God has graced our struggle abundantly. God's most beautiful gift bestowed on us is

---

*SP, p. 131.
†DL, p. 156.
‡M/F, p. 83: the 1921 speech cited by F, p. 221; also GQ, p. 73.

the hate of our enemies, whom we in turn hate from the bottom of our hearts.' "

Hitler was a desperate man, while at the same time, he was a visionary of a new, heroic, pagan, and scientific world. He was an unhappy child and an unhappy adolescent, spurred by shame and resentment, surely after 1918. That his hatred issued from the sad and painful memories of a humiliated child is plausible; that, as happens to many people, he compensated for certain feelings of inferiority is plausible, too.* But not too much should be made of this; there were and are millions of humiliated children who turn out to be neither desperate nor brutal. As Schramm put it, "Hitler can be explained neither in terms of his social origins nor in terms of the influences of early environment, and not on the basis of the fact that he originated among a particular people."†

He was a strong man; and a fundamental source of his strength was hatred. Yet his hatreds did not coagulate until he was thirty years old. Before that he remained a boy; at thirty, he became a man suffused with vengeance. And what is vengeance but the idea of causing suffering in order to heal one's own suffering? The German word for vengeance is "Rache." There are few more threatening guttural words in the German language.‡

---

*One example: his frequent statements, indeed, exclamations: "I have never had a feeling of inferiority!" (On one of these significant exclamations, carefully noted by Churchill, see DL, p. 38.) In the 1920s, Hitler liked to carry a whip of water-buffalo leather. As a boy, he was a rambunctious leader in war games. Yet the only instance when Hitler physically attacked someone (an editor of the party newspaper) occurred in 1927.

†SCH, p. 125. Also: "Hitler broke loose from the social level from which he came without settling into another. He belonged to no 'class' or 'estate.' Social history, therefore, cannot provide us with the sort of essential insight we need in order to understand Hitler." SCHRB, p. 124: "A still more serious mistake would be to try to derive Hitler's way of thinking from the Catholic Church." Yet the Catholic Heer (HR, p. 406) wrote: "Especially the falling away of the remains of his Christianity shows, from decade to decade, the specific Catholic structures of his psychic mentality, as his anticlericalism, too, is specifically Catholic in its origins and formulations."

‡The German word "Hass," too, is more declaratory than the English "hatred."

OF THE FOUR—POSSIBLY FIVE—great turning points in Hitler's life, 1919 in Munich was the most important. But before saying anything about the others, we must consider two conditions. The first is that a turning point is not identical to a milestone, surely not in a person's life—a milestone is a visible event, whereas a turning point takes place in a person's mind; in the case of Munich 1919 in Hitler's life, however, it was both. The second, more complex but perhaps equally important, condition is a matter of mind, too: the importance—by which we mean the consequences—of his ideas. There is a very wise sentence by an English historian, H. C. Allen, in his *Sixteenth-Century Political Thought* that I have thought about, and used, often: "Men are constantly engaged in an, on the whole highly successful, effort to adjust their ideas to circumstances and also in an effort, very much less successful, to adjust circumstances to their ideas."* Perhaps Hitler's most astonishing achievement was his ability to achieve the latter. And (unlike Dostoyevsky's heroes and villains), it was not so much ideas that led to his thoughts but the reverse (which is relevant to the Vienna/Munich question). It was most probably in Munich that his thoughts crystallized into his principal ideas: They became, by and large, the same.

By and large: because, after all, thoughts and ideas are not exactly the same things—or, rather, they do not always remain the same. (Behind Hitler's discovery of his ability as a speaker is another, at least partly unanswerable question: What made him speak?) But let us not spin this out further. The first important turning point of his life was his coming to Vienna, in 1908. The second was his return to Munich, in 1919. The third, in 1924, was in Munich, too, when he was released from prison. His putsch, his attempt to spearhead a revolution, had failed, but had brought him to recognize something else:

---

*To which I would like to add: "of which two processes the first has been, by and large, ignored by Dostoyevsky and by many modern intellectuals." Consider, too, Heiden's startling generalization concerning the difference between talent and genius (HD, p. 44): The former fits himself propitiously into the world; the latter transforms the world in accordance with his needs—or, I should say, ideas.

that he possessed not only oratorical but political power, not merely great demagogic but great democratic abilities. He would achieve power in Germany not by a violent revolution that appealed to the imagination of people but by impressing them through a political (and thus legal and respectable) process.* And in 1938—which was the most successful year of his entire career—came another turning point, eventually leading to a catastrophe—his catastrophe.

What occurred then was another change in his mind. His concern with his health reached a critical stage. Unlike Bismarck, Hitler was often in a hurry. He feared that Fate, or Providence, would not allow him to fulfill his great tasks for Germandom. Throughout his life he had minor ailments. While not a hypochondriac, he was often worried about his health. Soon after his triumphant progress to Vienna, he dictated a detailed private will (2 May 1938). Throughout the rest of 1938, there was a marked change in his habits. He now shunned the least physical exercise; he drastically changed his eating and drinking habits; he withdrew from the convivialities of his cohorts. His subsequent concentration on foreign policy, his preparation for a war, was a consequence of this. There was no time left.†

---

*In this respect, the conclusion of the American historian Harold C. Gordon, at the end of his fine book (see above, p. 39) on Hitler's 1923 putsch, is worth considering (pp. 618–19): "By sheer determination and sense of mission Hitler transformed himself from the frenetic revolutionary who had been shattered and silenced by the Putsch into a political leader ready to accept years of careful building and constant struggle as a prelude to power. Rossbach, Ehrhardt and Ludendorff all failed to turn this vital corner and perished politically. Hitler took it in stride and left them far behind. The Putsch had transformed the old Hitler into the new, just as World War I and the revolution had turned the bohemian would-be artist of Vienna and München into a revolutionary leader—and of the two transformations it was perhaps the greater. [This is debatable.] Hitler's first crisis made him a revolutionary. His second made him the undisputed leader of a serious political movement. The third crisis brought him to the helm of Germany, while the fourth led him to conquest, defeat, and death."

†We know many important details of his medical history. (See PH, p. 83; also M/A, chapter 8.) "His belief that he was ill and there was little time left, henceforth rules all of Hitler's thoughts, plans, and acts." (M/A, p. 331) Perhaps not "rules" but "influences." Deuerlein and Fest recognized this even earlier; see F, p. 536, where there is a reference to "Wesensänderung," a change in personality. So did Speer recall the change in Hitler, to whom he was very close at that time. An important

During this year, 1938, this change in Hitler's mind became complete. From that year onward, he thought he was more ill than he actually was.* Yet "actually," in this context, is an imprecise word. His increasingly frequent gastrointestinal ailments were, to use a modern and not very satisfactory term, at least to some extent psychosomatic. Their etiology, indeed the etiology of many such illnesses, was existential, not merely functional—and this was bound to be an exaggerated condition in the life of a man whose force of character had its source in his belief in the power of the mind and of the will. Perhaps we may detect God's hand in the development of this paradox: This man, who so often spoke of the primacy of mind over matter, and of will over flesh, now began to move downhill and eventually into catastrophe—because of the developing state of his mind, which affected his body, whose symptoms, in turn, impressed him with a deep inner sense that he had not long to live. His belief in mind over matter had raised him to the highest power on earth; and this belief would destroy him in the end.

To this we may add the last—albeit arguable—turning point, in November 1941, when Hitler (much earlier than we have been accustomed to think) realized that he could no longer win *his* war in *his* way. But the discussion of this must be left to chapter 5 of this book.†

---

example: In January 1938 Hitler suddenly ordered Speer to build the New Reich chancellery, to be ready within a year (for the annual reception of the diplomatic corps scheduled for 9 January 1939—it was actually completed two days before that). SP, p. 103: "The haste with which Hitler was urging the building . . . had a deeper cause in his anxiety about his health. He seriously feared that he did not have much longer to live." (Destroyed in 1945, the New Reich chancellery was Speer's—often unjustly maligned—finest building.) See also Leon Krier, *Albert Speer: Architecture 1932–1942*, Brussels, 1985 (hereafter: K).

*At least until 1944, when his condition *was* aggravated by Parkinson's disease.

†In SP, p. 472, see also Speer's observations about the last years of Hitler's life: "In addition he had again become more amiable and more willing to drop into his private mood. In many ways he reminded me of the Hitler I had known at the beginning of our association twelve years before, except that he now seemed more shadowy. He centered his amiability on the few women who had been with him for years."

3

Reactionary and/or Revolutionary?

A problem of definitions—Hitler's revolutionary rhetoric—
His appeal to conservatives—His revolutionary achievements—
The question of a duality—A revolutionary of a new kind

T HE HISTORY OF POLITICS is a history of words. The word
"revolutionary," applied to politics, is a little more than two
hundred years old. "Reactionary" is more recent: According
to the *Oxford English Dictionary*, its first appearance in English is
1858. ("Nationalist" and "capitalist," too, are more recent than we
are accustomed to think—they appear around 1850.) However,
150 years is a long time, during which—indeed, from the very
beginning of the usage of these words—"reactionary" has had a uni-
versally bad connotation, while "revolutionary" has had many connotations, often positive ones. The reasoning (rather than reason)
behind this should be obvious. A revolutionary is a promoter of
Progress—perhaps dangerously, at the expense of law and order,
but an advocate of Progress nonetheless, while a reactionary is not.
The latter not only denies the benefits of "Progress" but reacts
against it: he wants to turn the clock back, indeed history backward.

This is why many, if not most, people (even now) have thought
of Hitler as a reactionary, given his statements about race, or Jews,
or women, or political liberty, or nationalism, or the philosophy of

the Enlightenment. But we have a problem here. It involves not only the extraordinariness of Hitler but the slowly eroding meaning of our political vocabulary. As early as 1835 the young Tocqueville, returning from America, wrote that "a new science of politics is necessary for a new world." It has not been forthcoming. The terms "right" and "left" (which appeared shortly before Tocqueville's birth) and the application of the words "conservative" and "liberal" to parties and politics (which did not occur in England until the 1820s) are still prevalent, even though we live in a very different world from that of the 1830s, and when not only "conservative" and "liberal" but also "right" and "left" have changed and inflated their meanings to such an extent that they are almost—though not wholly—useless. Already during Hitler's lifetime, the terms "right" and "left" did not properly apply to him. Was he to the right or to the left of, say, the Pope? Or Franco? Or even Churchill? That he was a radical (which is the oldest of English political adjectives) is obvious. That he was not a conservative is also obvious. But we have reached a stage where we must rethink not only the appropriate meaning of some of these now often antiquated terms but also the very idea of such older and larger terms as "progress" and "modern."

This brings me to the central theme of this chapter: Was Hitler reactionary or not? Or was he a compound of a reactionary and a revolutionary? This is not a semantic question, and it is not addressed to the kind of intellectuality that tends to substitute vocabulary for thought. We may glimpse the confusing nature of it in two dramatic statements issued at the most dramatic moment of World War II, at the highest moment of Hitler's career, June 1940, when France was collapsing and he seemed to be the victor of the war. A few days before the French surrendered, their—by no means unintelligent—premier Paul Reynaud made his last broadcast: "If Hitler wins," he said, "it would be the Middle Ages again, but not illuminated by the mercy of Christ." That is, Hitler the reactionary—a new kind of reactionary, perhaps, but someone who is turning the clock, and history, backward. A few days later (on 18 June 1940), Churchill saw differently. The prospect he evoked was not that of a *return* to the Middle Ages but that of an enormous lurch *forward*, to a new Dark Age. If Hitler wins and we fall, he said, "then the whole world, including the United States, including all that we have known and cared for, will sink into the abyss of a New Dark Age made more sinister, and perhaps more protracted, by the light of perverted science." Note the words "protracted" and "science." Churchill did not consider Hitler a reactionary. To the contrary, he knew that Hitler represented a revolutionary force in the world, one that carried a new revolutionary appeal to many people—especially in the event of his victory. Hitler was thrusting the wheel of History forward,* in a new and sinister direction—which was why he had to be stopped—and reacted against.

Now this question does (and did) pose particular difficulties in Germany for Germans. Among other things, the meaning of "reactionary" and of "reaction" are, at least slightly, more condemnatory in Germany than in England. One reason for this is the failure of a liberal-democratic revolution in Germany in 1848 (and the compromised character of their November revolution in 1918). There is the inclination of many Germans to see the Hitler era as a dreadful and unnatural chapter, or episode, in modern German history, a veritable lurch backward, disrupting the—belated—progress of Germany in a liberal and democratic direction, to conform to the Western and Atlantic democracies. This perception (or, rather, the insistence on its validity) lay underneath some of the arguments of many of the functionalists in the functionalist-intentionalist debate among historians mentioned in chapter 1. Consider the question posed by Hans Mommsen, a principal historian among the functionalists: "Is it proper [*sinnvoll*] to give National Socialism the adjective 'revolutionary,' and therefore array it with those developments in the history of Europe that had begun with the French Revolution of 1789?" As Schreiber put it in his historiographical survey, many Germans, and of course such "functionalists" as

---

*I found Hitler's own use of that figure of speech *after* I had written the above, in JHH, p.171, note 28, citing a statement by Hitler in 1931: "If once more World Jewry wants to turn the wheel of History backward, then it will be crushed by the same wheel."

Mommsen, are still reluctant to call Hitler a revolutionary; "historical research is still unwilling to rethink the meaning of what is 'revolutionary.' " Mommsen "refuses to include Hitler in the group of world-historical revolutionaries (Bracher is more ambivalent and careful: he sees in the Third Reich a previously unknown combination of traditionalism and revolution)." Thus Schreiber concludes: "The answer to the question whether it is permissible or not to describe Hitler as a revolutionary depends, first of all, on the determination of the meaning of 'revolution.' About this the historical-scientific debate is still undecided."*

However, there is something unnecessarily cautious and pedantic about this kind of semantic reluctance. From the very beginning, all kinds of biographers and commentators of Hitler recognized—indeed, emphasized—the revolutionary character of his ideas, his rhetoric, his plans, and their execution. Among them we may list such very different interpreters as Rauschning (with all due consideration to the liberties of his "reconstruction"), as well as Irving. Both Deuerlein and Fest referred, more than once, to Hitler as "a real [wirklicher] revolutionary."† A significant, and valuable, contribution to Hitler historiography is the work of the German literary historian L. P. Stern, *Hitler, the Führer and the People* (I., 1975), in which Stern argues that Hitler's worldview was not at all reactionary or even bound to nineteenth-century ideas but was specifically German and new.‡ A very substantial work is that of the American historian David Schoenbaum (*Hitler's Social Revolution*, NY, 1966), a cogent and convincing summation of the transformation of

---

*SCHRB, pp. 250, 252, 253, 263: "The dilemma of the definition seems to be unsolvable."

†F, p. 238.

‡There were, as we shall see, German conservatives who—some cautiously, some not—welcomed the Hitler movement as "counterrevolutionary," especially before and in 1933. There were virtually no such German interpretations after 1945, whether cautiously apologetic regarding Hitler or not (except, of course, by some Marxists in East Germany). One exception, and definitely not an apologetic one: Christian Graf von Krockow, *Scheiterhaufen, Grösse und Elend des deutschen Geistes* (B, 1983), in which Krockow insists on the counterrevolutionary, antiegalitarian element in Hitler, the very opposite of the ideals of the French Revolution.

the German social structure that Hitler and the Third Reich had brought about.*

A remarkable, and recent, contribution was made by Rainer Zitelmann. At the early age of twenty-five, Zitelmann had already produced a substantial dissertation (at the time only available in typescript), in which he argued that the social revolution in the Third Reich had been planned by Hitler, and that it was not (as many historians reluctantly explained) the largely unplanned consequence of Hitler's otherwise confused and confusing social ideas.† Already, at that time, Zitelmann indicated his intention to prepare a larger work on this topic; and he was as good as his word. In 1987, ZIT/A was published. In the very last sentence (p. 404) of the second (1988) edition of his historiographical survey, Schreiber praised Zitelmann's "consistent and convincing" definition of Hitler as a "revolutionary." "A provocative book, and one of the rare studies that has achieved an essential advance in the historical research [about Hitler] since 1984." There have followed, during the last six years, various works of the prolific Zitelmann, including his Hitler biography (ZIT/B), several collections of studies under his editorship, including Michael Prinz and Rainer Zitelmann, eds., *Nationalsozialismus und Modernisierung*, 1992 (expanded ed., Darmstadt, 1994).‡ Note the wording: "National Socialism and Modernization." There were many things in National Socialism and in Hitler's ideas and plans that were *modern*.

It is not surprising that this, perhaps somewhat bold, explication of the Third Reich and of Hitler as "modern" would shock those historians, especially in Germany, who preferred to regard Hitler,

---

*Similar perceptions (though seldom categorically defined or expressed) exist in a great variety of monographic and special studies, especially since about 1970. One good example is VFZ, January 1983: Horst Möller, "Die nationalsozialistische Machtergreifung. Konterrevolution oder Revolution?," in which Möller quietly but convincingly comes out in favor of the latter assertion.

†See SCHRB, p. 250, no. 290: "an outstanding work." Also: Zitelmann, *Soziale Zielsetzungen und revolutionäre Motive in Hitlers Weltanschauung als Forschungsdesiderat*, Darmstadt, 1983. The very title suggests its author's insistence that his theme ought to be researched and studied further.

‡Hereafter: ZIT/PR.

if not as "reactionary," then as opposed to "modernity"; that is, to the progressive, liberal-democratic world whose ideals and practice Germany had failed to adopt until it was too late. Still it behooves us, at the end of the twentieth century, to rethink not only the meaning of Hitler but also the very meaning of the idea of "Progress" and of "modern." I shall come back to what was "modern" and "social," and perhaps even "progressive," in Hitler's views and plans for his people later in this chapter and also in other chapters—not for the purpose of mitigating his record but, to the contrary, to emphasize the abiding dangers of their past (and at times at least potentially present) attractions.* Some of the functionalists, especially Hans Mommsen, have emphasized the responsibility—personal, political, rhetorical, and ideological— of the "older elites" in Germany for allowing, or even abetting, Hitler's coming to power; and this, in many instances, was indeed true. But in that particular historical instance it was the Sorcerer who was young, and his Apprentices who were old; and by this I do not only mean their respective ages but their respective ideas as well.

HITLER HIMSELF SAID—AGAIN and again—that he was a revolutionary. Again and again, he said that he was to be the leader of a national revolution. These were not simply rhetorical devices or habits. So he saw himself throughout his entire political career; that is, throughout the last thirty-six years of his life.† Here again the Munich turning point of his life is significant. There is no evidence that he thought of himself as a revolutionary (or that he saw his congealing ideas as revolutionary by nature) before 1919. There was a short period in his political career—before he gained the chancellorship and for some time afterward, to which we shall return—when he did not often employ the words "revolution" and "revolutionary." This was part of his political calculation: to establish and solidify his

---

*See especially chapter 9.

†Except that his own notion as a Leader, Führer, of a movement appeared only in 1921–22.

respectability among the conservative nationalists, the army—indeed, among a mass of the German people. But he never denied—either to himself or to others—his view of himself and his conviction of his destiny in the history of Germany as the fulfiller of a national revolution. In any event, a reactionary he was not. As he himself said on many an occasion: reactionaries, as well as Communists or Marxists or Jews, were his main enemies, within Germany as well as abroad. Indeed (he said this often), within Germany the reactionaries were his most dangerous enemies. The well-known line in the "Horst-Wessel-Lied," the National Socialist fighting and marching song, expressed his own views: Avenge "Kameraden, die Redfront und Reaktion erschossen"—comrades killed by the Red Front and by the Reactionaries.

We must accept his word in order to understand him. At the same time, we must direct some attention to its meaning. A revolutionary does not only wish to change the direction of the ship of state; he wishes to remake its society. We have no evidence that before 1919 Hitler showed any deep dissatisfaction with the order of German society, except perhaps for his desire to see certain elements (Socialists, Jews, internationalists) excluded from influential positions within it. But when his resentments and desires for revenge erupted in 1919, these were not directed primarily against the enemies of Germany abroad but against those he thought were within: not only, and not even primarily, against the Versailles Treaty but against a political and social order in Germany that he saw as destructive, corrupt, hopeless, and weak. Soon he found that he had many potential allies, many of them from the nationalist and conservative middle classes.

To "nationalist" and "conservative" we must add "counter-revolutionary." That was a very acceptable and logical term then, and for some time thereafter. Whatever the deeper roots of nationalism, and conservativism, and anti-Marxism, and anti-Semitism in the minds of these people were, their then-present convictions were the result of their experience and their reactions against the leftist revolutionaries in Munich and elsewhere in Germany in 1918–19. Between 1910 and 1923 the term "counterrevolutionary" in Bavaria and Germany, as well as many other places in Europe, was almost identical with the Radical Right. Almost: but not quite.* Hitler, as we saw in chapter 2, knew that he could profit from his alliance with the counterrevolutionaries, and from his acceptance by certain social circles in Munich. But soon—latest after 1920—he began to have reservations; indeed, he began to despise many of his potential (and even some of his actual) allies. This happened even before his failed putsch in November 1923: a rising that failed because of the—at first reluctant, then, in the last moment, determined—decision of the counterrevolutionary and the traditionalist elements of the German state and social order to reject him. Or, rather: his leadership of a national revolution. After that came the next turning point of his life and career: his decision to achieve power in Germany not through an armed revolution but by acceptable (and, in the broadest sense of the word, democratic) means; not by a dramatic uprising against the state and the social order but by convincing the masses of the German people, reminding them that in their hearts they would know that he was right.

He achieved this. As many of the electoral and sociographical studies of the 1928–33 period show, the novelty of his National Socialist Party did not reside only in its organization and propaganda. Unlike all other political parties in Weimar Germany, the National Socialists were a true people's party, a *Volkspartei*, since they gained adherents across the board, from all elements of German society. They were neither a typically lower-middle-class nor a predominantly Protestant or decisively capitalist-supported party (the latter, the explication of Marxist historians and political scientists, was insubstantial and has largely been disproved). As a matter of fact, the general tendency and result of research of the last fifteen years at least indicate that, surely after 1928, a significant movement toward the Hitler camp came from the German working classes. Hitler realized this long before 1930. More important: true to him-

---

*Within Germany (and Austria), the positive meaning of "counterrevolutionary" had largely disappeared by 1933; in some other European nations (Hungary, Spain, the Baltics), it lingered on until about 1938. But there, too (as indeed in Austria after 1930), the main struggle developed between the two "Rights"—between a conservative and a populist one, between a traditionalist and a radical Right.

self as a revolutionary, his main sympathies and loyalties were directed to the German workers. There are historians who describe Hitler as a typical man of the lower middle classes, a petit bourgeois turned fanatic. That picture is largely wrong. There *were* a few petit-bourgeois elements in his preferences and in his manners (how could there not be: no one can shed his origins or his childhood entirely). But much more significant was his loathing of the bourgeoisie, of the traditional German *Bürgertum*, of their "reactionary" values.

This he discovered early, well before the "counterrevolutionaries" deserted him on that bloody morning in November 1923. He had become repelled by the traditionalist values of the German bourgeoisie. He was contemptuous of their caution, of their thrift, of their respect for the monarchy, of their social aspirations, of their desire for safety, of their class-consciousness, of an entire range of their characteristics, from bourgeois "Gemütlichkeit" to the old-fashioned standards of patriciandom.*

These were antiquated remnants of a time now long past. Instances of this from Hitler's very statements are too numerous to detail here. As early as 1920, he was impressed by the revolutionary antibourgeois hero of a play by Hanns Johst (one of the few prominent German writers who became an admirer of Hitler) entitled *Der König*, where the protagonist hero revolts against the traditionalist

---

*Here I must draw attention to another, now unfortunately confusing, terminology. This is the still extant (though now somewhat fading) identification of "bourgeois" with "middle class." The two terms are not the same. On the one hand, the inflation of "middle class" has been such that it has become increasingly devoid of its once meaning. On the other hand, "bourgeois" has lately begun to lose the pejorative meaning attributed to it not only by Marxists but by bohemians, artists, and aristocrats (or by their admirers) in the nineteenth century. (See a discussion of this in my essay "The Bourgeois Interior" in *The American Scholar*, September 1970; also in *The Passing of the Modern Age*, NY, 1970.) To this we must add the specifically German meaning of "Bürger," suggesting not only "middle-class" or "bourgeois" but also "citizen," "townsman," "freeman of a city"—the latter with a patrician tinge. Hitler's ideal was "Völkisch"—that is, populist: a largely (though perhaps not entirely) classless Germany, resting on the strength of the National Socialist convictions of its people. That the German *Bürgertum* shared some of the "Völkisch" ideology did not mean that they were "populists," surely not in Hitler's sense.

classes, coming to a tragic end, for eventually he is betrayed by the reactionaries and the bourgeois, and prefers to die by his own hand. When Hitler first met Johst in 1923 (in the patrician apartment of his friends the Bruckmanns in Munich), he told him that he had seen *Der König* seventeen (!) times in the previous three years, that it was his favorite drama, and that perhaps his own life might end that way.* Whatever the significance of this—in retrospect startling— remark, there can be no doubt that in his rejection of the bour- geoisie Hitler remained consistent throughout his life. One example, from one of his table conversations on 5 September 1941: "The cowardice and the stupidity of the educated Bürgertum filled him with such revulsion in those times that now, too, when the Bürgertum run after him because of their opportunities, he has had enough of them. Had he not had his followers from among the people he would have despaired of the Germans."† There was more to this than rhetoric; it was an expression of one of his deepest con- victions. According to Zitelmann, Hitler's outbursts and objurga- tions against the older bourgeoisie were seldom merely emotional; they had a rational fundament.‡ Perhaps. But what remains true is that after his failure in 1923, Hitler learned a lesson: he realized that he had to bring both German *Bürgertum* and conservatives to his side. He needed—at least for some time—an alliance with them, "not *despite* his understanding of their ineffectiveness and weakness but *because* of it."**

AT LEAST DURING the ten years from 1924 to 1934, Hitler was consciously willing and able to attract conservatives with an anti- revolutionary rhetoric—even as expressions of his exaltation of the workers and his rejection of the "selfish" upper classes remained fre- quent. The Sorcerer's mastery in politics now included the occa-

---

*SCHO, p. 734.

†Koeppen notes, p. 2 of the manuscript in the IFZ.

‡ZIT/A, p. 146. Cf. HD, p. 11, in which Heiden, who in this instance was wrong, wrote: "Hitler's entire life is his singular and unhappy love for good bourgeois [guten bürgerlichen] society."

**ZIT/A, p. 84.

sional intonation of the "conservative" side of his ideology. The most important—and effective—element here was his anticommunism; but there were, too, more than occasional presentations of himself and of National Socialism as being antirevolutionary, and even many positive declarations in favor of Christianity.

The psychology of anticommunism (more precisely, the history of its appeal) still awaits treatment by a master historian. Its appeal was not restricted to those who, no matter how briefly, experienced brutalities and misdeeds of a Soviet-like rule (as had the people of Munich in the spring of 1919). Nor was it restricted to the upper or to the property-owning classes, who had much to fear from the expropriations of a Marxist revolution. The main appeal of anti-communism has seldom been economic. There was the fear of revolution, yes; but even when and where the prospects of a Communist revolution were minimal, the stronger current was the respectability of nationalism, including the rejection of an internationalist doctrine, and of people who seemed to be among its proponents.*

Hitler was, of course, a *National* Socialist; of the two adjectives, the former was more important, and decisive, than the latter. But he was an opponent of *international* capitalism, as well as of *international* socialism. As a matter of fact, he had more of an appreciation of Communists and even of certain Socialists than of capitalists and reactionaries. There are many statements of his in that regard. Not many of them were made in public. He knew that in order to come to power, he had to appeal to the anticommunism of the German conservatives. In November 1932, he told Hindenburg: "The Bolshevization of the masses proceeds rapidly." He knew that this was not true. He also knew that this kind of argument would impress Hindenburg and the conservatives. Unlike nine years before, when

---

*Hence, for example, the frequent anti-Marxism among the working classes in many parts of the world: a thorough refutation of Marx. It may also be of interest to notice that anticommunism was often most popular not when the power of the Soviet Union or when the local Communists or Marxists were strongest but when they were weakest: thus in many European countries in the 1930s and in the United States in the 1950s—for instance, during the McCarthy years.

his revolutionary attempt was shot down in the Munich streets, he would become the ruler of Germany legally, constitutionally, democratically, and not against but with the support of the most respectable people in Germany—at least in part because of their anticommunism. It is significant that he continued using this theme even after he became chancellor, and even after the election campaign that finally led to his consolidation of power. On 14 October 1933 (and in a speech justifying Germany's departure from the League of Nations), he said: "The Red revolt could have spread across Germany like wildfire. . . . For eight months now we have been waging a heroic struggle against the Communist threat to our people. . . ." (This at a time when the Communists in Germany had been annihilated, their leaders in prison or in exile.) On 27 June 1934 (three days before his move against Röhm, the "Night of the Long Knives"), he received three Catholic bishops, to whom he declared: "The defense of Europe against Bolshevism is our task for the next two or three hundred years."*

He knew how to appeal to the conservatives. Already in *Mein Kampf* he praised the Christian-populist Karl Lueger, "who knew how to use the existing structures of power and authority, using such older elements and institutions to the advantage of his own movement." We saw that he sought, and gained, entry to conservative circles in Munich as early as 1920–21. In 1926, he fought and won against the radical Gregor Strasser within the party, agreeing to vote in favor of a restitution of properties to the former German princes that had been taken from them in 1918—a cause dear to the older German conservatives. In 1930, he said: "Against us stands an older Germany. It is no longer our world, but we do not wish to be torn away from this older Germany, because to it belong

---

*Cited by Klaus Scholder, *Die Kirchen und das Dritte Reich*, B, 1985, I, p. 246. He would, of course, return to such arguments after his invasion of the Soviet Union in June 1941, but at that time he would no longer do so in the service of domestic politics but as an instrument of his statesmanship; while at the same time (again, privately), he often expressed his admiration for Stalin, together with his contemptuous hatred of the reactionary capitalists Churchill and Roosevelt. For more details about this, see chapter 5.

millions of most decent people. . . ."* As late as 1934, Hitler said that "the agitated age of the nineteenth century is finally over with us. In the next one thousand years there will be no more revolutions in Germany."† It was because of such statements—and not only because of opportunistic political calculations—that this Sorcerer gained the support of his older and old-fashioned Apprentices, men such as Papen, fellow travelers whose inclinations mirrored those of fellow travelers of Communists ("No enemy on the Left"). For the former, there would be no enemy on the "Right"; and they saw Hitler as a man of the Right, which is how *he* wanted them to see him.

Just so did the antireligious and anti-Catholic Hitler know how to gain the—at least partial, and at least temporary—support of the German Catholic hierarchy, and the partial support of the German Catholic masses. While Friedrich Heer was wrong in overstressing the importance of the residual Catholic elements in Hitler's mind, what remains true is Hitler's conscious appreciation of—and his appeal to—the religious factor in ideology and in politics. In *Mein Kampf*, he wrote in detail about his admiration for George von Schönerer, the anticlerical leader of the Austrian pan-German movement; but he wrote that Schönerer, unlike the Catholic Lueger, had made the mistake of being outspokenly antireligious. In this respect, too, Hitler's searing experience in November 1923 marked a turning point. He turned away from the anti-Catholic Ludendorff (and, indirectly, against a memory of the Bismarck period): In the future, there must be no "Kulturkampf" in Germany. In *Mein Kampf*, there are many passages that warn against a campaign against religious believers in Germany. A political leader must not touch the reli-

---

*Cited by Heiden, HD, p. 228. To this add Heiden's remarkable insight: "What is certain: Hitler as speaker gives the impression of an honest man. At the highest moments of his speeches he may be deceiving himself, and whether he says true things or the thickest lies, he is still what he says, [they are] fully the expressions of his own self. . . . The unity of man and his words is the [second] secret of his success." (HD, pp. 101–2) Also: "No matter how contemptible his ideas may be, his achievement is a proof of the old adage: genius results from diligence [*das Genie fleiss ist*]. Through his indefatigability Hitler defeated his opponents." (HD, p. 103)

†Cited by Heer, HR, p. 273.

gious teachings of his people: "For, if so, he must be not a politician but a religious reformer, if he has it in him!"* And later: "In the ranks of our movement there is a place for the believing Protestant sitting next to the believing Catholic, without the slightest conflict of their respective consciences with their religious convictions." Speer recalled that when in 1937 Hitler heard that many of his followers had dropped their church membership upon the urging of party and SS leaders, he forbade his close collaborators, including Göring and Goebbels, to do so; and that in 1942 he insisted upon the absolute necessity to maintain the churches. He "condemned sharply the struggle against the churches: a crime against the future of the people: to substitute a 'Party-ideology' is an impossibility."†

This Hitlerian politic explains—at least partly—the at first reluctant and later consenting support given Hitler by not only the Catholic Papen but by the Catholic Center Party in 1933. It was the only party, Hitler later said, whose firm opposition he had feared; the only party where a mass of voters had not gone over to the National Socialists in the previous elections.‡ Before the national election in March 1933—indeed, immediately after his assumption of the chancellorship—Hitler knew what to say: The national government "will preserve and defend the fundaments on

---

*HR, p. 235. Also pp. 220–21: "Rereading *Mein Kampf* in 1938 I find something very significant: Adolf Hitler takes here extraordinary consideration for his Christian, Catholic, clerical, Bavarian, conservative believers. That is the hard truth: very much in *Mein Kampf* could be unquestionably accepted by these very Christian, Lutheran, Catholic and conservative faithful: the attacks against Jews, Freemasons, democracy, the call for the destruction of the Soviet Union, the 'necessary' struggle against France." And: "In *Mein Kampf* Adolf Hitler expressly distances himself from the . . . neo-Pagan, 'Germanic religion' ideas. In many places a present reading of *Mein Kampf* gives the impression of his wish . . . to appease and calm his Christian followers."

†SP, p. 95. "Undoubtedly . . . the church would learn to adapt to the political goals of National Socialism in the long run, as it had always adapted in the course of history. A new party religion would only bring about a relapse into the mysticism of the Middle Ages. The growing SS myth showed that clearly enough, as did Rosenberg's unreadable *Myth of the Twentieth Century*."

‡Hitler in one of his table talks, 18 September 1941 (Koeppen notes, p. 13): "Brüning, a man of some talent . . . my most dangerous opponent was undoubtedly the Center Party."

which the strength of our nation rests. It will be the strong pro-
tector of Christianity as the basis of our common moral order, and
of the family as the basic cell of the people and body of our nation."*
And on 15 February 1933, in Stuttgart: "They say today that Chris-
tendom is imperiled, that the Catholic faith is in danger. To this I
answer: 'Finally there are Christians and not international atheists
who are in charge in Germany.' " After his electoral empowerment
Hitler went on with this theme. He spoke of the "Christian fundament of the state." On 1 May 1933: "We do not ask the Almighty:
'Lord, make us free!' We want to work, in brotherly understanding,
struggling together, so that the hour comes when we may face the
Lord and say: 'Lord, we have changed!' "† It was thus that Papen—
perhaps sincerely but wrongly—could say that the Third Reich was
"the Christian countermovement to 1789"; that is, the counter-
revolution to the French Enlightenment.

This is not the place to detail the complicated and melancholy
history of Hitler's relationship with the leaders of the German
churches. It has been studied often, and described at times carefully
and well. What belong here are a few examples of Hitler's continued acknowledgment of the importance of that relationship.
During the previously mentioned June 1934 meeting with three
archbishops (Gröber of Freiburg, Berning of Osnabrück, Bares of
Berlin), Hitler said, "Never in this life will I lead a Kulturkampf."
He was even able to impress anti-Nazi princes of the Church. (Thus
Cardinal Faulhaber of Munich, after meeting Hitler in 1936: "The
Führer is a master of diplomatic and social manners, as if he were a
born monarch, if not better.")‡ In August 1941, Hitler ordered that
no move should be undertaken against Archbishop von Galen of
Münster, who had openly attacked the euthanasia practices of the
government during a Sunday sermon. In the same month Hitler
threatened the Gauleiter of Bavaria with removal and imprisonment

---

*Cited in ZIT/PR, p. 13.

†Cited in HR, pp. 250, 262.

‡D, p. 119. Cardinal Faulhaber in his sermon on New Year's Eve, 1938, praised
Hitler's "example of a simple, sober way of life, free of alcohol and nicotine. . . ."
Cited in Lothar Gruchmann, "Korruption im Dritten Reich," VFZ, October 1994,
p. 577.

because of the latter's stupid attempt to have the crucifixes removed from Bavarian schoolrooms. That year Bormann, in a party directive, included a sentence: "Christianity and National Socialism are not reconcilable." Hitler ordered the removal of that sentence and the instant cancellation of the directive.* Yet at the same time, and often during the war, he told his circle that the business of taking the churches to task would have to wait until the end of the war. Then they would be properly dealt with, and German youth would be liberated from their influences.

He knew what he was doing, and whereof he was speaking. Whatever duality may have existed within him, he was aware of the duality within the German people. After all, the same Archbishop (later Cardinal) von Galen—still sometimes hailed as a leading figure of Christian resistance against Hitler—in the same, now-celebrated sermon in August 1941, praised the German crusade against Russia and Bolshevism. Here, however, our concern is not with the ideas—including the religious ideas—of the people of Germany; it is with the ideas (and the rhetoric and politics) of Adolf Hitler.

IN 1934, AFTER HIS EXPULSION from the party and his exile from Germany, Otto Strasser predicted that Hitler would "flee into war" in order to avoid choosing between "reaction" and "revolution."† Strasser's prophecy of Hitler going to war was correct, but his analysis of Hitler's purpose was not. Strange as this may sound, foreign policy was secondary in Hitler's intentions—or, at least, consistent with his primary and principal intention: that of forging a new kind of unity of the German people. In this his vision was different from that of the great German historian Leopold von Ranke, who wrote of "Das Primat der Aussenpolitik" (the primacy of foreign policy in the histories of nations).‡ It differed, too, from Bismarck,

---

*FR, p. 33.

†SCHRB, p. 152.

‡The important element in this was Ranke's (and also Hegel's) view of the supreme importance of *the state*—which for Hitler was superseded by the primacy of *the nation*. (See chapter 4.)

whose main concern with a potential national disunity came after his great achievement of establishing a powerful German state. As early as 1923, Hitler decided (and instructed the party accordingly) that the struggle against the then French occupation of the Ruhr was secondary; the first task was to achieve the national revolution at home before driving out the foreign occupier—and not only because in 1923 Germany was too weak to risk a war with the French. His political realism, especially after 1923,* was apparent in his continued priority of "Innenpolitik." Reminiscing about the years 1930–32, he said that Chancellor Brüning was "a man of some talent; but his greatest mistake was to attempt successes in foreign policy and thereby increase his popularity, whereas he [the Führer] proceeded exactly in the opposite way, knowing that foreign policy can never be successful when the domestic political conditions for it are not at hand."†

Notwithstanding all of the necessary reservations about Rauschning's authenticity, his attribution of the following statement to Hitler sounds like a true and clear reflection of Hitler's mind. Upon the question of whether he was planning to nationalize German industry, Hitler is supposed to have said: "Why should I nationalize the industries? I will nationalize the people"—a trenchant expression of his political principles. To the assembled industrialists in Düsseldorf on 27 January 1932, he said: "It was not that German industry had triumphed world-wide, after which came the development of German state power [*Machtentwicklung*]; then, too, German power had achieved the main conditions for the later blossoming of German industry." And in a speech in 1937: "If the German industrialists were to tell me: 'We cannot do this,' then I would say to them: 'Good—so I will take this up, because it has to be done.' But

---

*Bullock (BU, p. 314) recognized Hitler's realism in 1923: His insistence that the first task was to overthrow the republic "rather than to waste German strength in a fight with the French which the Germans were bound to lose" was sound; but Bullock was wrong (p. 93, note 1) in drawing a parallel between Hitler and Lenin ("both wishing to achieve the revolution at home before driving the foreign invader out"). In F, p. 430, Fest remarked on the primacy of domestic policy, though he did not sufficiently emphasize Hitler's successful anti-Communist propaganda.

†Koeppen notes, 18 September 1941, p. 13.

when the industry tells me: 'We can do that," then I am very pleased not to have to take it upon myself."* *Summa summarum:* It made no difference whether Krupp was nationalized. Irving was probably right when he wrote that Hitler "had a sounder appreciation of economics than people believed," though Irving added, exaggeratedly, as has been his wont: "Over the first few months Schacht and the Reich Cabinet came to regard Hitler as a genius."† Zitelmann, more convincingly, produced considerable evidence that Hitler was not ignorant of economics; and that his amazingly rapid elimination of German unemployment was made possible only through "a gigantic rearmament program is only partly true."‡ All of this was clearly seen by Simone Weil, as stated in an unpublished paper, in 1942: "If Hitler despises economy, it is probably not simply because he understands nothing about it. It is because he *knows* (it is one of the notions of simple common sense that he clearly possesses and that can be called inspired since such ideas are so little understood) that economy is not an independent reality and as a result does not really have laws, since in economy as in all other spheres human affairs are ruled by force. . . . It seems to me difficult to deny that Hitler conceives, and conceives clearly . . . a kind of physics of human matter. . . . He possesses an exact notion of the power of force."**

From the revolutionary drummer to the political leader and then to the head of the state and of its armed forces in war: these were stages in Hitler's career. Many people thought, and hoped, that after his assumption to power he would become more moderate because of the exigencies of government and of statecraft. We have seen that he was willing to grant some credence to such hopes and

---

*The first quote by Heer, HR, p. 247; the second by Zitelmann, ZIT/A, p. 118.
†I/W, p. 21.

‡Haffner, HF/AN, pp. 28–29: "Was the German economic miracle of the Thirties really Hitler's achievement? In spite of all conceivable objections one will probably have to reply in the affirmative. It is entirely true that . . . economic matters, prior to 1933, had played virtually no part in his plans or political thinking." And the economic miracle was not simply due to rearmament. HF/AN, p. 31: "In actual fact, the Third Reich was producing guns *and* butter, and a great many other things."

**Quoted by Simone Petrément, *Simone Weil: A Life,* NY, 1976, pp. 510–11. See also Peter Drucker, *The End of Economic Man,* L, 1939, a book that was supposed to have been read by Churchill with interest.

beliefs; but none of this meant that he had changed his own radical and revolutionary views. He was more than a demagogue; he was a populist. Often Hitler insisted that he was not a dictator. Dictators were petty tyrants,* often dependent on small coteries supporting them by force. He saw himself as the leader not of a determined minority but of a majority. "We National Socialists are the better democrats," he said several times during the years 1933–1935.† He agreed with Goebbels when the latter pronounced (in 1934) the existence of a "new Germanic democracy." While he was contemptuous and dismissive of parliamentary democracy and of the democratic "pretensions" of Great Britain and the United States during the war, in his speech on 30 January 1941 he said that "the National Socialist Revolution defeated democracy through democracy!"

Shocked and stunned as he was in 1918 by witnessing and living through the collapse of the German empire, Hitler was not a monarchist—even though before 1918 we have no evidence of his hostility to the Hohenzollerns (as contrasted with his consistent hostility to the Habsburgs). Because of his need for conservative support there were few—if any—antimonarchical statements by Hitler during the period 1929–33, or until well after his assumption of the chancellorship. There were German (especially North German) conservatives who as late as 1934 hoped that Hitler would consent to a restoration of the monarchy in Germany. But after Hindenburg's death, with his consolidation of the chancellorship and the presidency, his dismissals of the—for him long-antiquated—hereditary idea and the monarchical principle (and not only in Germany) began to accumulate. A significant—and, for him, revelatory—event was his state visit to Italy in May 1938. He was repelled by what he saw as the creaking ceremonials of the Italian royal house, the precedences of court society, the corruptions of the Roman aristocracy, the personal weaknesses of the Italian king. By having

---

*"I am not a dictator and will never be one . . . any popinjay can rule as a dictator." Cited by Fest, F, p. 572.

†ZIT/A gives many instances of such Hitler statements: p. 569, note 189. See also BU, p. 191, Hitler's "open letter" to Brüning, 13 December 1931: "You refuse, as a 'statesman', to admit that if we come to power legally we could then break through legality. Herr Chancellor, the fundamental thesis of democracy runs: 'All Power From The People.' "

allowed its continued existence, by sharing his rule of Italy with the monarchy, his friend Mussolini had made a grave mistake. That is what Hitler saw, and thought, and found it now proper to express to many of his confidants. Then he decided to raise the pension payments of the surviving Social Democratic ministers of the Weimar period; it had, after all, been their great merit, he said, to have freed Germany from the Hohenzollerns in 1918.*

The Kaiser, William II, was living in exile in Doorn, in Holland, when the German army invaded Holland in May 1940. Churchill offered him refuge in England, but William refused. Not by a single act (or word) did he demonstrate compassion for his Dutch hosts under the German occupation. When France capitulated, William sent a congratulatory telegram to Hitler, repeating the pious sentimental phrase that his grandfather had uttered in 1870: "Welche Wendung durch Gottes Fügung!" ("What a turn of events ordained by God!") Hitler was contemptuous: "Didn't anything newer occur to him?"† As far as he was concerned, the Kaiser could return to Germany if he so wished. In June 1941 William died. Hitler allowed a special train with the imperial relatives to travel to Doorn for the Kaiser's funeral.

IN THE PREFACE OF HIS great biography in 1973, Joachim Fest speculated: had Hitler suddenly died in 1938, he would have been—and would perhaps still be—regarded as one of the greatest Germans in history.‡ Such a statement may have shocked some readers, but the reality of it would be recognized by others.** For Hitler's achievements—domestic rather than foreign—during the six years of his leadership of Germany *were* extraordinary. Not only did he

---

*HR, p. 417. In 1/w, p. 65, Irving cites Hitler on 23 November 1937: "Monarchies are at most capable of hanging on to what has been conquered. World empires are won only by revolutionary movements."

†Hermann Giesler, *Ein anderer Hitler*, Leoni am Starnberger See, 1977 (hereafter: GR), p. 393.

‡F, p. 25.

**Especially by a German generation to whom, of course, Fest's *Hitler* was mainly addressed, but also by many biographers who preceded Fest (Heiber, Deuerlein, and others); by Haffner later; and, more recently, by Zitelmann.

make Germany the greatest—and the most respected and feared—power in Europe; not only did he bring the Germans of Austria and Bohemia and Moravia, most of them enthusiastically willing, into a Greater Germany—surpassing the achievements of Bismarck, and all of this without a single shot fired, without a war. He brought prosperity and confidence to the Germans, the kind of prosperity that is a result of confidence. The thirties, after 1933, were sunny years for most Germans: something that remained in the memories of an entire generation among them. The concentration camps, the suppression of German Jews, the raucous vulgarity of Nazi propaganda were there, painfully sharp in the minds of an embittered minority; but how could they stack up against Hitler's creation of Prosperity, Greatness, Unity? After the war, shortly before he was hanged, Hans Frank wrote of the thirties in his memoir: "Über alles lagen Sonne, Glück, Jubel und Freude."* ("Above everything there was sunshine, happiness, rejoicing, cheer.") A sentimental exaggeration: but not without some substance.

This is neither a history of the Third Reich nor a biography of Hitler, and this particular chapter is directed to the question of whether he really was a revolutionary; that is, to the character of his ideas and how they have been seen by historians. But ideas do not exist in the abstract; they are incarnated by human beings (contrary not only to the views of many intellectuals but contrary, too, to Hegel or Dostoyevsky, what men do to ideas is more important than what ideas do to men). Hegel's famous "Zeitgeist" may have assisted Hitler's coming to power; but in the end he created his own Zeitgeist, and pragmatically indeed. That was already true of his achievement of power.†

---

*FR, p. 320.

†Fest (F, p. 370): "Hitler's extraordinary ability to recognize situations, to see through conflicting interests, to realize weaknesses . . . his tactical sense [was at least as important] as were his rhetorical powers, to convince people. . . ." I find this more convincing than the otherwise judicious Kershaw, KER, p. 37: [In 1930–33] "the personal role played by Hitler is greatly overshadowed by matters and events beyond his control." Also KER, pp. 38, 45, 52: "External events—the Young Plan to adjust reparation payments, the Wall Street crash, and Brüning's entirely unnecessary decision to have an election in the summer of 1930—put

Thereafter he could boast that his "Socialism of Action" was replacing his erstwhile opponents' "Socialism of Words." As Zitelmann wrote (about Hitler's decision to make May 1 a national holiday for German labor): "Not for the last time the National Socialists were [actually] realizing demands for which the workers' movement had fought for long and in vain." Also: "It is not debatable that in various social matters National Socialism made remarkable advances, for example in the improvement of the protection of the young, of others, and of social security."*

The optimism and the confidence: For every two children born in Germany in 1932, three were born four years later. In 1938 and 1939, the highest marriage rates in *all* of Europe were registered in Germany, superseding even those among the prolific peoples of Eastern Europe. The phenomenal rise of the German birthrate in the thirties was even steeper than the rise of the marriage rate. It is unreasonable to slur over these figures by simply referring to Hitler's populationist policies. Of course he encouraged large families, and offered social and financial benefits to them. But no national leader

---

the Nazis on the political map." And: ". . . without the onset of the world economic crisis from 1929" the extreme Right "reduced to a tiny rump of electoral support . . . might have remained so." Also: "Without the Depression [Hitler] would have continued to be an insignificant minority on the lunatic fringe." I do not believe this was so. But Kershaw is right in KER, pp. 46–47: "Hitler combined the fixity of basic points of dogma with maximum pragmatism in political maneuvering. . . ." And 112: ". . . far from revealing a naïveté and an incapacity which would have made him putty in the hands of the traditional power groups and would rapidly have rendered him dispensable, he showed a quick and sharp appreciation of the realities of governmental power."

*ZIT/A, pp. 87, 122. What remains debatable: "Unfortunately the area of [Hitler's] social policy, unlike National Socialist foreign policy, has not yet been researched [studied] well enough." This, not unlike some other statements by Zitelmann, at least suggests some special pleading; though less so than Toland. For example, TO, p. 405: "Tuberculosis and other diseases have noticeably diminished. The criminal courts never had so little to do and the prisons have never had so few occupants. It is a pleasure to observe the physical aptitude of the German youth. Even the poorest persons are better clothed than was formerly the case, and their cheerful faces testify to the psychological improvement that has been wrought within them." Not entirely untrue—but note that this is a quote from a German propaganda book in 1938, used by "Sir Arnold Wilson, M.P." Toland failed to say that Wilson was a notorious British Naziphile.

can force fathers to beget children (or mothers to bear them); and confidence in the future had much more to do with national perspectives than with economics. Social conditions are not material conditions, just as social history is not economic history.* From 1932 to 1939, the number of suicides committed by Germans under twenty dropped *80 percent* during the first six years of the Hitler regime (from 1,212 in 1932 to 290 in 1939). Consider, too, not only Hitler's autobahns but his agricultural reforms, the extraordinary popular outpouring of support for the "Winterhilfe" ("No German must be hungry or cold"), Hitler's special interest in providing inexpensive vacations for German workers.† Hitler's National Socialist Germany demonstrated that it was possible to achieve a high standard of living under a rigid dictatorship.

It may be argued that many of these achievements were not "revolutionary"; but they were surely modern. Hitler's interest in and respect for technology were considerable. Schramm cited Hitler: "Just as the bird represents, in comparison to the flying fish, a higher stage of development, the ship is a preliminary stage of the airplane. The future belongs to the airplane." Hitler on 3 October 1941: "[He] thinks that the automobile is the most beautiful invention of man, as long as he really uses it for his pleasure. The automobile opened up the landscape for people. . . ." Of Hitler's city planning, Toland wrote: ". . . there would be automated underground parking, a traffic-free center, numerous parks and green areas, and strict pollution control."‡ Some of this is imprecise; it was developed in better detail by Zitelmann, with evidence culled from Hitler's written and spoken statements of the 1926–30 period. In the ZIT/PR volume of collected studies, Hans-Dietrich Schäfer

---

*LEW, pp. 175, 176, 177. Also 177, note 5: "It is perhaps significant, too, that in 1939 among German cities, Danzig and Gleiwitz, on the Polish border, registered phenomenally high birthrates, over 24 per thousand (the average of German cities of comparable size was 17.5 per thousand); even more phenomenal was the marriage rate in Linz, this then prototypically Nazi town, the cradle of Hitler as well as of Eichmann, with 25.8 marriages per 1,000 inhabitants, more than twice the national average."

†There's a good general summary in HB, pp. 96–97.

‡SCH, p. 86; TO, p. 405; also Koeppen notes, p. 41.

presented two interesting theses. One of these suggested a kind of historical continuity: "In harmonizing [social differences] the regime achieved more than the social policy of the Weimar Republic . . . there was a levelling of classes, the formation of a large middle-class society which earlier researches have attributed only to the 'Economic Miracle' of the [West German] 1950s." The other was Zitelmann's and Schäfer's presentation of Hitler's "Americanism." Zitelmann: "Hitler did not let himself be governed by backward [that is, reactionary] visions of a medieval social order. In many ways his model was the United States. Although he rejected capitalist economics and the democratic order of the USA, he nevertheless admired its technological-industrial development which he often saw as a model for Germany." This even included American methods of advertisement. Schäfer: ". . . National Socialism calculated the wishes and anxieties of the majority rationally, bending the psyche of people without their noticing it. It knew exactly how to attract and lead Germans freed from their consciousness of class."[*] Some of this had been noted earlier by Fest. He described the superior effects of Nazi marches and parades compared to those of the German Communists before 1933; and also that Hitler understood the popular effect of the cult of the "star"; in incarnating that role, "he was certainly the most modern phenomenon in the politics of his time."[†] Earlier the philologist Klemperer noted the National Socialist preference for the words "organisation" and "organisieren" [to organize], which appealed to younger Germans. "This simplistic mechanization of the human person was typical of [a new] language."[‡] It affected everyday life, and it had a powerful attraction for many young people.

Modernization does not necessarily mean a cult of youth; but for

---

[*]zit/pr, p. 214 (Schäfer); p. 16 (Zitelmann); pp. 210–11 (Schäfer). The latter cited a book published about advertisement [Werbung] in Berlin in 1939: "For advertising to have a total effect . . . it is necessary to consider people *totally*" (italics in text). But already Viktor Klemperer in *LTI: Notizbuch eines Philologen* (Leipzig, 1960) noticed many of the Nazified Americanisms in the language of the Third Reich.

[†]F, pp. 399, 410

[‡]Klemperer, pp. 126, 191.

Hitler the latter was dominant. Revolutionaries often claim to be representatives of youth; this was true of Fascists as well as National Socialists, including Mussolini and the Spanish José Antonio Primo da Rivera, whose emphasis on youth was even stronger than Hitler's. But Hitler put much more of his cult of youth into practice than Mussolini did. Oddly enough, the impression he gave of himself was seldom (surely not after 1923) that of a particularly youthful person. But his party and his movement *were* youthful: In 1931, in Berlin 70 percent of the SA were men under thirty, and in the Reichstag in 1930, 60 percent of the National Socialist deputies were under forty, while only 10 percent of the Social Democrats were. The German exile Karl Otten wrote an incisive paragraph about Hitler's appeal to German youth: "The young truly love Hitler, in almost limitless ecstatic admiration. Not only because he understands their childish impulses and even encourages them. The Wild West games [*Indianerspiele*] of the young serve as a preparation for war."* Hitler seems to have been the creator of a free country of the young. Before them he plays not the role of a severe father but of a mother, a source of many pleasures and of love. He allows them pseudo-revolutionary freedom for their biological and sexual impulses, adding to his appeal.†

Yet much of the new order depended on an increase of administration, the cult of youth notwithstanding. In 1939, Hitler wanted every young German to spend at least one month each year at manual labor, preferably on the land—a clear break with the sedentary bourgeois era. Still, the portion of the people who lived on the land and were engaged in agriculture was falling (it was 30.5 percent in 1925 and 26.1 percent in 1939). The portion of those who were employed in industry was exactly the same in 1939 as it was in 1925 (42.1 percent); what increased was the section of the population employed in administration and services, from 6.6 percent in 1925 to 10.4 percent in 1939. A new amorphous middle class was coming into being whose competences were not always clearly categorizable but whose style of life became increasingly modern.

---

*About Hitler and the American Wild West, see p. 155.
†Cited by Scholdt, SCHO, p. 660.

THERE WERE DUALITIES in the history of the Third Reich, as there were dualities in Hitler himself. That, too, is a normal condition (one that is often understood and described better by intelligent biographers than by psychoanalysts). One basic duality in Hitler resided in his dual ambitions: the Leader and the Artist; or—again, more precisely—the national leader and the national artist.* He was no Nero, for whom art was a game, serving his vanity; he took art more seriously than that. And it is in his preferences in art that we can detect both modern and conservative, revolutionary and reactionary elements.

Hitler's interest in art was evident throughout his life. He wanted to be a painter; and then an architect. Unlike his great adversary Churchill, whose discovery of the pastime of painting occurred suddenly, at the suggestion of a lady friend, at the age of forty during a depressive break in his career, and for whom painting turned out to be a diversion, superb relaxation, a pleasure (and who was interested in literature and poetry but in music not at all); in sum, unlike a statesman one of whose hobbies was painting, Hitler saw himself as a statesman *and* an artist (the word "Künstler," too, in German has a more serious tone than the English term "artist"). Until the very end of his life, Hitler made remarks regretting that the great burden of his tasks as a national leader did not make it possible for him to build.

He would destroy people and cities, if need be. But it was in architecture, and architecture alone—not at all in literature or painting or music—that he and the Third Reich made some remarkable achievements.† I know that this statement may be debated or dismissed, and that this is not of course the proper place to sustain it further. Allow me only to cite a principal historian of the

---

*See also Gert Kalow, *Hitler—das deutsche Trauma*, M, 1976.

†This issue is, of course, inseparable from the memoirs and from the extant remnant of materials of Speer (also of Troost), including the complicated relationship of Speer and Hitler. About this see SP, and also Gitta Sereny, *Albert Speer: His Battle with the Truth*, L, 1995.

artistic and cultural policies of the Third Reich, Hildegarde Brenner: "During the years 1934 to 1940 . . . one cannot deny the 'historical uniqueness' . . . in architecture. In this field National Socialism succeeded in reaching a form of self-expression that cannot be doubted."* (In support of this summary statement, Brenner also cites Bruno Zevi, *Poetica dell'architectura neoplastica* [Milan, 1953], and Nikolaus Pevsner, *Europäische Architektur* [M, 1957], two of the most eminent European architectural historians, both of whom, incidentally, were serious and respected scholars of Jewish origin.)

It is in Hitler's artistic preferences and appetites—more than in his ideological and even literary preferences—that we may detect both bourgeois-conservative and modern-revolutionary elements. Especially in his preferences in music and painting, besides sculpture and architecture. This duality is there in his very statements. In his speech at Nuremberg on 1 September 1933: "It is better to imitate the good things than it is to produce new bad things." (Note, however, that this was the political period, when he found it necessary to appeal to German conservatism.) At the same time, there was his respect and admiration for supermodern technology. To Speer he said that the autobahns would be his Parthenon.† Again to Speer: "The popes of the Renaissance and the rulers of the Baroque era considered buildings as pastimes. For [Hitler] it was part of the political will of the National Socialist movement."‡ He thought that he and his architects might achieve a new kind of architectural unity of what was best in the old and in the modern. Hence his preference for the neoclassicism of the architects Tessenow and Troost and Speer, different and better than the neoclassical architectures of Mussolini or Stalin: "It had been the declared will of Hitler and

---

*Hildegarde Brenner, *Die Kunstpolitik des Nationalsozialismus*, Hamburg, 1963, p. 118.

†"Road-building had always been the sign of powerful governments, he said, from the Romans and the Incas down to Napoleon." (I/W, pp. 22–23)

‡Krier, K, p. 213, citing Speer. About the autobahns-Parthenon analogy, see F, p. 527 *et seq.* Also, Hitler to Abel Bonnard (a French intellectual admirer of his) in 1937: "A man must be considered anew, spiritually and not only professionally. . . . It is not enough to build him a house but to have a light shine out from it." (HR, p. 319)

Speer not to copy historic styles but to create a new style which was itself to become historical."* When the architect Giesler (Speer's rival and competitor) presented Hitler with his model of a rebuilt central Munich (Speer's grand model was the rebuilding of central Berlin), Hitler said that he saw it "as a monument of the new technology of our times—and I add that the 'Grosse Strasse' [the Grand Avenue] . . . will be the most modern Strasse of our times!" He foresaw the need to avoid masses of cars in cities, and for giant underground parking garages. The building of the first U-Bahn (subway) in Munich was begun on Hitler's orders (the first element in a modern public-transportation system that is among the best in Europe today). Hitler often used the word "modern" approvingly. According to Maser, there is evidence that, unlike Mussolini and Stalin, Hitler did not dismiss abstract painting entirely (though Maser does not produce such evidence); on the other hand, Maser is right: "Not in every field of creative art was [Hitler] conservative and traditionally bound."†

Hitler's duality was apparent in many other elements of his thinking. About women, for example, his insistence on the revival of traditional practices of German motherhood, on the unbridgeable differences between women and men (and on the inevitable superiority of the latter in certain areas of life) went hand in hand with his promotion of the physical education of German girls, equal to that of boys; of their modern and sportive training. Yet when, later in the war, Goebbels proposed the total mobilization of German women, Hitler was reluctant; he did not approve it. He both admired and rejected elements of the Prussian tradition. Bavaria and Munich were the center of his political career, yet he rejected the anti-Prussianism of the Bavarians, though his ideology was not Prussian; Prussia and Prussianism were not the models for his vision of a new Germany.‡ Nor was his frequent dismissal of intellectuals and rationalists ("Ver-

---

*K, p. 226.

†M/A, p. 103.

‡Wolfgang Wippermann, "Nationalismus und Preussentum," *Das Parlament* (26 December 1981), p. 127. "In this he differed essentially from most of the Prussian and Protestant conservatives of the Weimar Republic."

standesmenschen") typical of the older, anti-Enlightenment traditions of German thinking. It was post- (if not anti-) -conservative, -populist, and -modern. In his mind, at least, there was no conflict between the older and the newer elements at hand. To the contrary, he thought that he represented and incarnated a new kind of German unity. He showed respect for some of the old things; but a conservative he was not, and a reactionary not at all.*

ADOLF HITLER was not the inventor of National Socialism, but he recognized the compatibility—indeed, the marriageability—of two great movements. This was a worldwide phenomenon. For a long time, nationalism and socialism seemed to be incompatible, indeed hostile to each other. Socialism was, after all, international, given its belief that entire classes, rather than entire nations, mattered and that the struggle of classes carried history forward. What happened in many places after about 1870 was that the nineteenth-century antithesis and debate between conservatives and liberals had begun to lose its meaning. For two reasons: Because of the developing democratization of societies, conservatives were becoming more liberal, while some liberals were becoming more conservative. But what was at work here wasn't the development of some kind of a transcendent Hegelian solution. The alternatives were not about to be superseded by a synthesis. They were increasingly overshadowed by two new forces on other planes: by nationalism and socialism. Throughout the twentieth century the relationship (or the compound or mixture) of nationalism and socialism would

---

*Contrary to the famous "Is Paris Burning?" idea in 1944, he did not order Paris to be destroyed. At the time of the German retreat from Rome that year, he also ordered Rome to remain unharmed and untouched; but that order of his was made public for propaganda purposes, to impress some people worldwide, including Catholics. On the other hand, the destruction of London or Budapest did not bother him at all. He did not, of course, order the destruction of the great cities of Germany—the air war of his "barbaric" Anglo-American enemies was doing that— but he rigidly refused to visit or even look at the destroyed cities. He sympathized with Goebbels's argument, according to which this may have had a positive side— i.e., the destruction of the last remnants of an old bourgeois order. On one occasion he also said that in less than thirty years the destroyed cities would be rebuilt.

prove to be the dominant political configuration throughout the world.*

Of course the German, and Hitler's, National Socialism was almost sui generis. It was not only that for him nationalism was the dominant partner in that marriage; he was convinced that modern populist nationalism can—and indeed must—be socialistic. There was also the condition that the propagation of that marriage had deeper roots in Germany than almost anywhere else. Many followers and at least some later opponents of Hitler believed in its desirability. A Germany that was both nationalist and socialist (meaning socialist in a particularly German way) was a frequent desideratum of conservative political thinkers in the 1920s, its expressions ranging from Oswald Spengler's *Preussentum und Sozialismus* (1923) to the perhaps even more trenchant and significant *Der Arbeiter*, Ernst Jünger's book in 1932.† Yet these—always anti-liberal, often conservative, and sometimes (but only sometimes) traditionalist—thinkers were one thing; Hitler the revolutionary was another.

In Germany the failure of international socialism was crassly evident already in 1914. When the kaiser appeared in the Reichstag on 2 August, calling for national unity, the great majority of the German Socialist deputies rose with the others and voted for the war credits. In the hot skillet of nationalist emotions the essence of international socialism melted away, like a pat of cold margarine. (And this happened elsewhere in Europe, too, at least partly because of the democratization of societies; for democracy nationalizes even more than it internationalizes, and by 1914 a German factory owner already had more in common with his workers than with a French

---

*About this see chapter 9. (Also my article "American History: The Terminological Problem," in *The American Scholar*, Winter 1992.) Consider, too, the turning point in Mussolini's life. Unlike Hitler, Mussolini in 1929 was the founder of his movement of "Fascism." Yet earlier, in 1911–12, he had already discovered that he was a *nationalist* Socialist. Mutatis mutandis, consider that this applies to Stalin, too (one of the reasons that, about 1932, he forbade the use of the term "National Socialism," insisting that Communists use the term "Fascists" or "Hitlerites" instead).

†"Der Arbeiter [the worker] is also a fighting soldier [*Frontsoldat*]. "Looking back at a century of German history, we may assert *with pride* that we were *bad Bürger* . . ." (reprinted in Jünger, *Essays*, II, p. 17, s, 1965). See also the useful compendium, Armin Mohler, *Die konservative Revolution in Deutschland 1918–1932*, s, 1950.

factory owner.) In 1917 occurred the first Communist revolution, in Russia; but, unlike the French or the American or many other great revolutions, it failed to achieve power anywhere outside the—defeated and diminished—Russian empire. (Had the first Communist revolution in Europe succeeded in Germany, not in Russia, its influence would have been immeasurably greater—but that is another story.) This is not the place to describe the failures of Marxism (not to speak of the failures of International Communism) except to say that the Marxist—as also the liberal-capitalist—belief in a deterministic materialism, in Economic Man, rested on a view of human nature that was flawed from the beginning—besides the fact that Marx, as well as many of his followers, was blind about the importance of the nation (which Marx almost entirely ignored, confusing it with the state).*

Hitler understood this very well. He understood the weaknesses of the Marxist view of human nature and of society, even as he knew how (and why) to preach about its dangers. We ought to pay respect to the German Social Democrats who opposed Hitler in 1933 (they were the only party voting against his investment with full powers at the memorable Reichstag session of 21 March 1933). But in 1933 Hitler knew that masses of Socialist and Communist workers were deserting their parties in droves, many of them coming over to him easily and early; and that the only serious threat to him would exist on the "Right," not on the "Left."†

It was a national mentality, not a class-consciousness, that at-

---

*The otherwise judicious Marlis Steinert, sT, p. 174: "Compared with Marx's conciseness, [Hitler's] ideas seemed very vague. . . ." This is incorrectly put. See also Klaus-Dietmar Henke, *Die amerikanische Besetzung Deutschlands*, M, 1995, pp. 624–25 and 819–21: "Through Hitler's propaganda the natural opposition of Capital and Proletariat was washed away; the masses no longer reacted to it. . . ." Many things led to a "fundamental acceptance of the Hitler regime by the working class."

†HF/AN, 58: "The only opponents or rivals whom Hitler had to consider seriously and whom at times he had to fight in the domestic political arena between 1930 and 1934, were the conservatives. The liberals, Centre people or the Social Democrats never gave him the least trouble, and neither did the communists." (And this was a worldwide phenomenon. The same applies to Franklin Roosevelt in the 1930s, whose most dangerous rival was Huey Long, and opponents such as Father Coughlin. See also "The Two Rights" in LEW, pp. 286–96.)

tracted people to Hitler. Again, there was something particularly German about this—but something more universal, too. The German element was both apparent and inherent in the word (and the definition, ideology, and cult) of the *Volk*, going back more than a century before Hitler. Here some distinctions are in order. The words "Volk" and "völkisch" are not identical with the English terms "folk" and "folkish";* their usage is slightly different from the Scandinavian "folk" too, as well as from the French "peuple"† (though, oddly enough, not very different from the Russian usage of "narod"). However, during the nineteenth century and well into the twentieth, "Volk" and "völkisch" in Germany (and Austria) were conservative terms—anti-international, anti-Marxist, anti-Jewish, anti-French, and "Christian." It might even be said that in many places in the nineteenth century "völkisch" could be patriotic as much as nationalistic. (On this essential and grave difference see chapter 4.) But after 1890 at the latest, in Austria as well as Germany, there came a change. The conservative (and occasionally patriotic) meaning and attraction of "völkisch" was beginning to dissipate, while, simultaneously, its radical and nationalist meaning began to grow.

In the history of the twentieth century, this was more than a German phenomenon. In the late eighteenth century, the cult of "the people" had begun. Throughout the nineteenth century, "people" and "popular" were leftist words and titles and political slogans. But in the early twentieth century this changed. It was more than a rhetorical device when Mussolini in 1914—having broken away from the Socialists—titled his daily newspaper *Il Popolo d'Italia*.‡ Hitler's main newspaper, too, was the *Völkischer Beobachter*. There was more to this than the titles of newspapers. Throughout

---

*Bullock, BU, p. 123, note 1: *Volk* is "a difficult word to translate: it combines the idea of nationalism with those of race and anti-Semitism"—to which we may add the populist idea and element.

†In the Latin languages "folk," as such, does not exist. Consider, too, the mostly nineteenth-century, pejorative German word "Pöbel" (meaning "mob"), derived from the French "peuple" and, at least implicitly, condemnatory of it.

‡*L'Ami du Peuple* was Marat's rabble-rousing radical paper in 1791; in the 1930s, it was the title of a French Fascist weekly.

the twentieth century, people's parties became rightist rather than leftist: anti-international, anticapitalist, and, on occasion, anti-Semitic. With few exceptions,* populism moved from the Left to the Right—including in the United States.

And Hitler was a populist—a believer in the sovereignty of the people; a modern populist, and not an old-fashioned demagogue. Yes, there had been populists before him. But the very idea of who "the people" were changed during the last few centuries.† Among the earlier populists, nationalism, as such, was only latent; but Hitler realized—among other things—that modern populism, by its very nature, must be nationalist, and—more important—that nationalism must be populist.‡ The words "Volksgemeinschaft" and "Volksgenossen" ("people's community" and "folk-comrades," inadequately translatable in English) were basic to Hitler's principles. The relationship between the Führer and the people was quite different from that of the kaiser and his citizens: "not a respectful acceptance of hierarchy but the voluntary and unlimited acquiescence of the people." Also: "In the Hitler movement Germany experienced its only genuine revolution, even though that did not entirely conform to the theoretical model of 'revolutions.' "** Or Fest: "Dismissing Revolution, he [Hitler] had become in reality

---

*For a while, Communists stuck with their populist terminology: "People's Democracies," for example (as different from "Capitalist Democracies"). Yet these were often not much more than leftovers of an earlier political terminology.

†About this see Lukacs, HC, p. 69 *et seq.*

‡This is evident in the political history of the United States in the twentieth century, though it is lamentably seldom recognized thus: populism *is* nationalism, in more ways than one; while populism and (true) conservatism are entirely incompatible (no matter what our recent "conservatives" say). A conservative and antidemocratic nationalist such as Ernst Jünger recognized this, though only after his disillusionment with the Third Reich. The populism that began with the democratic propaganda of the French Revolution—he wrote during the war—has now produced "all kinds of new spirits and new evils" (*Strahlungen*—his diaries— 27 March 1944, cited by Scholdt, SCHO, p. 542). Also in his *Auf den Marmorklippen* (published in Berlin, in 1939!): "What happens when the weak misread the laws [of history] and, half-blind, they unlock with their own hands the gates that were closed for their own protection?"

**Lothar Kettenacker, "Sozialpsychologische Aspekte der Führer-Herrschaft," in *Der Führerstaat: Mythos und Realität. Studien zur Struktur und Politik des Dritten Reiches*, S, 1981, pp. 124, 130.

the German phenomenon [*Erscheinung*] of Revolution." Further: "His place in history is much closer to the great revolutionaries than to the conservative despots." And: "He may have [seemed] anachronistic; but he was more modern and more devoted to modernity than all of his domestic political opponents."* The fact that during his election campaigns Hitler did not outline a program for his future government was neither due to a cautious calculation nor to the condition that he had no precise economic program. It accorded with his plan to appeal to all social strata "in the name of the Volksgemeinschaft, an entire people's community."† Even at that time of great unemployment and social distress, his populist nationalism was more influential than any economic appeal.

He carried the revolutionary theme into the war. On 8 November 1940, he said in a speech: "Every soldier knows and must know that the armies now marching under our flags are the revolutionary armies of the Third Reich." And in one of his table talks (21 September 1941), he said that William II should have destroyed the Habsburg monarchy: "As neither the emperor, nor his circle, nor the German people had recognized this task, there remained no historical justification for the existence of Hohenzollern monarchy, and its fall was a historical necessity. That the monarchies were terminated by the Marxists . . . and not by National Socialists the Führer finds a special gift of Destiny."‡

Destiny . . . Hitler did believe in God, in a God (perhaps Stalin did too).** Hitler was a new kind of revolutionary, transcending

---

*F, pp. 1035, 1037.

†M. Rainer Lepsius, *Extremer Nationalismus. Strukturbedingungen zu der national sozialistischen Machtergreifung*, s, 1966, p. 11.

‡Koeppen ms., pp. 23–24.

**HR, p. 343, cites FR: Hitler told Frank that in the hospital he had hoped in Providence; if he recovered, he would see that as a sign, to be a politician; and when he regained his sight, "I was really stunned and took it as a call from Heaven for me." Speer (SP, p. 570, note 19) cites Hitler's speech to industrialists on 26 June 1944: "It seems to me as if we must endure all of the trials of the Devil and Satan and Hell until we win the final victory. Perhaps I am not a pious churchgoer, that I am not. But deep inside I am still a devout believer [ein frommer Mensch], meaning that the laws of nature that a God has created correspond to this world: whoever fights bravely and does not capitulate but recovers again and again and advances anew, will not be abandoned by the Almighty but receive the blessing of Providence in the end. And that has been the lot of all great souls [Geister] of this world."

(and, in a way, melding) Germanic myths and German Christianity (as also "Right" and "Left"), uniting some of their doctrines within his own revolutionary ideology. But it is very significant that, as the Third Reich evolved, power became more decisive than ideology. Hitler himself knew that. Well before him, Proudhon had seen deeper than had Marx: People, Proudhon wrote, react less to ideas about social contracts than to realities of power. Two episodes of reactions during Hitler's career possess, I think, considerable significance. When in November 1923 the aggressive minority of Hitler's National Socialists rose in Munich, it is remarkable that neither the Communists nor the Social Democrats did anything: "There is no report of a single armed Leftist uprising anywhere in Bavaria during the Putsch."* Even more significant, to me, was the reaction of the German people, with their majority of anti-Communists and conservatives, to the news of Hitler's pact with Stalin in August 1939. There was not a single resignation from the party, not a single expression of disapproval from the conservatives, from those many millions who in 1932–33 and after had sided with Hitler because of their anticommunism. To the contrary, there were many expressions of wonder and felicitation at that unquestionable triumph of Third Reich diplomacy. (The same was true of sympathizers of National Socialism throughout the world.) This at a time when thousands of Communists worldwide were experiencing shock, confusion, and disappointment. Yes, compared with communism, Hitlerism was more modern. And popular.

Maser (m/a, p. 279, note 401) cites his 1971 interview with Eva Braun's sister: Hitler and Eva Braun prayed together before their suicide. Here the perceptive Haffner was partly wrong. hf/an, p. 92: "[Hitler] was, in spite of his customary rhetorical appeals to 'Providence' and the 'Almighty,' not only irreligious himself [true] but also had no perception of what religion can mean to others" [not so]. (About Stalin, see his reference to God in his talk with Churchill, August 1942; also his later treatment of the Russian Orthodox Church.) Hitler was no atheist. Here again we may encounter the particular danger of half-truths, and perhaps also St. John of the Apocalypse, who predicted that the Antichrist would not appear as Satan or Lucifer, not as an atheist but as someone who in many ways acts and presents himself as a believer and a Christian. (For further discussion, see chapter 9.)

*Harold J. Gordon, Jr., *Hitler and the Beer Hall Putsch*, Princeton, 1972, pp. 407–8, also p. 449.

ALLOW ME NOW TO RETURN to Tocqueville (whom Hitler had surely not read, and who would have been anathema to him). Three principal elements in Tocqueville's vision and in his writing are relevant to our theme here. The first is Tocqueville's prophetic perception of a new kind of tyranny peculiar to the coming democratic age, the tyranny not of a minority but of a majority; a tyranny not only established with the consent of but exercised by the majority on occasion. That new kind of "Caesarism" (as Tocqueville at times put it) was already apparent, here and there, in the nineteenth century, though not in Germany. Twenty years after Tocqueville first wrote about it in *Democracy in America*, it came to France through the plebiscitary triumph of Louis Napoleon. But the semi-authoritarian regime of Napoleon III was still very different from that of Hitler. In the Third Reich, the majority gave not only its passive but its active consent to the Führer. Hitler was more of a populist (and, in the broadest sense of the term, more of a democrat) than Napoleon III, more so than other dictators, such as those in South America or Mussolini or Kemal. As a matter of fact (as he himself said), Hitler was not really a typical dictator—but this was not, as some of the Functionalist historians argue, because he was hesitant, circumscribed by his bureaucracy, or "weak." He was more than a dictator; he was something else. "The old tyrants," Chesterton said, "invoked the past; the new tyrants will invoke the future."

The second element of Tocqueville's vision is his startling statement, again made first in *Democracy in America*, that the age of great revolutions may be a thing of the past, because in a democratized society the majority of people do not wish to be disturbed by revolutionary ideas, though they are wont to accept the presence of a vast bureaucracy in their everyday lives. Again, this applies to Hitler—though only to some extent. His 1934 statement to the effect that there would be no revolutions in Germany for a thousand years was more than an assuaging of the latent fears of German conservatives and ordinary people. From time to time, he still employed the adjective "revolutionary" in a positive sense—in the sense that what he established was a revolutionary "New Order," as opposed to disorder. Here again, an anti-Marxist epigram of the profound Simone Weil (1942) is telling: "It is not religion but revolution that is the opiate of the people"—and Hitler's usage of "revolution" was a kind of opiate for the New Order.

The third element is Tocqueville's vision of the last one thousand years. Aware and knowledgeable as he was of the classic division of European history into ancient, medieval, and modern epochs, he had another view that transcended these categories. This was the change from the aristocratic age to the democratic age; from entire societies ruled by minorities to societies ruled by their majorities (or, at least, in the name of their majorities). He thought that this was the deepest change in the history of the last thousand years. What we may then see now, at the end of the so-called Modern Age, is that this last great era, which began about five hundred years ago, may have been marked by the—sometimes uneasy but civilizationally and culturally fruitful—confluence of tradition and reform, of aristocracy and democracy, with the former weakening and the latter rising, until now, when we live in an overwhelmingly democratic age (and when we may have to rethink the very political terms associated with democracy). What this means for the future, I cannot tell; new divisions and new hierarchies will appear. But what it means for the recent past, a historian can—and ought to—recognize: that Hitler was a new kind of revolutionary; a populist revolutionary in a democratic age, notwithstanding all of the then still extant older elements of German institutions and German society, many of which he knew how to employ for his purposes.*

---

*A general tendency of most historians—and perhaps especially the German ones—has been to see the Hitler chapter of German history as a horrid but transitional one: something between (or a compound of) the old and the new, in part also because of the evident ambiguities in Hitler's character and ideas. There *is* truth in this vision, though, in my opinion, it does not go far enough.

4

State; People; Race; Nation

The insufficient category of "totalitarianism"—
Hitler and the state—His racism—Patriots and nationalists—
Hitler the extreme example of the latter

THE TERM "TOTALITARIANISM" has a curious history. It is not included in the *Oxford English Dictionary*, though it is included in its Supplement. It seems that the word first appeared in the late 1920s, in a designation of the single-party state of Fascist Italy. We may find it here and there during the 1930s, applied to Fascist Italy or to National Socialist Germany, though seldom to Communist Russia, even though the latter was at that time the most "totalitarian" state in the world. After World War II "totalitarianism" became a current and frequently used adjective, applied especially to Communist states but also—indiscriminately and, as we shall see, imprecisely—to most of the dictatorships of the twentieth century.* However, beyond this latecoming equation of

---

*An influential example of the employment of the term is Hannah Arendt's *The Origins of Totalitarianism*, published in 1951, which had a considerable impact on intellectuals, especially in New York, many of whom were for the first time (and belatedly) willing to recognize the totalitarian features of Stalin's dictatorship. This flawed and dishonest book (see my review-essay in the *New Oxford Review*, "Vital Works Reconsidered," April 1990) had been composed by its author in the

Hitlerism and Stalinism, what we ought to consider now is the incorrect application of "totalitarianism"—meaning total state rule—not only to the Third Reich but to the very ideas (and some of the practices) of Adolf Hitler.

To begin with what is (or should be) obvious: the *total* rule of the state is impossible. Even at the peak and at the maximum extent of a modern tyrant's rule, there remain people and islands of life that are surprisingly untouched by the police rule of the state. Still, the term "totalitarianism" may seem reasonable when it is the practical *intention* of the tyrant or tyrants ruling a state to exercise total control over its inhabitants. But there is room for a serious question whether that was Hitler's intention. His intention was to rule with the active consent of the majority of his people, among whom the potential opposition of—small—minorities would be insignificant and entirely ineffectual. It may even be said that while Stalin (not unlike other, mostly Oriental rulers) was exercised by the danger of *potential* opponents, whence his purges), Hitler (and also Himmler, the SD, and the Gestapo), while aware of the existence and the locus of potential opponents, were principally interested in discovering evidence of any *actual* opposition. For Hitler the only categorically and unquestionably potential opponents—people whose asseverations, indeed, whose very acts, of loyalty were unwanted because, to him, they could not be anything but actual enemies—were the Jews; and it is to this obsession of his that I shall have to return (chapter 6).

Of course, Germany was not Russia; and the Hitler revolution in Germany was not at all like the Bolshevik revolution in Russia. Except for Jews, there was more individual and even political freedom in National Socialist Germany than in Communist Russia—a greater variety of publications in the sciences and in the arts, and more

---

mid-1940s and originally referred only to the origins and practices of Nazism; unhistorical and shrilly verbose, the book illustrated its theses with quotes taken from an undiscriminating variety of books. After 1948, after the manuscript was rejected by various New York publishers, Arendt thought it politic to add two, extremely superficial, chapters expounding the totalitarian features of Stalinism. These were illustrated by citations from no more than two (then recent) books describing Stalin's crimes.

elbow room for individual endeavor. As one reads about the recon-struction of the various German opposition groups against Hitler, one is struck by their relative liberty of movement within that police state; by the relative ease with which some people flitted back and forth between Germany and abroad, or met foreign diplomats in Berlin, talking cautiously but almost freely. This kind of behavior would have been inconceivable in the Soviet Union (and in some other police states too). But then, Gestapo and sD notwithstanding, National Socialist Germany was both more and less than a police state.* The clever Carl Schmitt, the principal constitutional theorist of the Third Reich, wrote in 1935 that the National Socialist re-gime meant the end of the old Prussian "Beamtenstaat," with its Hegelian conception of a state governed by officials. It was, instead, a "Volksgenossenstaat," a state of the comradeship of the people: 'The state is the instrument of the people.' "† That was exactly what Hitler thought. The German working class, among others, felt something of this, too: Many of the steelworkers of Krupp were more reliable followers of the Führer than were some of the old Prussian civil servants. As late as March 1945, Speer was driven to despair as he overheard the talk of German workers who, unlike himself, were still confident of Hitler and of victory in the end.

In reality, the Third Reich was a mixture of "Volksgenossenstaat" and "Beamtenstaat."‡ But our concern is with the history of Hitler, not with that of the Third Reich. He—unlike Mussolini or, more often, Goebbels—seldom used the word "total." Bullock properly

---

*Schramm, SCH, p. 95: "It would be an oversimplification to characterize Hitler as a hyper-Machiavellian no longer inhibited by law. His concept of legality came from what he saw as 'the eternal laws of natural events.' " Kershaw, KER, p. 194: "Hitler was not a tyrant imposed upon Germany. He was in many respects, until well into the war, a highly popular national leader." At the same time Speer (SP, p. 359), on the subject of Hitler's pragmatism, cites him as saying: "For there can be only one single rule, and this rule, put succinctly, is: That is correct which is useful in itself."

†See Lukacs, LEW, p. 324. Note, too, the difference from Spengler, in *The Decline of the West*: "The state is the form of a people." The "elitist" Spengler still saw "the state" as being of a higher order than "the people"; Schmitt sometimes; Hitler never—except when circumstances forced him to do so (about this see chapter 5).

‡This is the essence of the important argument of Edward N. Peterson, *The Limits of Hitler's Power*, Chicago, 1968.

cited his speech in Munich in November 1934: "In Germany bayo-
nets do not terrorize a people. Here a government is supported by
the confidence of the entire people. . . . I have not been imposed by
anyone upon this people. From this people I have grown up, in the
people I have remained, to the people I return. My pride is that I
know no statesman in the world who with greater right than I can
say that he is representative of the people."* Fest's insight is considerable: "Hitler never wanted to establish a tyranny [Gewaltherr-
schaft]." And: "A mere hunger for power is insufficient to explain
the Hitler phenomenon, which cannot be studied as [yet] another
form of modern tyranny."† We have seen that Hitler himself said
that he was not a dictator and did not wish to be one. Kershaw
expressed this, in a judicious sentence: "To suggest that Hitler's
power rested on 'totalitarian terror'—leaving aside difficulties with
the concept of 'totalitarianism'—is to state only a partial truth."‡ In
HF/AN, Haffner made the bold suggestion that at least until 1938
the Third Reich was not a totalitarian but an authoritarian state,
thus at least comparable to other dictatorships in the Europe of the
1930s, including Italy.

THERE IS (OR, RATHER, WAS), of course, a difference between
"totalitarian" and "authoritarian" regimes, between, say, Hitler's on
the one hand and Franco's or Salazar's or Pilsudski's or Metaxas's
on the other—a difference that is more than one of nuances. Most
of these dictators did not intend to maintain total control over personal and family lives. But by fixing our attention on *the state*, we
miss the essential difference that separates Hitler's vision—and his
intentions—from that of all other contemporary dictators, including
Mussolini and Stalin.

Consider that the state, as we know it, was a creation of the
so-called Modern Age, arising first in Renaissance Italy and then
in Western Europe about five hundred years ago; in an age marked
by the roiling and evolving mixture of monarchy, aristocracy, democ-

---

*BU, p. 404.

†F, p. 571; also p. 572.

‡KER, p. 62.

racy—and that Hitler's vision of history and of the future entailed a radical break with the institutions of the Modern Age. He would have agreed with Tocqueville on one thing: that the age of democracy was now irreversible. One hundred years before Hitler's assumption of power, Tocqueville projected a new kind of tyranny, peculiar to the democratic age: the tyranny of a majority. What was perhaps peculiar to Hitler was his establishment of a tyranny not so much *of* but *through* a majority.* "The state"—i.e., state interests, the security of the state—was a sacrosanct term in the modern world, even in Stalin's Soviet Russia, at the latest by 1939.† But already in *Mein Kampf*, Hitler had written that "the state is but a means to the end" ["Der Staat ist ein Mittel zum Zweck"]. And—with all of the compromises he had to make for the sake of the state—he remained consistent about this priority till the end. In March 1929, he said: "For us the idea of the Volk is higher than the idea of the state." On 10 May 1933: "It is not an accident that religions are more stable than forms of states." On 6 April 1938, he put it tersely in a speech in Salzburg: "In the beginning was the Volk, and only then came the Reich." Or, in his significant speech to officers in the Platterhof in May 1944: "The state is only an enforced framework" [eine Zwangsform].‡ On 5 September 1934, in Nuremberg:

---

*Zitelmann (ZTT/B, p. 85) cites Haffner: In 1933, among the German majority there existed a widespread feeling of freedom, of being "relieved of [parliamentary] democracy." He adds: "Hopes for a revival of national greatness were joined with utopian aspirations for a better, more socially minded society. It may sound paradoxical: but the end of [parliamentary] democracy seemed to mean to many the beginning of true popular rule."

†The term *the state*, originally anathema not only to Marx but also to Lenin, had become sacrosanct in the Soviet Union by 1939. (It may even be argued that Stalin's 1936–39 purges signified in large part the transformation of a party bureaucracy into a state bureaucracy.) In any event, Stalin (who, the very opposite of Lenin, was not a revolutionary but a statesman) discovered the supreme importance of the state at the very time when Hitler found that supreme importance to be outdated—another example of the backwardness of Stalin's Communism compared with Hitler's National Socialism.

‡Jäckel (JHW, p. 99) also cites MK: "The question of the external structure of the state . . . is not of principal importance, it only serves certain practical purposes." Haffner (HF/AN, p. 86) goes further—in my opinion, correctly—recognizing the significance that "in Hitler's political system the state plays an entirely subordinate part."

"Foreigners may say that the state created us. No! We are The State! We follow the orders of no earthly power but those of God who created the German people! On us depends the state!"

Here was one of the differences between Mussolini and Hitler, or between Italian Fascism and German National Socialism. In the Fascist Manifesto of 1932 Mussolini said, "It is not the people who make the state but the state that makes the people."* Mussolini was a populist, but less so than Hitler. Campaigning against the individualism of the Italian people, Mussolini tried to institutionalize and enforce the submission of the individual to the state—harking back, at least in some ways, to the ideal of the state of the Italian Renaissance. He occasionally used "totalitarian" as an adjective. Yet his Italian regime was authoritarian rather than totalitarian, and not only because of his acceptance of the monarchy, the church, and many other minor exceptions to Fascist "totality." To describe Hitler and National Socialism as one of the forms of Fascism, as Ernst Nolte did, is wrong—as is the imprecise and mistaken leftist practice of applying the adjective "Fascist" to all movements and regimes of the radical right.†

At the same time, Hitler's political realism compelled him to consider the primacy of state interests on many an occasion. Already in 1926, he put the necessity of good relations with Mussolini above the nationalist desires of many Austrians and South Germans to reclaim the largely German-inhabited South Tyrol, which the Paris peace treaties had awarded to Italy. He had some trouble convincing some of his followers of this. The decision not to imperil his potential relationship with Mussolini, whom he admired and respected at that time, may have been ideological as well as realistic. I find Hitler's reaction to Mussolini's acquiescence in his occupation of

---

*Cited in a study by Horst Zimmermann in Manfred Funke, ed., *Deutschland und die Mächte. Materialien zur Aussenpolitik des III. Reiches*, D, 1977, p. 817.

†Haffner, HF/AN, p. 60: "Nothing is more misleading than to call Hitler a Fascist." Fest, who was sympathetic to Nolte, used the term "Fascist" in F, on occasion; but as Bracher wrote in his complimentary review of F, this happened seldom, and it had no influence on Fest's interpretation, according to which Hitler, unlike other "Fascists," did not depend on historical reminiscences but worked for revolutionary change.

Austria in March 1938 perhaps more significant: "Mussolini, I shall never forget this!" Hitler fired this emotional, and revealing, message to the Duce when the latter had accepted the Anschluss, meaning also the presence of a Greater Germany at the crest of the Alps. That was months, even years, after Mussolini had proclaimed a Rome-Berlin Axis and his friendship for Hitler, and after a large accumulation of most reliable evidence of Mussolini having written off the independence of Austria. Yet Hitler was relieved. He had feared that, after all—or in the end, or at the crucial moment—Mussolini's Italian *Staatsräson*, *raison d'état*, would kick in, more important than their ideological comradeship.

It was to solidify his position and authority within the German state (even more than within the National Socialist Party) that Hitler moved against Röhm in the brutal coup of June 1934—after which he made one of his few speeches sanctifying the cause of the state: "The nation must know that its existence—and this will be guaranteed by its internal order and security—will not be endangered with impunity by anyone! And everyone must know for all the future that if he raises his hand to strike at the state, then certain death is his lot."* There was—obviously—*some* political calculation behind such a statement, but it was not altogether contrary to his own realistic beliefs. Bullock was astute in writing that Hitler's "originality lay in his realization that effective revolutions, in modern conditions, are carried out with, and not against, the power of the State: the correct order of events was first to secure access to that power and then begin his revolution."† But already in 1932 Ernst

---

*Cited by Fest, F, p. 644. He adds: "Repellent as the circumstances of the murder of Röhm are, we may yet ask whether Hitler had any other choice at all. . . ." Hitler's successor Dönitz did not comprehend this well enough. In 1945 (in captivity), he said that in June 1934 Hitler had to navigate between two opposites: According to the radical Nazis (Röhm), the National Socialist revolution had not gone far enough; according to the conservatives (Papen), it had gone too far. But there was more than this kind of calculating navigation in Hitler's mind. As long as Röhm was alive, Hitler could not count on the unquestioning obedience of the leaders of the army, which was the only strong element in the structure of the state that was not yet *entirely* subordinated to him.

†BU, p. 257.

Jünger wrote, "It makes no difference whether power is achieved on the barricades [that is, through a revolution] or in the form of a sober takeover of the administration of the state."*

In February 1945, a friend came to see Albert Speer. He placed on Speer's desk two excerpts from *Mein Kampf*: "It is the task of diplomacy not to allow a people to go under heroically but to preserve it practically. Any way to this is allowable, and the lack of such an effort must be described as criminal negligence." And, "The authority of the state as the highest purpose ["Selbstzweck"] cannot be, for in that case every tyranny on earth would be untouchable and sanctified. When a people is led to disaster through the instrument of governmental power, then the rebellion of every member of such a people is not only a right but a duty."† It was that night, after reading this, that—if we may believe Speer—he for the first time thought of killing Hitler by some means (his idea was the injection of poison gas into the ventilation system of the Führerbunker); but I think that he had read Hitler wrong. Hitler's priority was not the cause of the state; it was the cause of the German people—more accurately, *his concept of the German people*—till the end.‡

AND NOW: WAS HITLER'S CONCEPT of the German people identical with his concept of race? It was not. Yes, Hitler was a racist—

Der Arbeiter, B, 1932, p. 270.

†The quotes are from the 1935 edition of MK, II, p. 603.

‡Worthy of mention—and encouraging—are the reminiscences of the West German Heinz Krekeler, expressed in the Colloquium of the IFZ, *Deutscher Sonderweg: Mythos oder Realität?*, Munich/Vienna, 1982, p. 65. Krekeler was a member of the West German Parliament and of the constitutional commission of the state of North Rhine-Westphalia in 1946–50. He opposed the fundamental sentence: "All state power derives from the people" in the West German constitution, "fervently . . . and I succeeded. With a simple argument that my colleagues found very convincing. The making of popular sovereignty absolute—interestingly, only the Communist faction wanted it—means that the sovereign people may then again dispose of democracy and introduce a dictatorship again. There must exist something that limits popular sovereignty, and these are the basic values and basic rights of [our constitution]." An edifying instance of true conservatism, inspired by the then recent memories of Hitler and the Third Reich.

in the sense in which many people (all kinds of people, including Benjamin Disraeli) have recognized the unavoidable influence of race in the conflicts of humanity. He did write in *Mein Kampf* that "the racial question was the key to world history." That he was not consistent in his racial preferences is obvious. When the occasion demanded, he chose, or sought, alliances with Japanese, Chinese, Romanians, Arabs, and so forth, while remaining committed to fighting or even destroying his "Nordic" or "Aryan" opponents. This may, of course, be attributed to the exigencies of his state-craft, especially during the war. But that was not all. We have no evidence that—even during his formative years, in Vienna—Hitler read or took seriously the late-nineteenth-century French or German racialist philosophers, such as Gobineau, Vacher de Lapogue, Lagarde; or that the hysterical racist pamphleteers of the "Ostara" type had a strong or definite influence on him. Not many of his biographers have noted or emphasized this. Haffner did, however. Aware of the above-cited sentence in *Mein Kampf* about race being the key to history, Haffner noted that race was "never defined by him and often equated with the concept of 'nation' . . . A supreme race as a master nation shall, according to Hitler, rule the world one day—but which, a race or a nation? the Germans or the 'Aryans'? This is never entirely clear with Hitler. Equally unclear is whom he regards as Aryans. Only the more or less Germanic nations? Or all whites except the Jews? This is nowhere clarified by Hitler." The real racial differences among white, black, and yellow-skinned people did not much interest Hitler. What interested him was "the struggle *within* the white race, between the 'Aryans' and the Jews."* Only about Jews did he remain consistent, to the very end of his life. Yet even on the subject of what the Jewish race meant, he changed his mind, as we shall see in a moment.

For, whether race was the key to history or not, there was an

---

*H/AN, pp. 80, 82. This is more solid than Fest's citation of the often unreliable Rauschning in F, p. 939. Hitler allegedly said to Rauschning: "Race is a higher concept than nation. With the idea of nation the French led their revolution beyond their frontiers. With the idea of race National Socialism will carry out its revolution to a new world order."

evolution of his thinking in that regard. There were many committed and rigid racist and racial dogmatists among his early allies
and followers. The dogmatic racists among the higher members of
the Third Reich's hierarchy, such as Himmler, were numerous and
important; their racial philosophy led to the establishment of
various institutions. Yet Hitler did not share Himmler's "primitive
biologism" (well put by Marlis Steinert). Schramm noted that he
"had serious reservations about the glorification of the early period
of the Germanic peoples—unlike many of his followers."* Speer
cited Hitler's dismissal of Himmler's racialist mysticism: "What
nonsense! [W]e have . . . reached an age that has left all mysticism
behind it, and now he wants to start . . . again. We might just as well
have stayed with the church. At least it had tradition." A number of
historians noted that Hitler did not take Alfred Rosenberg seriously
at all, and that he was contemptuous of Rosenberg's cloudy book
Myth of the 20th Century. According to Speer, Hitler said, "a relapse
into the mysticism of the Middle Ages."† Heer cited one of Hitler's
1942 table talks, in which he expressed his pleasure with Cardinal
Faulhaber's public protests against Rosenberg's screed.‡

Hitler's many—and there were many—statements about races are
really statements about what he saw as national characteristics.
There *was* a racist element in his thinking (as is true of almost every
nationalist), but his governing obsessions were not biological. He
knew of the relative lack of response among the German people to
the racial propaganda put out in streams by Rosenberg and
Himmler. National sentiments of superiority, where and when they
existed among the German people, were cultural rather than racial.
This is a subject of enormous significance and delicacy which lies
largely unexplored. There was (and remains) a superficially slight
but essentially profound difference between a *folkish* and a *racist* type
of thinking.** The response that Hitler wished to evoke was the
result of the former rather than the latter. And that reflected, too,

---

*sch, p. 77.
†sp, pp. 94, 95.
‡hr, p. 406.
**See lew, p. 397.

the evolution—if that is what it was, if not a gradually hardening recognition—of his own beliefs.

In May 1944, to officers in a remarkable speech at the Platterhof, Hitler said: "We have this people of ours that is not to be identified with a race, and this is now clear to millions. . . . But when I began [speaking] about twenty-five years ago this was not so. I was told by [counterrevolutionary-*bürgerlich*] circles: Yes, Volk and Race are one and the same! No! Volk and race are not the same. Race is a component of blood, a hematologic [*blutmässig*] kernel, but the Volk is very often composed not of one race but of two, three, four or five different racial kernels. . . . Each of these racial kernels possesses particular talents."* And in the Bormann records, on 13 February 1945, Hitler said: "Pride of race is a quality which the German, fundamentally, does not possess. We use the term of Jewish race as a matter of convenience, for in reality and from the genetic point of view there is no such thing as the Jewish race." *There is no such thing as the Jewish race. . . .*†

NATIONALISM AND RACISM are not easily definable terms. (Nor is there a first-rate general history of either nationalism or of racism. One reason for this is that nationalism may differ from country to country more than internationalism or socialism does.) And this is not the place to expatiate on their differences or on their origins, except to emphasize three matters: (1) that Adolf Hitler was more of a nationalist than a racist; (2) that nationalism can be even more exclusionary than racism—mostly because of its attribution of cultural,

---

*Speech of 26 May 1944, published and annotated by Hans-Heinrich Wilhelm, in *Militärgeschichtlich Mitteilungen*, 1976 (2), pp. 149–50. In this speech Hitler did *not* insist on the superiority of the Nordic racial "kernel": "The strongest of these racial kernels, with a commercial but no creative talents, would have been the Jews among us, in the long run, and with the difference that this Jewry would not have been absorbed racially by the German people but that it would have destroyed the German Volk gradually, step by step."

†*The Testament of Adolf Hitler*. The Hitler-Bormann Documents, L, 1961 (hereafter AH/B). In these last recorded monologues, Hitler also referred to Jews as "a spiritual race."

linguistic, and even religious elements;* and (3) that nationalism, more than racism, is a modern, and populist, phenomenon.

Modern, and *populist*. When Samuel Johnson made his celebrated pronouncement "Patriotism is the last refuge of a scoundrel," he meant *nationalism*, since that word did not yet exist in English. Patriotism (as George Orwell noted in one of the few essays extant on its distinction from nationalism) is defensive, while nationalism is aggressive; patriotism is rooted in the land, in a particular country, while nationalism is applied to the myth of a people (indeed, to a putative majority); patriotism is traditionalist, while nationalism is populist. Populism is folkish; patriotism is not. This phenomenon— or, rather, tendency—is almost universal in the twentieth century. The nineteenth century was full of liberal nationalists, some of them inspiring and noble figures. In the twentieth century this has seldom been so. One hundred years before, Orwell's (1943) distinction between nationalism and patriotism would have seemed labored, it would have made relatively little sense. Even now nationalism and patriotism often overlap within the mind and the heart of the same person. Yet we must be aware of the differences between them— because of the phenomenon of populist nationalism, which, unlike old-fashioned patriotism, is inseparable from the myth of a people. One can be a patriot and, at least culturally, cosmopolitan. But a populist is inevitably a nationalist of sorts. Patriotism, too, is less racist than is populism. A patriot will not exclude a person of another race from the community where they have lived side by side and whom he has known for many years; but a nationalist will always remain suspicious of someone who does not seem to belong to his kind of people—or, more likely, to his way of thinking. "The jingo nationalist"—Alfred Duff Cooper said it well—"is always the first to denounce his fellow countrymen as traitors."

This difference between patriotism and nationalism Hitler exemplified. About its meaning he was explicitly clear. Early in his youth, as he put it in *Mein Kampf*, "I was a nationalist, but not a patriot."

---

*Few, otherwise racist, Southerners would deny that American-born blacks are Americans; many German Nazis denied that German-born Jews were Germans. (Other examples: Ulster, Yugoslavia.)

He desired to unite himself and the Austrian Germans with a Greater Germany, at the expense of the multinational and dynastic Habsburg imperial state that he wished to see broken up. He developed this theme often. Thus in a little-known speech in Munich, on 6 April 1927, reported in detail in the *Völkischer Beobachter* two days later, "Nationalism and Patriotism" was the very title of his speech.* A few excerpts: "We are not [merely] national; we are nationalist!" "A decisive settlement of accounts with that national sentiment of the German Bürgertum that has petrified into a patriotism." "Our young and socialistic nationalism has nothing in common with the older outdated patriotism." "The German Bürgertum does not yet have a true national goal. [Their] nationalism and ours are two absolutely different things. Their nationalism is at best a means to allow the past to continue a little longer." Throughout his public career Hitler was aware of the tremendous attraction of nationalism. He made good use of it. He understood, for instance, the reluctance and the occasional opposition of the German Catholic hierarchy, clergy, and lay people to National Socialist racialist propaganda and racial institutions when at the same time he knew how to profit from their unqualified nationalist sentiments.†

Patriotism is not a substitute for religious faith, whereas nationalism often in, it may fill the emotional—and at least superficially spiritual—needs of people. It may be combined with hatred. Görlitz-Quint made telling observations about this: "Hate as the initial impulse [Ausgangspunkt] . . . was characteristic of [Hitler]‡ and of his movement, which grew on the pavements of the big cities. . . .

---

*The subtitles of the lead articles (which Hitler himself edited) are a summary of his speech: "The curse of the small German states—The dynastic patriotism—The guilt of the Bürgertum—The international cosmopolitanism of the upper ten thousand—The nationalist state."

†Example: In the mostly Catholic Saar, in 1932 the Nazis polled less than 7 percent of the vote, while in 1935—supported by the clergy—91 percent voted for union with the Third Reich. In Austria, the cruelest and most brutal ss leaders—Eichmann, Globocnik, Kaltenbrunner—identified themselves with Germany, while the *Austrian* National Socialist Leopold was rejected by Hitler in 1938–39. It may also be telling that in 1940 Hitler referred to the right-wing "isolationists" in the United States as "radical nationalists"—a term much more accurate than "isolationists."

‡See chapter 2 for a discussion of Hitler's cultivation of hate.

The human reservoir of the movement were soldiers, workers, and people uprooted in the big cities, artisans and lower-middle-class people . . . [but] the peasantry was quite alien to Hitler. All of those later ideals of a revival of the peasantry, of the creation of a new landed class of 'blood and soil,' were not among his original ideas, and they did not correspond to the origin of the movement which sprang up not from blood and soil but the masses of the cities."* Unlike many of the populists of the nineteenth century who had risen from the peasantry, nationalists in the twentieth century have often preached an abstract love for the peasantry and the land. The early speeches of Hitler and early National Socialist propaganda included little or nothing about peasants and agriculture. Heiden, too, noted this: "It is a program for hungering city people. . . ,"† to which he added that Hitler had realized this, and began to appeal to the German peasantry with success only after 1928, during the great agricultural depression. In Munich (10 April 1923), Hitler said: "For the liberation of the people more is needed than an economic policy, more than industry: if a people is to become free, it needs pride and willpower, defiance, hate, hate and once again hate." Whatever the deeper source of Hitler's hatreds, he projected them outward, in the service of his extreme nationalism and racism.‡ Hitler may have understood something that Chesterton knew when he wrote that while love is always personal and particular, it is hatred that unites otherwise disparate men.

Neither the "racist" nor the "Social Darwinist" designations explain Hitler sufficiently. He believed in the Survival of the Strongest,

---

*GQ, pp. 126–27.

†HD, p. 88.

‡There is evidence of occasional sentiments of inferiority (or, more precisely, compensations for such a feeling) in some of Hitler's expressions. (Churchill was acutely aware of some of them: See DL, pp. 41–42.) See also Hitler's speech in Kassel, 4 June 1939: "Not for a moment will I admit that our Western opponents have a right to think or to consider themselves superior . . . I do not suffer in the least from any sort of inferiority complex." (LEW, p. 390.) His remarks (9 January 1939) to the assembled workers and architects of the New Chancellery, cited by Speer (SP, chapter 5): "Why always the biggest? I do this to restore to each individual German his self-respect. . . . I want to say to the individual: We are not inferior; on the contrary, we are the complete equals of every other nation." Krier, K, p. 214: "Hitler's gigantic buildings were intended to impress the people with their power."

but was there anything new in that? The principle of the triumph of the Tough over the Weak goes back even beyond Machiavelli, perhaps to Cain and Abel themselves.* Hitler understood that people respond to—indeed, that they will respect—the realities of power.† Moreover, unlike many Social Darwinists, Hitler was not a materialist, convinced as he was of the power of ideas.

He was an extreme nationalist—perhaps the most extreme nationalist of all the principal figures of the twentieth century. And while nationalism is atavistically human, deeper, and stronger than class consciousness, the trouble is not only its latent inhumanity but the—perhaps surprising—abstractness of its assumption about human nature itself. "Love of the people": but who *are* the people? Nationalism is both self-centered and selfish, because human love is not the love of oneself, it is the love of *another*. Patriotism is traditional and not merely biological, because charitable love is human and not merely "natural." Nature has—and shows—no charity.‡ That Hitler believed. He also believed that charity does not have a function in the history of mankind. Whether that amounted to his belief in Social Darwinism is arguable. What is not questionable is that his hatred for his opponents was both stronger and less abstract than was his love for his people.** That was (and remains) a distinguishing mark of the mind of every extreme nationalist.

---

*Zitelmann—as well as others—overemphasized Hitler's Social Darwinism. Hitler often made references to Marx but seldom, if ever, to Darwin.

†In February 1924, before the court: "The psyche of the people is such that it respects the existence of power, first of all." (ZIT/A, p. 47.)

‡It is therefore that the dignity of human life must proceed from a denial of Darwinism, and from the recognition that, no matter how biologically small, there *is* an essential difference between human beings and all other living beings. Both Christianity and Western civilization are humanist in that sense, in the sense of their requisite denial of the survival of the fittest as a principle governing humanity.

**And yet consider: Hatred is a *human* inclination, as is love. Just as human love is something more and different from an animal's instinctive affections, hatred in humans is something different from the "red tooth and claw" of nature. And while human love is always a love for another, human hate is inevitably self-centered; for we often hate in others something that we hate in ourselves. (That, too, is true less of racism than it is of nationalism.) And what did Hitler hate in himself? That is a secret that he died without divulging.

5

Statesman and Strategist

The attention directed to Hitler's statesmanship has been generally slight—
His abilities as statesman and strategist—Questions about Munich
and the Russian enigma—His goals during the war—
His decision to attack Russia—His consideration of the United States—
The "Friderician" turning point—His ability to recover—
His aim of splitting the Allied coalition—Confronting the
final defeat: obstinacy or consistency, or both?

WITHIN THE VAST AMOUNT of biographical literature about Hitler the treatment of Hitler the national leader is much larger than the treatment of Hitler the statesman and the strategist. A division of his life and career into two periods seems obvious and logical: his astonishingly successful rise until 1939, and the six years of the war, ending with catastrophe and suicide—an end result, though dramatic, well nigh foreordained in retrospect. That is probably the reason for the tendency of many of his biographers to devote little space to the last six years of his life.*

---

*Maser, for example, has but a short chapter (No. 9: "Der Feldherr und Stratege") in M/A; Jäckel, in JHH and JH, does not go beyond 1941; GQ, though otherwise insightful, is weak on Hitler's foreign policy; Zitelmann in both ZIT/A and ZIT/B is much more detailed and convincing about Hitler's domestic than about his foreign policies (when describing Hitler's decision to attack Russia he relies almost entirely on Goebbels's Diaries, even though Goebbels was *not*, at that time, closely connected with Hitler's planning). In ZIT/A, p. 103, Zitelmann denies that Hitler wanted to dominate the world: true, but he then says nothing about the limits of Hitler's geopolitical aims. In F, p. 186, Fest rightly warns against

This tendency is not unreasonable; their emphasis is on Hitler's career leading to a war that he could not but lose, dragging millions to death and destruction before the end. This widely and generally held view still remains acceptable, except for two things. One is that in 1940 and 1941 Hitler came close to winning his war. The other is that his ultimate defeat may have been foreordained (even though "foreordained" suggests a determinism that historians ought to avoid) because of his hubris; but then hubris is a fault of character rather than of vision; and Hitler was not blind.* As Pascal said, love is not really blind; and neither are other kinds of passion. They are, more than often, a compound of a startling clarity of vision with a startling blindness (a compound that, like "half-truth," is not fixable within the categories of mathematics). And since vision involves purposes rather than motives, we ought to direct some attention to what Adolf Hitler's purposes were before and perhaps especially during the war.

They are not easy to ascertain.† (Or perhaps I should write

---

the "to this day widely prevalent representation of [Hitler] the man of instincts . . . ignoring the rationality and the boldness of planning that were basic to his behavior and which governed his rise not less than all his other apparent abilities"—very true, but then Fest does *not* apply the same judgment to the war years and to Hitler's foreign policies (about which we may find the few mistakes in his otherwise excellent book). Steinert, who is very good on the German people during the war (in ST/HK/D) in ST, is weak on Hitler's statesmanship and strategy, with a share of minor errors; also unduly dependent on Goebbels. The most extreme disproportion between the space and treatment devoted to the war and the prewar years is in Davidson. (See chapter 1, p. 22*n*.)

*Kershaw in KER, for instance, p. 121: ". . . a deepening hubris of power, the early stages of what was to develop into catastrophic *folie de grandeur* and detachment from reality." (Not entirely untrue, but the last three words are debatable.) KER also tends to exaggerate Ribbentrop's influence on Hitler (pp. 144, 146); and he does not treat Hitler's aim and wish to split his enemies after 1941. Yet Kershaw is correct when he states (p. 177): "Hitler's decisions in the military arena were by no means all as absurd as they were sometimes retroactively painted."

†Schramm, in SCH, p. 31: "Hitler hardly ever lost control of himself completely, even though in time his nerves were taxed to such an extent that most men, operating under a similar burden, would not have been physically equal to it. Consequently, it is very difficult to come to grips with what Hitler really thought and perceived, difficult to clarify the extent to which he was motivated by logic or impelled by instinct."

"understand," rather than "ascertain"—since, unlike in the natural sciences, the purpose of historical knowledge may be understanding even more than "certainty.") There exists a substantial body of his own statements about his purposes—not only in his public speeches and his "private" table talk but well before that, in the hundreds of pages directed to what the aims of German foreign policy and German expansion should be, in *Mein Kampf* and in *Hitler's Secret Book*, as well as in the many articles he dictated or wrote during the years before his coming to power.* But here may be a case of not seeing the trees for the forest. To think (as, for example, Bullock does) that Hitler's aims were clearly set forth in *Mein Kampf*, and that therefore there was a frightening consistency in his purposes and their execution, is too simple. Recall, too, that he was also a very secretive man.† Whatever his basic ideas were (and we have also seen that there was, at least in some of them, an evolution), there were instances when he, like every other human being (not to speak of a politician or a statesman) had to adjust them to circumstances beyond his direct control. We have also seen that many of his statements were meant for public purposes, including the purpose of influencing not only large groups of listeners but men around him, and his conversants. Of course, no historian—and surely no biographer—possesses the mental powers (and, consequently, ought not to have the intellectual arrogance) to define and divide and nail down two categories of proof: (a) this was what his subject said he thought, (b) this was what his subject really thought.

Hitler's Secret Book, NY, 1961 (hereafter: H2B). Deuerlein is very perspicacious about this (D, p. 76): ". . . *Mein Kampf* is not . . . a 'Timetable of a World Conqueror'; rather a summary of what Hitler himself said; lead articles for [a] 'Völkischer Beobachter.' "

†Gerald Fleming, *Hitler and the Final Solution*, Berkeley, Calif., 1982 (hereafter: FL), p. 18, citing Hitler's words to General Halder when appointing the latter as chief of staff of the army, September 1938: "You should know first of all that you will never be able to discover my thoughts and intentions until I give them out as orders. . . . In politics things are entirely different. You will never learn what is going on in my head. . . ." (Halder confirmed this personally to Fleming.) See also Schramm (SCH, p. 130), Hitler to Admiral Raeder, admitting his own "three ways of keeping secrets."

We may say—at the risk of some imprecision—that his purpose was to make Germany one of the greatest powers of the world, certainly the greatest in Europe. The fundament of this was the achievement of a new and unprecedented unity of the German people (which involved the expulsion of the Jews among them), and the eventual unity of nearly all German-speaking people in Europe in a single Reich. We may essay the statement that this was probably his minimal aim,* even though he did not (and could not) follow it with any great consistency. Especially during the war, his policies would evolve and change. We shall see, for example, that his policy of expelling Jews from Germany eventually evolved into the aim in 1940) of expelling them from most, if not all, of Europe; then (in 1941), when emigration and expulsion were no longer possible, to have masses of them exterminated, and then (in late 1944) the mass extermination of the remnant millions in the death camps was suspended (a complicated matter to which in chapter 6 I shall have to return). There is, of course, ample evidence that the presence of Jews (at least in Germany and Europe) was a fundamental obsession of Hitler's. There is also ample evidence of his desire for "Lebensraum": to obtain, or conquer, if need be, more lands for German settlement in the east of Europe, including Russia. But while obsessions and intentions may overlap, they are not altogether the same thing; and, despite Hitler's innumerable and often categorical statements and directives concerning the latter, his Lebensraum policies were less consistent than his Judeophobic ones.†

This is the main reason why we must qualify the widely accepted view, according to which anti-Judaism and the conquest of European Russia leading to *Lebensraum* were not only the two fundamental but

---

*"God writes straight with crooked lines." Paradoxically, his defeat and death achieved this (except for Austria and the South Tyrol). In the last year of the war, millions of Germans abandoned their lands and fled westward, into what remained of Germany; after the war, millions more were expelled from Poland, Czechoslovakia, Hungary, Romania, and Yugoslavia. Thus, for the first time in eight hundred years, there were few Germans left in Eastern Europe beyond the Oder River— which was perhaps the most enduring, and historic, consequence of Hitler's war.

†Schreiber (schrb, p. 65) mentions that Hitler used the term "Lebensraum" in mk only twice. (The term came from the German geographer Ratzel and others, as early as 1897.)

the two unchanging elements in Hitler's strategy. Among his many historians and biographers, two widely read writers (one a respected professional historian), David Irving and Andreas Hillgruber, have devoted most of their interest to Hitler's strategy and statesmanship during the six years of the war. Because of Irving's tireless collecting of papers (mostly, though not exclusively, from people who had lived close to Hitler), his work has lately received some grudging recognition from military historians. But while some of Irving's "finds" cannot be disregarded, their interpretation (as I indicated in chapter 1, and to which I must return in chapter 8) is, more often than not, compromised and even badly flawed because of Irving's aim of rehabilitating Hitler. Anyone, of course, has the right to admire a historical personage, no matter how unpopular. But there exists no "fact" in history that is separable from its statement; and every statement, in turn, is inseparable from its purpose. Apart from (or, perhaps, in addition to) moral judgments, there are two main reasons why Irving's researches on Hitler the statesman and the strategist should be treated (and read) with considerable caution. The first is the evidence of his frequent "twisting" of documentary sources not only through their interpretation but through the inadequacy of their actual references.* The other is that Irving's portrait of Hitler as statesman and strategist is achieved with undiscriminating strokes of his brush. He is satisfied with presenting the warrior Hitler as having been not only more able but also superior in character to all of his opponents. Consequently in Irving's works a discriminating historical reconstruction of Hitler's decisions and purposes hardly exists at all.†

---

*There are innumerable instances of this, both in 1/w and 1/H. One telling instance: a verbatim citation of a Stalin speech of 5 May 1941, including a toast: "Drink to the new era of development and territorial expansion that has begun! Long live the active policy of aggression of the Soviet nation!" (1/H, p. 240.) There is absolutely no proof of this. Or 1/w, p. 147, about the British ambassador in Washington, July 1940: "[He] was openly conceding that Britain had been defeated and must expect to pay." This is an egregious and willful misreading of Lord Lothian's statements at the time.

†An important example: In 1/w, Irving pays almost no attention to the crucial turning point, the change in Hitler's mind and personal habits, during the winter of 1937–38.

More serious than Irving (and not only because of his qualifications as a professional historian) are the two thoroughly researched works of the political and military historian Andreas Hillgruber (especially HST). This volume is a very important secondary source for Hitler's statesmanship and strategy in the crucial years of 1940 and 1941. There are, however, questions about Hillgruber's interpretation of Hitler that must be raised.* One is his categorical assertion that Hitler had but two fundamental objectives, the conquest of European Russia and the elimination of Jews, which he pursued consistently. One cannot entirely disagree with this view, but that consistency is open to question because of circumstances that may have forced Hitler to change his aims from time to time. More important—at least for the purposes of this chapter—is the questionable (and consequent) Hillgruber thesis of the step-by-step timetable of Hitler's Grand Strategy: Hillgruber's "Stufenplan."† According to this, the conquest of Russia was, and remained, Hitler's main intention throughout; and the defeat or acquiescence of France and Britain was but secondary to that aim. After the elimination of opposition in the West, the real campaign in the East would begin; and, after that, a future struggle with the United States, perhaps not even in his lifetime. This general scheme of Hitler's Grand Strategy may be intellectually convincing, especially in the case of a grandiloquent and fanatical dictator; yet it is debatable, not only because of Hitler's complex nature but on the basis of actual evidence. Yes, Hitler wanted to conquer European Russia; but after 1940 his main intention was to force the British (and the Americans) to recognize the senselessness of continuing a war against him after he had eliminated the Soviet Union. Moreover, he had not contemplated, let alone desired, a war against the United

---

* We may also detect an evolution during the forty years of Hillgruber's professional work, from a sometimes—consciously or not—concealed positive appreciation of Hitler's statesmanship (evident here and there in HST) to his categorical condemnation of some of Hitler's misdeeds.

†Jäckel in JHW inclines to such a "Stufenplan" (". . . the great war of conquest against Russia could take place during the third and final phase"), though less so in JIIII (written twenty years later).

States. We shall return to these crucial matters in the course of this chapter.*

MUCH THAT WAS SUCCESSFUL in Hitler's career was due to his opponents' underestimation of his abilities. The head of the small party that Hitler joined in 1919 underestimated his capacity to attract people and power to his side;† the German politicians (and not only politicians) woefully underestimated his political abilities; and after he came to power many people throughout the world derided his talents as a potential European statesman. Yet he proved to be an alarmingly effective statesman—not only in peace but also in war—and an often alarmingly successful strategist.‡ From a provincial demagogue, he rose to a successful politician and an awesomely respected leader of a great nation, and then—at least for some time—to the director of the greatest war machine in the world. In that capacity, the world—including his leading opponents—finally learned not to underestimate him, even though there

---

*I must also state another disagreement with Hillgruber, who was a proponent of the—to many Germans still attractive—two-war theory: that the war in the West (which was a "normal European war" [ein europäisches Normalkrieg]) was regrettable, a tragic development to which Hitler had decisively contributed, whereas the war with Russia, at least in its latter stages, amounted to a heroic defense of the German land, the German people, and Western civilization. I understand the sentiments of this native of East Prussia; but I must abide by the answer that Field Marshal Montgomery gave in May 1945 to the exclamation of the German generals who wished to get from him a partial surrender: "The Russians are savages!" Whereupon Montgomery: "You should have thought of that in June 1941."

†Fest, F, p. 203: "With a mixture of coldbloodedness, calculation and determination as well as [his] readiness to take great risks for the sake of limited aims—and this he demonstrated in all kinds of crisis situations—he succeeded in getting the Party in his hands." Also, p. 206: His later demonstrated ability to master crises included, too, his repeated tendency "to endanger his triumphs through their further exaggeration."

‡Some of his biographers shy away from the word "statesman," mostly because of the positive connotations of the word. Thus Heiber in HB, p. 117: "No. Hitler was a very clever leader of a party, a dedicated demagogue, an inspiring speaker, and even about Hitler the military commander there will be something to say: but *a statesman* he was not."

was little in Hitler's past that suggested a character comparable to a Caesar or a Napoleon. But the evidence had come, and the world had learned a bitter and hard lesson.

One—perhaps the main—source of Hitler's political and military, diplomatic and strategic, abilities may be summed up briefly. He had an ability—mostly, though not entirely, instinctive—to recognize the weaknesses of his actual or potential opponents. (And also those of his actual, or potential, allies or followers.) He did not always know with certainty what they would do; but he was reasonably confident (and often rather accurate) in understanding what they were loath to do. This stabbing comprehension of the weaker sides of human nature carried him far; but it also led to some of his greatest failures when he underestimated some of his adversaries and therefore failed to understand them.* Still a powerful understanding of human nature may be a principal instrument, serving not only a statesman but a strategist as well.† Napoleon Bonaparte knew this when he quipped that there are two human occupations where an amateur is often better than a professional, one being prostitution and the other war.

In Hitler's case we may have to carry this a little further, evoking Napoleon's contemporary Clausewitz, the great German theoretician of war.‡ His famous maxim that war is but the continuation of politics by other means, surely applies to Hitler. (It is of course a truism: even a tyrant prefers an opponent who surrenders rather than fights.) But Clausewitz was thinking and writing about the many dynastic wars of the eighteenth century and of Napoleon, and

---

*Churchill, for example. Also, not being an optimist, Hitler was wont to expect the worst from his enemies. This went beyond attributing weaknesses to them.

†Schramm (SCH, p. 32, note 2) cites Dr. v. Hasselbach ("the most critical and reliable of Hitler's doctors"): "Hitler repeatedly asserted that one of his essential capacities, which he could depend on absolutely, was the ability to judge men. Even a brief impression was sufficient for him to be able to say what sort of a person a man was and how he could best be used."

‡Görlitz-Quint cite a Hitler statement in GQ, p. 482: "Strategy is not a secret science. It is the application of a healthy knowledge of human nature. Its basis [ihre Grundformen] may be studied at a boxing match. Armies are nothing but gigantic bodies." This corresponds to Hegel's idea according to which the state is but a human being writ large, a "Macroanthropos."

Hitler's wars were so very different. (Also, Hitler was a Clause-witzian in the reverse sense, too, waging politics as if it were war.)

In addition—superseding both Napoleon's and Clausewitz's realistic recognition of the supreme importance of morale in war—Hitler was an idealist determinist, which is perhaps a peculiarly German inclination. He believed (as had Schopenhauer and Nietz-sche) in the supreme importance of will; and also in the supreme power of ideas. He thought that in the streets of German cities as well as in the arena of politics, his National Socialist storm troopers must, and would, win: that one National Socialist street fighter was worth two or three of his Communist or Socialist opponents, not only because he was better disciplined and trained but because of the superior force of his convictions and ideas. He believed that the war in Europe was but the repetition on a larger scale of what had happened within Germany in 1928–33: that a German fighting man was worth two English or three French or four Russian soldiers because of the superior nature and strength of the idea which he incarnated. And that was why Germany had to win this war against her numerous enemies, just as the National Socialists had had to win, and indeed had won, their war against their enemies within Germany.* This conviction carried Hitler very far: but not far enough. Yet this was one instance in which there was probably no difference between his publicly expressed and his most private beliefs; in this kind of determinist idealism he seems to have believed till the end.†

At the same time, Hitler's convictions were sustained, assisted,

---

*Fest cites Hitler on the British appeasers (F, p. 801): "meine Hugenberger," "the likes of Hugenberg" (or "my Hugenbergs"), Hugenberg having been the German nationalist conservative who went along with Hitler hoping to get his own way, and then was easily discarded.

†He was, like most successful military leaders, an innovator; but, true to himself, he was more convinced of the importance of military morale than of that of new weapons. In this respect there was, again, a difference between his public statements and his private beliefs. It was to others that he would occasionally suggest the decisive importance of "wonder weapons," while there is little evidence that he privately shared the breathless expectations attributed to them. Steinert (ST, p. 538) exaggerates Hitler's trust in new weapons (his "puerile illusions"). Jäckel (JHW, p. 149) is probably right: There comes a time when Hitler "no longer believes in what he says," though Jäckel does not apply this to the 1943–45 years.

and served by a knowledge of historical and technical matters, in which he was not wanting. His knowledge of history, though selective and incomplete, was not insubstantial. His memories of his military service during the First World War served him in good stead. He was a fast reader of books and of all kinds of reports.* Perhaps most important, he had an astonishing memory, capable of absorbing and retaining a remarkable array of technical details, that would sometimes amaze his generals during their conferences.† There were campaign decisions when his generals were right and he was wrong; but there were many others when the reverse was true,

---

*A few examples. Lukacs, LEW, p. 371, note 95: "Hitler, who seldom read his ambassadors' dispatches, was nevertheless much interested in secret information culled from spies. In early July 1940 he wanted to read *all* reports of all kinds from agents and the transcripts of monitored telephone conversations from London. In the spring of 1941 he wanted and got a series of confidential reports gathered by agents working within the Soviet embassy in Berlin. Much of this involved trivia, but Hitler was acutely interested." He read many reports and articles about American opponents of Roosevelt during the war. In 1944, he commented in detail upon an article from an issue (March 1944) of the British *Contemporary Review*. Irving describes the "Forschungsamt" reports as the key to Hitler's political successes; but this is an exaggeration.

†Schramm (SCH, p. 104) cites Jodl on Hitler's astounding command of technical details: "It was due to him personally that the 75 mm. antitank gun replaced the 37-mm. and 50-mm. guns in time, and that the short guns mounted on the tanks were replaced with the long 75-mm. and 88-mm. The 'Panther,' the 'Tiger,' and the 'Königstiger' . . . were developed as modern tanks at Hitler's own initiative." p. 106: "This degree of technological aptitude is all the more remarkable considering that Hitler had never had any technical education nor the opportunity to gather practical experience in industry." SCH, p. 70: "His remarkable memory, together with iron diligence and a strong power of concentration." (Yet that kind of self-discipline Hitler began to impose on himself only after December 1941.) Carr, c, p. 78: "It is quite clear that Hitler was no ignoramus pontificating about [military] matters beyond his ken. On the contrary, Hitler had in fact an astonishingly broad grasp of military strategy and an eye for operational tactics in offensive warfare that one would not expect in a layman. . . ." About this the otherwise very judicious Kershaw is less convincing. KER, p. 171: "In many respects, his conception of weapons derived from the technological developments of the First World War and the 1920s. Moreover, he was scarcely equipped to cope with the sophisticated scientific and technological principles of modern weapons systems." See also Speer, SP, *passim*, about many examples, including Hitler's design for the Atlantic coastal bunkers: planned by Hitler to the last details "by himself at night. They were sketches, but well developed."

even when he had to impose them against the judgment of the best-trained general officers in Europe.*

There was one important—and historic—realization that Hitler made, and which served him well. This was the return of the supreme importance of land power. Sea power was the prime key to history, wrote the American Admiral Mahan (who was respected in Germany as well as in Britain) in the 1890s. That may have been true for centuries, perhaps, but no longer. The motorization of military movement changed that. In Napoleon's time the English, if not necessarily victorious, were unconquerable while they could sail rings around Napoleon's European empire, landing here or there with ease. But latest by the 1930s, armies could move faster on land than amphibious forces at sea. Hitler knew (and he said so on many occasions) that the horrible and senseless trench warfare of World War I, million-man armies struggling on the Western front in the mud for a few miles gained or lost, would not return. He was fascinated by the automobile, in many ways. The mobility of armor was even more important than its firepower.† Among his opponents the French, with the exception of Colonel, later General, de Gaulle, almost entirely failed to comprehend this; Franklin Roosevelt, as late as 1941, insisted that "naval power was the key to victory," which was still true in the Pacific and the Atlantic, but not in Europe; Winston Churchill had learned this quickly. All the superiority of the Allies at sea (and even in the air) was not enough; Hitler had to be defeated and Germany conquered on land. Perhaps Stalin knew it; but then the Russians have always been land animals.

---

*Schramm, SCH, p. 147: "It would be a mistake to belittle Hitler as a strategist, or to deny that during the first half of the war he developed conceptions regarded as masterly even by many skeptical experts." P. 190: "Undoubtedly Hitler was able, by his methods, to get much more out of the German Wehrmacht than even the most sanguine optimist would have believed possible." Bullock, too (BU, p. 588): "Hitler, the outsider, who had never been to a university or a staff college, had beaten the Foreign Office and the General Staff at their own game. It is customary to decry this achievement. . . . [But] if Hitler . . . is justly to be made responsible for the later disasters of the German Army, he is entitled to the major share of the credit for the victories . . . the German generals cannot have it both ways."

†Yet he studied naval handbooks in great detail. He was able to recall many details about the speed, armor, tonnage, and gunnery of enemy warships. Fest (F, p. 306) recognized Hitler's realization of the passing predominance of sea power.

On 30 January 1933, Hitler became the chancellor of a dark and depressed nation whose depression, however, was unusual, because it was not lethargic. On the contrary, millions of Germans felt themselves gripped by a strange kind of agitation, not knowing what to anticipate. Except for a minority who, with every reason, envisaged the worst, most Germans soon accustomed themselves to a new order that was both more and less radical than they had expected. There was a radical break with their immediate political past—this in spite of Hitler's proud insistence that a national revolution was being accomplished without turmoil and bloodshed. There was, however, a continuity—of sorts—in Germany's relations with the rest of the world.

It was not only that the immense importance of Hitler's assumption of power was inadequately understood by almost all foreign observers. (This is evident from the articles and commentaries of foreign newspapers during the week following 30 January 1933.) Despite the Depression, despite the very high rate of German unemployment, despite the recurrent electoral and political crises through which Germany passed in 1932, that year German foreign policy became more assertive than at any time since 1918. The Lausanne agreement in July 1932, which virtually put an end to all German "reparations," was acknowledged both by the Wilhelmstrasse and by German public opinion with a shrug of the shoulder; and at the more and more desultory disarmament conferences in Geneva the German delegation was increasingly stiff-necked and demanding. There is every reason to believe that the power and prestige of Germany would have risen in the 1930s even without Hitler; but a detailed exposition of this argument does not belong in this book. What does belong is a brief discussion of how Hitler, in the service of his statesmanship, made good use of the traditional and conservative personnel of the German Foreign Ministry during the first five years of his rule*—

---

*On one occasion, Goebbels criticized Hitler's foreign minister Neurath: Not a Nazi, "he belongs to an entirely different world." Hitler: No. "[Neurath] is seen in the Anglo-Saxon world as a [gentleman]." (sp, p. 162.) Also p. 217: " 'Gentleman' was an unusual word for Hitler to use."

even as he also took care not to alienate that other traditionalist and conservative element of the former republic: the army. Only one or two German diplomats resigned from the foreign service after 1933 and before 1938. Still Hitler's belief in his ideology remained fundamental. It would be too simple to think that he had subordinated his revolutionary ideology to the interests of the state (something that Stalin would do in a crass and brutal manner, misunderstood by anti-Communist ideologues to this day). It would be more accurate to say that Hitler's Realpolitik* was a compound of ideological convictions and calculations of state interest, indeed to the very end—a compound in which he, at least, saw no contradictions.†

Those of Hitler's serious biographers who have felt compelled to acknowledge, and describe, the startlingly successful first six years of his chancellorship have concentrated mostly on his domestic achievements without, of course, ignoring those of his statesmanship in foreign policy—reasonably so, since the two were not separable.‡ While, on the one hand, his forging of a German national unity was the basis on which his foreign moves had to depend, on the other hand his popular support was steadily enhanced by his people's admiration of his foreign policy, which had led to such a

---

*The word "Realpolitik" was coined by the Heidelberg writer A. L. von Rochau in 1853, in his book *Grundsätze der Realpolitik*.

†Thus, for example, he would appoint the same Papen, for whose political ideas and tactics within Germany Hitler had little respect, to important foreign posts (in Vienna and Ankara), where Papen's canny abilities served Hitler well (at least until 1944). As a matter of fact, there were crucial occasions (such as in July 1940) when Hitler would call for Papen, if not for advice, then to hear him out. LEW, p. 334, note 15: "On one occasion, in 1939, Ribbentrop forbade members of the ministry to talk directly with Papen [GD, D, VIII, p. 330]—yet Papen continued to function under Hitler's protection."

‡Görlitz-Quint, GQ, p. 513: "He applied the image of the party struggles [of the Weimar Republic] literally to foreign policy. He never realized that domestic and foreign policy are two entirely different matters." But are they? In this respect Irving's summary statement is, for once, more telling (I/w, p. xxiii): "In Hitler's view, Germany's [former] statesmen had put domestic strength too low in their priorities. . . . First he restored Germany's psychological unity; on this stable foundation he rebuilt her economic strength; and on that base in turn he built up the military might with which to enforce an active foreign policy."

great rise of German power and prestige abroad. Yet again, it would be erroneous to assert that before 1939 Hitler's statesmanship was, by and large, successful, because he had not yet broken with Realpolitik; and that thereafter the war and its catastrophes were the results of ideology overwhelming whatever "realpolitical" talents for statesmanship he may have possessed.* Ideology, even in the 1930s, was not something apart and different from his cold calculations, but part and parcel of them. Thus, for example, in his most difficult year, 1934, when National Socialist Germany and Fascist Italy seemed, at least for a while, to oppose each other, Hitler knew that this would not continue. His first meeting with Mussolini in June 1934 may have been inconsequential; but, contrary to the views of some of his biographers, it was not altogether a failure. It may have, at worst, delayed the pronouncement of a Rome-Berlin Axis that Mussolini would then declare in 1936, but it neither compromised nor obstructed its eventual development.† A compound of ideology and statesmanship governed Hitler's decision to actively support Franco in the Spanish Civil War, and also Germany's relationship with China and Japan.‡ It is true that both in *Mein Kampf* and in his 1928 "book" he had emphatically defined his realistic calculations, a German Reich needing good relations with England and Italy. But it was more than realistic calculation that made him arrive and rejoice at a naval treaty with England in 1935. He thought (and he had some evidence to that effect) that people in the governing circles of England would acquiesce in the rise of a new Germany

---

*Thus Fest, F, p. 836: "After 1939 Hitler departed from 'Politik' and he never returned to it." This is very debatable.

†Fest is not correct about Mussolini, "who, more than others, insisted on resisting Germany's further advance" at Stresa, in 1935. (F, p. 673.) He also exaggerates Hitler's Realpolitik during the Spanish Civil War. F, p. 685: ". . . here again he was a tactician and showed a cold rationality that was entirely [?] free of ideology: for years he did nothing to promote Franco's victory and wanted rather to keep [the civil war] going."

‡Toland, TO, p. 401: Hitler's persuading Japan to sign the Anti-Comintern Pact in 1936: "Admittedly spineless, the agreement was important as a propaganda ploy to justify German rearmament." It had nothing to do with rearmament, and everything to do with his calculation about the advantageous use of anticommunism.

because of their anticommunism and perhaps even because of certain racial sympathies.* Beneath this coursed his fundamental conviction of his ability to recognize and to profit from the weakness of his opponents. And so he was able to achieve something even greater than Bismarck and, unlike Bismarck, without war: the Saar, the remilitarization of the Rhineland, the incorporation of Austria, and the Sudetenland, creating a Greater German Reich such as the world had never seen. Even before he changed the map of Europe, even before he flung his armed power beyond the German borders for the first time in March 1938, he had already achieved a Diplomatic Revolution. He had, as yet, no fixed alliances—only a few treaties of nonaggression or friendship or anticommunism. At the same time, France had political and military alliances with Poland, Czechoslovakia, Romania, Yugoslavia, even Soviet Russia. Yet these no longer amounted to much; most of them were useless paper. That was a diplomatic revolution without precedent in the modern history of Europe.

But then, in the winter of 1937–38, there came a change. It was not a change in his objectives, or a result of his changing view of the European situation. It was a change within the man himself. He had convinced himself that he might not have long to live, that time was working against him—and, thus, against Germany. There is a concordance of evidence for this, ranging from changes in his personal and physical habits and his dictation of a private will and testament (in early May 1938) to his decision to appoint Ribbentrop as his foreign minister and dismiss General Fritsch as commander in chief of the army while he himself assumed the functions of minister of war and supreme commander of the Wehrmacht. Much has been

---

*Zitelmann, too (especially in ZIT/A), is mistaken about Hitler's foreign policy. He overemphasizes Hitler's affection for England, suggesting thereby that the British were responsible for not responding to that adequately. Other German historians have inclined to this, including Hillgruber, who respected Chamberlain but not Churchill. Also, Zitelmann explains Hitler's decision to move into the Rhineland in March 1936 as a reaction to the French Chamber of Deputies' ratification of the 1935 Franco-Soviet Pact "that Germany considered as a break of the Locarno Treaty." Not Germany: Hitler, who used it as a pretext.

written about the so-called Hossbach Conference of 5 November 1937, when Hitler, for the first time, told his military chiefs to prepare for an eventual war. It was less of a blueprint for war than an admonition to the generals that a resort to force might be necessary in the near future. Hitler described when and how Germany would move against Czechoslovakia and into Austria. Such eventualities included a conflict between France and Italy—civil war in France, for example. Because this did not happen, A. J. P. Taylor wrote that "Hitler's exposition was in large part daydreaming, unrelated to what followed in real life."* This is not very convincing. The important matter in the conference was Hitler's calculation that when his opportunity arose, France would be paralyzed by weakness: "Britain, almost certainly, and probably France as well, had written off the Czechs and were reconciled to the fact that this question for Germany would be cleared up in due course." This was a remarkably accurate statement of matters in November 1937; it was exactly what happened less than a year later.

But there is another element—or, more precisely, the absence of an element—in this November 1937 conference that has not received the attention it deserves. This is that Hitler made almost no reference at all to Russia. He said something to the effect that in the event of war over Czechoslovakia, Russia would be preoccupied with Japan (which was true), and then there is a cryptic sentence: "Poland—with Russia in her rear—will have little inclination to engage in war against a victorious Germany." In other words, if Poland were to move against Germany, Russia might move against Poland. Here was something like the pattern of German-Russian collusion against Poland nearly two years before it came about.

---

*A. J. P. Taylor, *The Origins of the Second World War*, NY, 1961. According to him: "The conference was a manoeuvre in domestic affairs." (Only in the sense in which some of Taylor's works were maneuvers in British academic affairs.) Bullock, in later editions of BU, pp. 367–70, adjusted his earlier statements about the Hossbach Conference in view of Taylor: "The significance of this meeting in November 1937 has been a subject of considerable controversy." It is true that the Hossbach record (like the record of another important Hitler speech to his generals, that of 22 August 1939) was not an exact verbatim transcript.

Was Hitler—the avowed champion of German and of world anti-communism—contemplating this as early as 1937? Sixty years later we still do not know. Hitler's lack of concern with Russia at that time is enigmatic; it remains perhaps the principal enigma in the international history of the origins of World War II.

His lack of concern with Russia during the Munich crisis in September 1938 was, again, startling—and insufficiently analyzed. Much has been written about Munich, which soon after that event began to be recognized as a disaster: "We have sustained a total and unmitigated defeat," as Churchill said in the House of Commons. Yet sufficient distance and evidence have accumulated during the last sixty years to reveal and revise some of the still-accepted views of that Western surrender to Hitler's demands. Enough evidence exists to suggest that—contrary to what most people, including even Churchill as late as 1948, believed and wrote—Hitler in September 1938 was not bluffing. Had it not been for the Munich agreement, he would have attacked Czechoslovakia on 1 October, as he had declared. The French, who, however reluctantly, had an alliance with the Czechs, *might* have declared war on him. The British, much more reluctantly, might have done *something*. But beyond a declaration of war, they would have done nothing—just as in September 1939 they stood by and took no military action while the Germans subdued Poland. These are speculations not unworthy of historians. The evidence is there. In 1939 it took the German army a few weeks to conquer Poland. In October 1938 it would have taken them a few days to conquer Czechoslovakia, a state riven by hostile elements, one half of them non-Czechs, many of whom wanted Czechoslovakia to break up or even cease to exist. But not only was that population divided; so were the people of Britain and France. They, including their governments, were not ready to face a second world war for the sake of Czechoslovakia—whereas in September 1939 they felt compelled to resist Hitler and go to war. Militarily, too, they were somewhat better prepared in 1939 than in 1938. After breaking the Czech resistance in a few days in October 1938, Hitler would have turned to the Western powers (as he did, in vain, in October 1939), offering peace on the basis of his fait accompli. There is every reason to believe that he would have succeeded. He knew that; on several occasions he later regretted bitterly that he had agreed to the Munich "settlement".*

But perhaps the most interesting question about Munich is that of Russia, and of Hitler's view of it. Stalin had signed an alliance with the Czechs in 1935. Yet it is amazing how little consideration Hitler gave to Russia during the entire Munich crisis. He discounted the Czech-Russian alliance almost entirely (though he would use the argument of anticommunism to justify his hostility to the Czechs). And we know something that even Churchill in 1948, in the first volume of *The Second World War*, either did not know or would not admit: that Stalin was as loath to go to war for Czechoslovakia in 1938 as were Chamberlain or Daladier—or even more so. Perhaps he would have moved against Poland, whose territory he might have had to cross in coming to the aid of the Czechs. Hitler would envisage this on occasion; we saw that he had done so already in 1937. But that was all. Was Hitler's dismissal of the Russian danger in 1938 simply due to instinct? Or did he have other information about Stalin's plans beyond the fragments of reports from the German embassy in Moscow or from assumptions of routine intelligence sources? We do not know.

It is not clear whether it was Hitler or Stalin who made—or allowed—the first cautious moves or signals for an improvement of German-Russian relations in 1939, eventually leading to their pact in August.† Yes, Hitler had made a remarkable statement at the Nuremberg Party Rally in September 1936: "If we had at our dis-

---

*One important argument *against* Munich is the existence of a plan of some German generals, including General Beck, to arrange a coup against Hitler if he went to war over Czechoslovakia. The news of Chamberlain's visits to Hitler and Munich then put an end to those plans. Yet there is little evidence that a military conspiracy against Hitler at that time would have been successful. The instruments of the party and of the ss, and, most important, the sentiments of the German people, were at least as strongly behind Hitler as they were in July 1944. Fest is wrong (F, p. 777): "Today it is undeniable that Hitler could not have withstood a military confrontation in the fall of 1938 for more than a few days."

†Stalin did make a cautious speech on 10 March 1939, suggesting—obliquely—some accommodation with Germany. But Toland (TO, p. 526) is entirely wrong in saying that the German press "seized upon [this] as a further overture to the Reich, and Soviet newspapers responded by congratulating them for their discernment." He is also wrong (pp. 522–23) about the course of German-Polish negotiations in the winter of 1938–39, and (p. 521) that in March the British Foreign Office was

posal the incalculable wealth and stores of raw material of the Ural Mountains and the unending fertile plains of the Ukraine to be exploited under National Socialist leadership the German people would swim in plenty." But in early 1939 he began to show his disinterest not only in the Ukraine but even in the Carpatho-Ukrainian portion of Czechoslovakia.

It is revealing that the first signs of a German-Russian improvement of relations occurred *before* March 1939, that is, before Hitler's sudden decision to march into Prague and occupy what remained of Czechoslovakia, which then led to a decisive change of British policy, including a British guarantee to Poland and the attempt to eventually reach a military alliance with Russia. Many things indicate that Hitler regarded a British-French-Russian alliance as unfeasible. In any event, during the summer of 1939 he demonstrated certain subtleties in the practice of his statesmanship. Reserve, rather than impetuosity or impatience, marked the *tempo* of his responses to the various signals from Moscow (except during the third week of August, when he insisted on a sudden increase of speed in the movement toward a pact; this then served him well). The record of the secret German-Russian contacts and negotiations of that time are one of the most fascinating chapters of modern diplomatic history, though they are more revealing of Stalin than of Hitler, including Stalin's prime consideration of Russian state interests—as well as of his respect for Hitler.*

What is also interesting and instructive is the triangular relationship of the principal powers in the summer of 1939. The British and the French, of course, made no secret of their wish to bring Stalin into an anti-Hitler alliance (even though the Chamberlain government was not above suggesting to Berlin that if Germany were only more reasonable about Poland, a broad British-German agreement

---

"warned by the Rumanian ambassador that secret sources indicated Hitler would take over Rumania and Hungary within the next few months." M. Tilea was not an ambassador, and the British instantly disbelieved him.

*The English wag who was supposed to have said at the news of the Hitler-Stalin pact that "all the Isms are Wasms" was, of course, largely right, but while International Communism was certainly a "Wasm," German National Socialism was not.

was still possible). Stalin was as secretive about his contacts with Berlin as behooved a sly Caucasian chieftain. It is significant that Hitler allowed hints to be dropped on occasion (as early as May) to the British and the French about the possibility of a German agreement with Russia.* Instructive, then, is his, often cited, conversation with the Swiss Carl J. Burckhardt on 11 August 1939, a few days before he approached Stalin directly. He told Burckhardt (who, he knew, was a partisan of some kind of German-British accommodation): "Everything I undertake is directed against Russia; if the West is too stupid and too blind to understand this, I shall be forced to seek an understanding with the Russians, defeat the West, and after its defeat turn with all of my forces against the Soviet Union. I need the Ukraine, so that they cannot starve us out, as during the last war." Many historians have described this statement as revelatory of Hitler's entire subsequent war strategy; Hillgruber described it as prophetic and farsighted [visionär].† In reality, it was Hitler's attempt (he knew that Burckhardt was listened to in London) to frighten the Western powers into abandoning Poland.

The attempt did not succeed. Nor did the news of the Hitler-Stalin pact eleven days later; nor his last attempts to "drive a wedge," as he himself put it, between the British and the Poles through his last, fraudulent, "offers" to Poland. Since the Poles refused to become German satellites, he would subdue them through war. With Britain and France he did not want war, and hoped that it might not come to that. But on 3 September 1939, Britain and France, however reluctantly, declared war on the Third Reich. Here was the first great and ultimately decisive failure of Hitler's statesmanship. Still, strategically it was not a decisive failure—at any rate, not yet. He knew that the British and the French were reluctant warriors. They might declare war, but beyond that, at least for the time being, they would do little or nothing. About that in the short run he was right.

---

*His ability to *divide et impera*—that is, not committing himself to one side or another for a time—existed already in 1921–22 and 1924–25 in the face of antagonisms within the party (and perhaps also in 1933–34, between the army and the SA.)

†HST, pp. 28–29. Also F, p. 801, and HF/AI, p. 224.

WAR IS AN UNPREDICTABLE THING; and there was no reason for him to go to war; certainly not in 1939. So here we come to the great failure of his statesmanship that was inseparable from the faults of his character.* He was in a hurry. This was not the result of a frenzied fanaticism. Throughout Hitler's career there had been many occasions when he knew how to wait, sometimes to the extent of prolonged hesitations. But we have seen that in the winter of 1937–38 he had convinced himself that he did not have long to live; that this led to a change of his physical habits, including his medications; that he had come to think that he was more ill than he actually was. And now he projected this feeling about himself onto the destiny of his nation. He feared that Fate, or Providence, might not allow him to fulfill his great tasks for Germandom. Already at the Hossbach Conference in November 1937, he said that he had to assume that Germany's "problems" must be solved before 1943–45, when time would turn against Germany, when the rearmament of the Western democracies against her would be completed. His friend Mussolini advised him against this—and not only because Italy was not ready for war in 1939. Time was *not* working for Britain and France, he wrote Hitler. They would not sustain a disciplined and severe program of rearmament against a National Socialist Germany and a Fascist Italy, strong and resplendent across Europe. Hitler, who believed in the innate superiority of National Socialism to the outdated liberalism of the West, should have listened to Mussolini, who was largely right; but for reasons peculiar to him, he did not. That was probably the most important miscalculation of his statesmanship, and led to his undoing. Two other mis-

---

*His barbaric mistreatment of the Polish people had much to do with his hatred of them for having dared to resist him and thus brought about a world war. Haffner (HF/AN, p. 162) shrewdly remarks: ". . . having won the war against Poland militarily, Hitler by no means used his victory for realizing his original objective, which was to force the Poles to enter the alliance they had previously refused." At the same time, there is plenty of evidence for the, potentially suicidal, character of his hubris. As Fest cites his statement on 23 November 1939: "In this struggle I will stand or fall. I will not survive the defeat of my people. For the outside [world] no capitulation, on the inside no revolution." So it was to be.

takes were his misreading of the British, especially in the summer of 1940, and his consequent conviction that he ought to attack his Russian neighbor no later than in the early summer of 1941.

HE FAILED TO CONQUER RUSSIA. But was his failure ordained from the beginning? He was stopped only at the gates of Moscow in December 1941. Not all of the mistakes of the German military strategy in Russia were attributable to him. If his decision to hold on to Stalingrad was wrong, his often-criticized directive, overriding his generals, not to drive directly on to Moscow in July 1941 is at least debatable,* and his determined order forbidding an overall retreat in December 1941 proved to be surprisingly effective. But these pages are directed to questions about his strategic statesmanship, not about his military tactics. Why did he choose to plan an invasion of Russia as early as July 1940? (The final directive was issued in December.) That was his supreme folly—thus the generally accepted opinion,† convincing because of what we know of its consequences. A strategic folly, motivated by his Lebensraum folly, aiming at something much more than the defeat of an opponent: to the permanent conquest of those lands for the purpose of settling Germans there.

But was *this* the reason why he chose to plan a war against Russia in July 1940? That, too, is debatable.‡ He took this step at the very

---

*Hillgruber (and others) make much of this. Yet as early as 5 December 1940, Hitler refused to make Moscow the main operational objective.

†"His ideology ["Weltanschauung"] now dominated his Realpolitik." GQ, p. 240.

‡It was—and it ought to be—debated. Hillgruber, in HST, repeatedly wrote that after July 1940 the war against England was of secondary [zweitrangig] importance to Hitler. This argument is not tenable. (About this see Lukacs, and LEW, *passim*.) The German historian Bernd Stegemann (1982) refuted it convincingly, in GWU, 1982, pp. 206–13 (also in 1987); also Hartmut Schustereit, *Vabanque. Hitlers Angriff auf die Sowjetunion 1941 als Versuch, durch den Sieg im Osten den Westen zu bezwingen* (Herford/Bonn, 1988). In Manfred Funke, ed., *Hitlerdeutschland und die Mächte. Materialen zur Aussenpolitik des III. Reiches* (D, 1977), Hillgruber (p. 100, note 18) criticized Broszat's article in VFZ, 1970, in which the latter wrote that Hitler's decision to go at Russia was not a "calculated plan to realize his [Lebensraum] ideas" but that he felt compelled [ein Zugzwang] to get out from waiting in the summer of 1940 and proceed to a decisive ending of the war." Broszat was right; Hillgruber's

time when he began to realize that the British were not giving in. As he said to the close group of generals at the Berghof on 31 July 1940, the British had two hopes left: Russia and America. Against America he could do nothing. But if Russia were knocked out, Churchill's—and Roosevelt's—hopes would be eliminated. The continental power of Germany would then be untrammeled and unconquerable, and sooner or later Churchill and Roosevelt would be forced to accommodate him. Their own people would be forced to realize the futility of an unwinnable war, and many among them would take at least some satisfaction from the liquidation of Communist power in the world.

This calculation was not entirely unreasonable. "Russia: England's last hope"—he repeated this among his generals and to his staff (including his secretaries), again and again; many records of that exist in 1940 and 1941, and even later,* and probably not only for

---

answer was weak: "In reality Hitler's decision for a war in the East [it was not yet a decision] came in July 1940, at a time when he was convinced of the possibility of reaching an arrangement with Britain." He was *not* so convinced then. The often superficial, but in this case insightful, Gisevius (GI, p. 516) wrote: "He took the detour to Moscow [in order to] defeat England." Bullock is not clear about this (BU, p. 598): On 31 July 1940, "Hitler still put the invasion of Britain in the front of his argument but he was already looking ahead to an attack on Russia in 1941, whether the British capitulated first or not." Jäckel sees a duality; but he is undecided. JHH, p. 86: "Since the 1920s Hitler wanted to conquer Lebensraum in Russia. That was always his main motive. Yet he did not emphasize this when he attempted to convince his circle about his plan." More clearly, p. 86: "Everything indicates that he had always kept [the *Lebensraum* plans] in sight. Whether he really believed the new strategic justification that he presented in July 1940 or whether he introduced it to win over his supporters for a new campaign of conquest is of course hard to determine. Probably both were the case."

*There are many such statements of Hitler's, among which is the one on 27 December 1940 to Admiral Raeder, who insisted on concentrating all German resources against England. Hitler: "This cannot be done until England's last continental hope is eliminated." To Hewel, 29 May 1941: When Russia is defeated, "this will force England to make peace. Hope this year." Halder's war diary, 14 June 1941: "After the attack on Russia and the evolution of his calculation that the collapse of Russia would induce England to give up the struggle." That same day: "The main enemy is still Britain." (From "an unpublished source taken by a Luftwaffe general"—no other reference or source, however—in Irving, 1/H, p. 266.)

purposes of self-justification. It was not to them but to his party cronies that he kept speculating about Lebensraum during his 1941 and 1942 table conversations (though seldom before the beginning of the invasion of Russia). And at the end, in one of his last "table" (i.e., Bormann-recorded) conversations, he said: "No decision which I had to make during the course of this war was graver than to attack Russia."

> For Time—and it's always Time, you notice—would have been increasingly against us. In order to persuade Britain to pack up, to compel her to make peace, it was essential to rob her of her hope of being able still to confront us, on the Continent itself, with an adversary of a stature equal to our own. We had no choice, we had at all costs to strike the Russian element out of the European balance sheet. We had another reason, equally valid, for our action—the mortal threat that a Russia in being constituted to our existence. For it was absolutely certain that one day or another she would attack us.*

"We had no choice"? "Absolutely certain"? Not at all. And what is significant: In Hitler's explanation of his decision there is not one word about Lebensraum.

It is of course possible that his emphasis on the English factor was meant to impress his generals. Possible, though not probable: for none of his leading generals showed the slightest reservations about

---

Hewel diary, 20 June 1941: "A long conversation with the Führer. Expects a lot from the Russian campaign . . . he thinks that Britain will have to give in." (Note that Hewel was *not* a general.) To Keitel on 18 August 1941 (ADAP/D/13/1, p. 346): "The ultimate objective of the Reich is the defeat of Great Britain." On 22 August 1941, with his armies at Leningrad, storming toward Kiev, and closer and closer to Moscow, Halder war diary: Hitler's aim is "to finally eliminate Russia as England's allied power on the continent and thereby deprive England of any hope of a change in her fortunes with the help of the last existing Great Power." Hitler to Admiral Fricke (KTB/SKL, 28 October 1941): "The fall of Moscow might even force England to make peace at once."

*AH/B, p. 15, February 1945.

the "Barbarossa" plan.* Indeed, they were more sanguine in their expectations than was Hitler himself, who, before the invasion of Russia, was suddenly beset by anxiety.†

We must keep in mind that while every human act arises from a multiplicity of motives, there is such a thing as a multiplicity, or at least a duality, of human purposes too.‡ It is wrong to presume that it was *only* Lebensraum, and ideology, that made Hitler choose to turn and plan his invasion of Russia in July 1940. It may also be wrong to assume that not only the principal but the *only* purpose of his invasion of Russia was strategic and political, to compel the British (and also the Americans) to recognize the hopelessness of the war against him. Both elements existed in his mind: to knock out the last potential ally of a Britain that he could not—yet—invade; and to achieve an—as yet undefined—Lebensraum in the conquered East. I incline to believe that of the dual purposes, the first was primary—without saying that the second was inconsequential.**

---

*Barry A. Leach, *German Strategy Against Russia 1939–1941*, Oxford, 1973, p. 100: ". . . this attempt to give the operations in the East some relevance to the war already being fought in the West was a rationalization for the ears of the generals. The true purpose of the campaign was the fulfillment of Hitler's *Lebensraumpolitik*." Not so. Haffner is more measured, but his conclusion is debatable, (HF/AN, p. 115): "One should not take these rationalization attempts of Hitler too seriously. Hitler's attack on Russia was not made *because* but *in spite of* the continuing war against Britain." (Haffner's italics)

†As early as 9 January 1941, KTB/OKW: "The Russians should not be underestimated even now." On 21 June 1941, Himmler to Heydrich: "The Führer is not so optimistic as his military advisers." Leach, above, p. 156. The night before 22 June, someone in Hitler's circle spoke of Russia as "a big bubble." The generals were, without exception, confident. Hitler suddenly became thoughtful. He said that Russia was rather like a ship in "the Flying Dutchman." He added: "The beginning of every war is like opening the door into a dark room. One never knows what is hidden in the darkness." (Lukacs, LEW, p. 139.)

‡Historians on the duality: Jäckel in JHW, p. 68; also p. 56: ". . . in the prevailing circumstances the Eastern campaign was also to serve a dual purpose. It was meant to lead to the conquest of living space as well as to discourage Britain once and for all." Haffner, HF/AN, p. 102: "It is always a mistake in politics to pursue two aims simultaneously." Perhaps. Zitelmann (ZIT/A, p. 147) writes that Hitler's purposes were not clear; he does not mention a duality but brings up Hitler's habit of amassing "every possible argument to justify his decisions."

**Consider that while Hitler did not speak much about Lebensraum before the campaign began, he kept talking about it to some of his circle in August and

THE SEVENTH OF DECEMBER IN 1941 was the turning point of World War II. The Russians halted the Germans in the frozen wastes before Moscow almost at the same moment that the Japanese attack on a tropical morning at Pearl Harbor thrust the United States into the war. Hitler's European war now became a veritable world war—which he could no longer win, or at least not in the way he had wished to win it. He himself realized this—a realization with many consequences, to which I must soon turn. But at this time something must be stated about his declaration of war on the United States on 11 December 1941. This has been defined and categorized as Hitler's supreme folly by many historians.*

It was, in some ways, an unusual event. Hitler himself said in June 1940—questioning Mussolini's stentorian declaration of war on France and Britain—that declarations of war belonged to the past, to the hypocritically chivalrous trappings of dynastic wars. However, in December 1941 he had Ribbentrop make such a declaration to the American chargé d'affaires in Berlin. Many historians have

---

September 1941—which at least suggests that this had begun to serve him for purposes of justification. Consider, too, that beyond Hitler's general speculations in his table talks, detailed plans for German settlements in the East were not made by Hitler but by Himmler and others (and in 1943 a Führer order led to the stoppage of these plans). Zitelmann in ZIT/A, p. 161: "The long accepted view that with the conquest of the Russian lands Hitler wanted to introduce a 're-agrarianization' of German society in order to realize an 'anti-modern' and 'anti-industrial' utopia is wrong."

*Emphatically—and wrongly—by A. J. P. Taylor. Bullock in BU, p. 662: "Hitler never supposed—any more than Hindenburg or Ludendorff in 1917—that he would have to reckon with a major American intervention in the European war." Not at all. Hitler to Jodl (KTB/OKW, I, p. 996) on 17 December 1940—that is, the day before issuing the definite Barbarossa directive: "We must resolve all continental-European problems in 1941, since from 1942 the U.S.A. will be in a position to intervene." Haffner in HF/AI, p. 229, on Hitler's decision to declare war on the United States: "This must be the most puzzling of any of his decisions in World War II. I cannot explain it. . . ." HF/AN, pp. 117–18: "There is to this day no comprehensible rational explanation for what one is tempted to describe as an act of lunacy . . . what induced Hitler to trigger America's entry into the German war, an entry which he had so far sensibly done everything to prevent, was not the Japanese attack on Pearl Harbor but the successful Russian counteroffensive at Moscow. . . ." An inadequate explanation.

claimed that this was but another example of Hitler's hubris, an unnecessary and disastrous act, since, Pearl Harbor notwithstanding, Franklin Roosevelt would have met some trouble in obtaining a declaration of war against Germany from Congress. This retrospective is unfocused. By December 1941, a virtual state of war existed in the Western Atlantic between American and German naval units. On 21 June 1941 (that is, the day before his invasion of Russia), Hitler gave a peremptory order to his naval commanders to avoid any hostile action against American units, even if German submarines or other vessels were being attacked by the latter. He knew that Roosevelt would wish to profit from a serious naval clash with the Germans in the Atlantic. He would not give Roosevelt such a chance, even at the cost of tying the hands of German naval commanders. But now these fetters could come off. Moreover, while he never doubted Roosevelt's willingness to go to war against him, he could hardly betray his Japanese ally by welshing on the principal item in their alliance,* which required them to go to war with the United States together and simultaneously.

Whether Hitler's declaration of war on the United States made Roosevelt's task easier may be debatable; whether his withholding such a declaration of war would have changed the main course of events is unlikely. But here we must correct an assumption that is widely held and more consequential than the somewhat jejune speculation about the formalities of the German declaration of war on the United States in December 1941. This is the widely accepted view that Hitler was woefully (woefully for him, of course) ignorant of the United States;† that he consistently underestimated the Americans as well as their military and industrial potential. Sufficient evidence to the contrary exists. Hitler was interested in America and things

---

*Jäckel is largely right in JH, p. 74: Before Pearl Harbor, "fear of American intervention and the desire to keep America out of the war were still the cornerstones of Germany's Japanese policy."

†It was not Hitler who was ignorant of the United States but historians such as Ernst Nolte, as he demonstrates in his absurd statement in his *Deutschland und der Kalte Krieg*, M, 1974, p. 160: "How can anyone seriously doubt that Roosevelt would have some sympathy for an anti-Communist and anti-Semitic movement in the United States . . . if the American Communist Party had played a role in American politics similar to that of the Communist Party in Germany?"

American from his early youth. He was an avid reader of the Western and Indian stories of the German writer Karl May, whose last public lecture and funeral he attended in Vienna.* We have also seen that Hitler often expressed his liking of and even admiration for American industry and its techniques. He was, in sum, not uninformed about the United States, including some American political currents. One of the few German military attachés whose reports he read assiduously in 1940 was General von Boetticher in Washington. ("He knows how to read behind the scenes.") He was attentive to all kinds of evidence of anti-Roosevelt and "isolationist" opinions, of American "radical nationalists." He and Stalin were the first foreign statesmen who wanted to include the American electoral timetable in their calculations (Stalin telling Molotov not to travel to Berlin until after the November 1940 American presidential election; Hitler telling Mussolini that he should have delayed his attack on Greece until after that election). Throughout the war, and well after December 1941, Hitler was aware of certain American currents of opinion; that, for example, in 1944 anti-Communist and at least indirectly pro-German currents were surfacing among some Republicans in Washington. In his last table

---

*Koeppen notes IFZ, 5 October 1942: "The Führer then told us that he acquired most of his knowledge of [American] geography from reading Karl May." Andreas Dorpalen, in his excellent article "Hitler, the Nazi Party, and the Wehrmacht in World War II," in Harry L. Coles, ed., *Total War and Cold War*, Columbus, Ohio, 1962, p. 72: "His generals lacked resourcefulness and imagination," [Hitler] began to complain; "they are too correct, their thinking is too conventional. They should have read more Wild West stories." Steinert in ST/HK/D, p. 545: "The false romanticism and anti-civilizational [philosophy] of a Karl May, reading of whom Hitler repeatedly advised." He said that as chancellor he reread all of May's books. In 1943 he ordered the printing of 300,000 copies of a May book (*Winnetou*), to be distributed among German soldiers. Klaus-Dietmar Henke, in *Die amerikanische Besetzung Deutschlands*, M, 1995, p. 133: In November 1944, "Himmler's chief of staff transmitted to the Gauleiters an exhortation from Guderian to prepare for cunning battle tactics and 'Indian-like' conduct . . . Karl May's books have proved to be educational in this regard." In Scholdt, SCHO, five solid pages (296–300) deal with this theme; see also Vappu Tallgren. Also Gertrud Willenburg, *Von Deutschen-Helden. Eine Inhaltsanalyse der Karl-May-Romane* (Köln, 1967). May's most famous protagonist, "Old Shatterhand," was a German-American. At the same time May was not a promoter of brutality. Many Germans liked his stories, including, for example, the radical artist George Grosz.

conversations he said that the war against America was "a tragedy"; and to the last moment he nurtured hopes of a break between Washington and Moscow from which he could then profit, at least to some extent. In this his wishes were in accord with the great majority of the German people. Even though in 1945 latent difficulties between London and Moscow were much more evident than any between Washington and Moscow, Hitler, again like most Germans, put some hope in a break not between the former but between the latter. (By that time he had given up all of his earlier illusions about the British, whose resolute anti-German strategy and policy filled him with hatred.)

It is true that in both his public and his private statements we may find enough evidence of anti-American statements and clichés, and of a generally condemnatory view of American civilization.* Yet these coexisted with a more informed and realistic view of America in his mind. In this as well as other instances, it may be too much to say that his wishes were the fathers of his thoughts; but it may not be too much to say that they baptized them.

As early as November 1941—that is, before the failure of the German army before Moscow, and before the event of Pearl Harbor—Hitler knew that he could no longer win the war: more precisely, *his* war, the war he had planned to wage and to win. There is evidence of this in General Halder's war diary of 18 November 1941 (that is, before the last attempt of Army Group Center to resume its advance on Moscow), quoting Hitler: "The recognition, by both of the opposing coalitions, that they cannot annihilate each other, leads to a negotiated peace." And: "We must consider the possibility that it will not be possible for either of the principal opponents to annihilate the other, or to subdue them entirely." This is corroborated by an

---

*See his statement in H2B that a conflict with America might come only after his lifetime. But then he made few such statements until they began to accumulate in his table conversations in the autumn of 1941—probably because he then foresaw that the war with America was soon to come. Thus, for example, his table conversations of 10 September, his statements to Ciano on 25 October, and to the Bulgarian foreign minister Popov on 27 November.

emphatic statement by Colonel-General Jodl, the man who was perhaps closest to Hitler during the war.* From prison in Nuremberg, he wrote that by the winter of 1941 Hitler knew that "victory could no longer be achieved." In a memorandum dictated to his wife about Hitler: Hitler's "military advisers—today one often hears it said—should certainly have made it clear to him that the war was lost. What a naïve thought! Earlier than any person in the world, Hitler sensed and knew that the war was lost. But can one give up a Reich and a people before they are lost? A man like Hitler could not do it."

Significant considerations arise here for a historian. One of them is obvious: The portrait of Hitler, blinded by his fanaticism, believing till the end that the war would not, because it could not, be lost is, at best, oversimplified and, at worst, false. The other, connected with the above, is the now growing discrepancy between Hitler's publicly expressed views and his private ones. ("Private" may not always be a useful term, since so many of his statements to his private circle were meant to impress them.) In other words, this man, who was at times capable of making circumstances conform to his ideas,† would from now on be increasingly compelled to adjust at least some of his ideas to circumstances that he could perhaps influence but not control. In other terms: the purpose of his military strategy now was less conquest than the forcing of at least one of his enemies to deal with him, preferably on his terms. But: this was not truly an admission of defeat. Invincibility now had a priority over conquest. The time for short, sudden victories ("Blitzkriege") may have been over; he and the Reich must now settle down for a longer war, during which German power would still be so strong that sooner or later one of his enemies—of that unnatural coalition of Anglo-Saxons and Russians, Capitalists

---

*Halder diary, 18 November 1941. Jodl's statements cited by Schramm, SCH, pp. 26–27 and 204. There are some signs that Hitler began to think that as early as mid-August. (Goebbels diary, 18 August 1941: "Separate peace with Stalin? Will Churchill fall?") Hitler considered the American entry into the war as practically inevitable.

†Hitler on 23 May 1939 to his generals: "The principle whereby one evades solving a problem by adapting oneself to circumstances, is inadmissible. Circumstances must rather be adapted to demands [*Forderungen*]." (IMT, xxxviii, 079-L, p 549)

and Communists—would be constrained to admit it. He might no longer be able to win *his* war on his terms, but he might still win a different sort of war, or at least not lose it.

This conviction sustained him almost until the very end. It was his final shift to a Friderician strategy; more, to a Friderician view of his own future. He had always admired Frederick the Great rather than Bismarck the Iron Chancellor—in this case the warrior-king rather than the statesman.* The result was his vision of—or, rather, his hopes for—a historic parallel. Frederick won because—unexpectedly—he defeated one of his main enemy powers, and then the whole group of enemy powers fell apart. It was not only that Frederick was brave and resolute, winning victories in the field against great odds; his resolution led to a break in the coalition of his enemies, a coalition less unnatural than that between Capitalists and Communists in *this* war. Elements of this vision inspired Hitler almost until the last week of his life.† What he failed to understand was that, yes, a break between Americans and Russians might come—but too late for him. This was not a war between eighteenth-century dynasties but a world struggle in which his opponents, no matter how disparate, were agreed on one thing: He and his Third Reich must be conquered and occupied, without conditions and without reservations. Even if Frederick had not won at Rossbach or Leuthen, his opponents would at some time have signed a peace with the Prussian king; but Hitler's adversaries would not make peace with Hitler.‡

However, we are running ahead of our main story. December

---

*A good summary of historians' comments about this is SCHRB, p. 133, note 252.

†On the night of 12 April 1945, Goebbels rushed to the chancellery bunker with the news of Roosevelt's sudden death. He brought champagne: "The Empress is dead!" (The sudden death of the Russian empress Elizabeth in 1762 led immediately to the dissolution of the anti-Prussian coalition and to Frederick's triumph.) This episode is often misread by historians. (BU, p. 781: "Goebbels's mood was fully shared by Hitler.") It was Goebbels, not Hitler, who was carried away by enthusiasm that night. (Hitler also disliked champagne.)

‡The American diplomatic historian Paul Schroeder, in his excellent book (*The Transformation of European Politics 1763–1848*, Oxford, 1994), p. 477, on the great coalition of 1813–14 against Napoleon: "Military victory was never the primary goal for the coalition as a whole, even in the final stages of the war. The allies, though they sometimes differed sharply over terms, always sought a negotiated

1941 not only marked the turning point of the war and a change in Hitler's view of it; it led to new decisions and to a change in his work habits. He ordered the entire German economy to be placed on a full wartime footing. (He was especially fortunate to find Albert Speer as a successor to the able Todt, who died in early 1942; Speer was neither an economist nor an administrator, but Hitler recognized his organizational abilities.) Hitler himself assumed the post of army commander in chief upon the resignation of the sick General Brauchitsch. But most important was his order superseding the suggestions and inclinations of some of his generals. He forbade a cautious retreat of the German armies (except at limited local salients) in spite of the awesome severities of the Russian winter and the hardly less awesome fighting abilities of the Russians. And after two months, at the latest by March 1942, it became evident that not his generals but he, with his unorthodox military directive, had been proved right. A catastrophe was avoided, and he could say in April: "We have mastered a destiny which broke another man 130 years ago."*

---

peace in one form or another and agreed that the war should be ended as soon as the right terms were attained. The reason the war lasted to a military decision, though not total victory, was Napoleon's persistent refusal to negotiate seriously. As soon as a French government agreed to negotiate, the war was ended, though at the time the French army was still capable of fighting and controlled most of France and vital areas outside it as well." This was not true of Hitler and World War II, certainly not after 1941.

*There was an astonishing recovery within the man himself. In November 1941 he sometimes gave the impression of being depressed. Now he changed his long-established habits of work. These had included a bohemian element; he was often unorganized in his daily routine. But now his disinclination for regular and continuous work disappeared. Speer was one of the first to notice this (SP, p. 293): "Instead, he regularly attended to an enormous daily mass of work. Whereas in the past he had known how to let others work for him, he now assumed more and more responsibility for details. As anxieties mounted, he made himself into a strictly disciplined worker. But such discipline ran counter to his nature, and this was inevitably reflected in the quality of his decisions." Also Fest (F, p. 917): "his great, desperate self-discipline." And Maser (M/A, p. 254): Deep down and secretly he no longer had illusions about a [final] victory, in 1941–42, and that "kept him from visiting the front line. [But] that was not the result of a fear for his own life." Two elements in his routine did not change: his habit of rising late in the morning and retiring very late at night; and his growing dependence on a great variety of medicines.

COULD HIS FRIDERICIAN strategy still succeed? For eight more months in 1942, he (and his Japanese allies) went from victory to victory.* But in November they were defeated on many fronts, always simultaneously: a German army was surrounded by the Russians at Stalingrad, another army in the Western Desert beaten by the British, the Americans landing in North Africa, the Japanese stopped at Guadalcanal. Thereafter it was retreat and retreat, interrupted only by some local and two great German offensives that failed. Still, Hitler's powers of recovery—and, more, of endurance—were astounding. In 1918, the kaiser's Reich collapsed less than two months after the first serious defeat of the German army in France, and only a few weeks after the capitulation of Germany's allies. In World War II, Hitler's Third Reich fought on for two and a half years after Stalingrad, and almost two years after its principal Italian ally deserted him. His great adversary Churchill understood this—which is probably why he told his people after the British victory in North Africa that this was not yet the beginning of the end but perhaps the end of the beginning.

We must not contemplate Hitler's endurance with wonderment—and not only because of the accumulating brutalities of his rule. (The matter for wonder is the largely unquestioning discipline with which most Germans—and perhaps especially the working class—trusted him and held out, demonstrating an astounding measure of national unity, until the last months of the war.) Our purpose, in this chapter, is to comprehend some things about his vision of the needs of his Friderician statesmanship, to which his entire strategy was now subordinated. He knew that he could no longer conquer his opponents—not even if he won at Stalingrad or Kursk or even on the Normandy beaches, or in Belgium in late 1944. But one decisive German victory in the field might convince one or the other of them to deal with him. Such a military blow might not

---

*The otherwise perspicacious Haffner (HF/AN, p. 49) wrote: "After 1941, indeed from the autumn of 1941 onwards, there were again no more successes." Not so. Kershaw (KER, p. 189) states: "From late 1941, defeat and destruction were the only possible outcome." Arguable.

reverse the entire course of the war; but it would be a turning point, forcing at least one of his enemies to ponder whether the cost of subduing such a tough and stubborn Germany might not be too heavy to bear. Again and again, Hitler insisted on this necessary precondition, when Goebbels or Ribbentrop or even Rommel tried to convince him to seek contact with one or another of his enemies. That would be useless, Hitler repeated, without having previously proved the power of Germany in the field. In this he was probably right. But he underestimated the importance of what bound the otherwise so disparate alliance of his enemies together: their resolution to put an end to him and to enforce the surrender of the Third Reich. In that he was most probably wrong.

THERE WAS ANOTHER feature of Hitler's statesmanship that differed from the Friderician or Clausewitzian pattern. In those eighteenth-century wars, the aims of the warring states were clearly defined; and when circumstances forced the rulers to adjust them, they remained essentially the same: territory. Yet Hitler's territorial aims—in this his thinking differed entirely from the German imperial aims during World War I—were vague, or, rather, willfully left pending. The armistice conditions he imposed on the French, for example (which showed a certain degree of calculating statesmanship that the British ambassador to France in June 1940 described as "diabolically clever"), left many territorial conditions undefined. Here and there (as in Poland in 1939 and Italy in 1943), measures akin to German territorial annexation were made, but these were the exceptions rather than the rule. One reason for this was, of course, calculation: the postponing of territorial redefinitions until the war was finally won—or until a settlement was reached with one or another of Germany's adversaries.

But there was another element in Hitler's brand of statesmanship. More than territory, he preferred vassalage. We may detect evidence of this inclination already in his domestic politics in 1933 and afterward. There was to be only one political party in the Third Reich; but former conservative politicians such as Papen or Neurath were allowed not only to exist but also to function, and serve, within the hierarchy of the National Socialist Reich, as long as they were obedient and subservient to him. In 1939, "Czechia" became a German protectorate under the name of Bohemia-Moravia, and Slovakia an "independent" state, yet entirely subservient to him. A. J. P. Taylor ("Only Danzig prevented cooperation between Germany and Poland") was entirely wrong: Hitler wanted a Poland that was a satellite or, at best, a junior partner of Germany, without any independence in foreign policy. These aims of a Hitlerian Realpolitik superseded his ideological preferences. All over Europe (for example, in Holland, Denmark, France, Romania, and in a few remarkable instances even in Austria), local National Socialist leaders were abashed when they found that Hitler did not support them and paid them hardly any interest at all. He preferred to work with the established pro-German governments of such provinces and states. The most telling example of this occurred in Romania in January 1941. There the National Socialist and populist Iron Guard (whose anti-Semitic ideology and practices were perhaps the most fanatic and radical in all Europe) got into conflict with the nationalist and military government of General Antonescu, whom Hitler respected and liked. When in January 1941 fighting broke out between the Antonescu and Iron Guard forces, the Germans unequivocally supported the former at the expense of the latter, on occasion with German armor and tanks.

Of course he had his reasons. While the war lasted, he needed order in the countries that were his allies or satellites—a kind of stability that must not be endangered by revolutionary experiments, and that assured undisrupted deliveries of necessary material supplies to the Reich. Thus he put up for a long time with allied chiefs of state— a Pétain, an Antonescu, Regent Horthy of Hungary, King Boris of Bulgaria—some of whom he knew were not wholly loyal or unconditional adherents of a National Socialist Germany. Still, it is significant that he did not offer the slightest promise or give the slightest indication to the effect that sooner or later, perhaps after the war, his foreign National Socialist followers would get their rewards.* In sum, a perfect conformity with the requirements of German foreign policy

---

*He would, of course, recognize and support some of them in 1944, when his former satellites or junior partners deserted him; but that was no longer important.

was a must, while a perfect conformity with the ideology and practices of German National Socialism was not—except in the case
of Jews.

THIS DISCREPANCY between ideology and statesmanship is most
startling when we observe Hitler's views and expressed opinions of
Stalin. Hitler respected (and, later, increasingly admired) Stalin.*
There are many recorded expressions of Hitler in that regard,
before the war and in many instances during it.† Yet none of this
can be found in his public speeches, or in the official propaganda
of the Reich as directed by Goebbels. The unavoidable struggle
against "Jewish Bolshevism" was the main theme, and the main justification of the war against Russia, as presented to the German
people and to the rest of the world until the end, with no diminution
or alternation in tone. There were many people outside Germany
who did not believe this, or did so only with reservations. Yet it had
lasting effects within Germany, as may be seen in the approval of the
war against Russia even by such anti-Nazi or non-Nazi personages
as Bishop (later Cardinal) von Galen in 1941, or by the continued
evocation of the "Bolshevik" terminology by the Dönitz government and by German generals even after Hitler's suicide. But there
is a good deal of evidence that Hitler himself did not believe this.‡

---

*In August 1939, he ordered his photographer Heinrich Hoffmann (whom he
also entrusted with a special personal message to Stalin) to retouch the photo
showing Stalin with a cigarette in his left hand. Gisevius (GI, p. 449) cites Hoffmann, who recalled Hitler's words: "The signing of a pact between two great
nations is a solemn act; one does not do that with a cigarette between one's fingers!
Such a picture does not show seriousness enough."

†Hitler to Mussolini in January 1940: ". . . since Stalin's final triumph Russia has
been experiencing a change from the Bolshevik [ideology] to a more nationalist
Russian way of life." Conversely, there is evidence of Stalin's admiration for Hitler
(as late as December 1944, he made a sympathetic remark about Hitler to de
Gaulle). There is also some reason to believe that Stalin's purges of some of his followers, beginning in 1935, were influenced by his perception of Hitler's liquidation
of Röhm in 1934.

‡Speer, SP, p. 306: As the war went on, Hitler "spoke admiringly of Stalin, particularly stressing the parallels to his own endurance. The danger that hung over

was obsessed with the influence of Jews on Roosevelt and , knew that Jews had no influence on Stalin; that, indeed, Stalin was an anti-Semite of sorts. Great Russian nationalism, and—perhaps—pan-Slavism made Stalin and Russia formidable. Near the end, in 1945, he even ruminated whether he should have attacked Russia at all; and that a nationalist Russia, purged of Jews, might be the greatest danger yet.*

WE NOW COME TO THE last year of the war and the last year of Hitler's life. Now the necessity of adjusting his ideas to circumstances, of subordinating what remained of his military strategy to what he thought were the requirements of statesmanship, had become absolute. Military and political decisions, and their purposes, are of course never entirely separable. This Hitler knew very well. Yet it is possible for a historian to list their respective evidence

---

Moscow in the winter of 1941 struck him as similar to his present predicament. [This in 1945] In a brief access of confidence, he might remark with a jesting tone of voice that it would be best, after victory over Russia, to entrust the administration of the country to Stalin, under German hegemony, of course, since he was the best imaginable man to handle the Russians. In general he regarded Stalin as a kind of colleague." As late as July 1944 (SP, p. 399), Hitler speculated that Stalin might have been right in the purges; perhaps the Moscow process against General Tukhachevsky was not a fake. Zitelmann in ZIT/A, p. 161: "The thesis spread by propaganda [it was not only spread by propaganda but expressed by Hitler on occasion] that "the issue was the defeat of Jewish Bolshevism Hitler did not himself believe"; he had concluded that Stalin pursued "a national-Russian policy, having freed himself from the Jewish influence through his purges." Yet the same Hitler, on 8 November 1941, in one of his *public* speeches (Heer, HR, p. 384): Stalin is "nothing else . . . but an instrument in the hands of an all-powerful Jewry"; behind him stand Kaganovich "and all those Jews who are [leading] that powerful state."

*AH/B, 26 February 1945: "The brutal manner in which [Stalin] decapitated the Jewish intelligentsia, who had rendered him such signal service in the destruction of Tsarist Russia, encouraged me. . . ." Also: "That Stalinist empire which, in all its essentials is only the spiritual successor to the empire of Peter the Great." 2 April 1945: "It is possible that under the pressure of events, the Russians will rid themselves completely of Jewish Marxism, only to reincarnate Pan-Slavism in its most fierce and ferocious form."

separately, while recognizing that their aims were, by and large, the same: to bring about a break in the enemy alliance.

Hitler's phrase in July 1943, exhorting the army before the great battle at Kursk, is telling: A German victory there must work as a giant torch ["ein Fanal"], a sudden, dramatic eruption of a flame, demonstrating to the world that Germany was still invincible, that it was still capable of great offensives, of winning a counter-Stalingrad. The defensive achievements of the army in Russia and Italy were important but not sufficiently impressive, for defense and invincibility were not quite the same thing.* It is remarkable how, in early September 1944 (that is, during the rapid German retreat from France and Belgium, and before the failure of the Allies' attempt to cross the Rhine at Arnhem), Hitler ordered preparations for a great German offensive to come in the Ardennes.† He knew, in what otherwise verily seemed a desperate situation, that the great American-British offensive was temporarily running out of steam, and that the Allies were not ready—yet—to thrust into Germany proper; but there was more to it. The aim of the great winter offensive was not to reconquer northern France or perhaps even all of Belgium (the ultimate goal of the offensive was not Paris but Antwerp) but to drive a wedge between the American and British armies in Belgium (whether he hoped to force Montgomery's army into a second Dunkirk was not clear); to shock and stun the Americans to such an extent that they might have to recon-

---

*He was, of course, impressed with Speer's achievement of German armament production. From 1942 to 1944, this had *tripled*. Speer, SP, p. 286: This seemed to support "Hitler's credo that the impossible could be made possible and that all forecasts and fears were too pessimistic."

†Carr (C, p. 105; also Schramm, SCH, p. 165) cites Hitler speaking to two of his generals on 31 August 1944: "The time is not yet ripe for a political decision . . . I shall not let an opportunity pass . . . but at a time of heavy military defeats it is quite childish and naive to hope for a politically favourable moment to make a move. . . . The time will come when the tensions between the Allies become so strong that in spite of everything the rupture occurs. History teaches us that all coalitions break up, but you must await the moment, however difficult the waiting may be. [I shall] continue to fight until there is a possibility for a decent peace . . . then I shall make it. . . . Whatever happens we shall carry on in this struggle until, as Frederick the Great said, 'one of our damned enemies gives up in despair.' "

sider the practicality of their avowed aim of forcing Germany to surrender unconditionally.*

"The Battle of the Bulge" failed. But—in this Hitler was in accord with the majority of the German people—he had begun to think that among his opponents the Americans might be the most amenable to making compromises.† Thus, for example, in June 1944 he not only

---

At that time Hitler was very ill. He told his favorite physician (Morell) that the weeks after the twentieth of July were the worst of his life. No one can imagine what he had to fight through. "Despite severe complaints, hour-long losses of balance, a dreadful condition about which he said nothing to no one, he stood fast and struggled through with an iron energy. There was the danger of a collapse, but he defeated it with his will." (Schenck, PH, p. 131.) Also: during September and October there were days when he had to cancel his daily situation conferences, and he was bedridden for almost two weeks. In mid-November (Schenck, PH, p. 396, relying in part on Goebbels's diary), Hitler stayed in bed, pale and thin, in his nightshirt under army blankets. He was advised to summon his generals to his bedroom and hold the situation conference there. No: "Heavily breathing he got up, stumbling, dressing himself without help, hobbled to the conference map table, sat down, wiped the sweat from his eyes, and asked for the generals to come in." While in their postwar prison in Spandau, Walther Funk told Speer that Hitler did not tell his doctors how he really felt ("he believed in his own lies"). Speer (SP, p. 367) is more plausible: People around Hitler "admired his composure in critical situations. . . . This self-command was an extraordinary achievement of his will till the end: in spite of his aging, in spite of illness, in spite of [Morell's medical experiments] and endlessly accumulating burdens. To me his will seemed unbridled and untrammeled like that of a six-year-old child who will not be discouraged or worn out; that was, in part, ludicrous, but it was also impressive."

*Haffner, HF/AN, p. 156: "Why did he insist [on the Ardennes offensive]? The answer is a riddle to this day." No. Henke (p. 314) cites Hitler's address to division commanders at his headquarters in Ziegenberg, four days before the offensive: "When we strike a few heavy blows here, then it may happen that at any moment [their] artificially upheld [alliance] suddenly collapses with a gigantic thud." (From Helmut Heiber, ed., *Hitler Lagebesprechungen. Die Protokollfragmente seiner militärischen Konferenzen 1942–1945*, S, 1952, p. 713.) Also: "The strategic calculation behind his orders for the great offensive in the West was not at all as wrongheaded or irrational as it is often said."

†Haffner (HF/AN, p. 52) does not see this: "In his struggle against the allied coalition of 1942 to 1945 he never showed even the glimmer of an idea of exploiting the internal tensions of the coalition with a view of splitting it apart." There were times when Hitler thought that his main chance might be a contact with Stalin (Goebbels diary, 5 March 1945), but that was not his main inclination.

allowed a peaceful German withdrawal from the city of Rome (from which he hoped to gain propaganda advantages) but allowed Field Marshal Kesselring to attempt negotiations with American generals. And when, in March 1945, SS general Karl Wolff entered into negotiations with the Americans about a partial capitulation of the German armies in Italy, Hitler not only was apprised of this but on 17 April received Wolff in Berlin and, in his way, wished him well in his endeavor.* Around the same time, he agreed to a proposal from Speer, to allow some of the Czech directors of the Skoda Works, "in view of their previous connections to American industry," to flee before the Russians and prepare a direct flight to American headquarters in Germany. By that time Hitler no longer believed that he had power enough to drive a wedge between his enemies. But he was still convinced that a break would come; indeed, the Dulles-Wolff negotiations did lead to a short but bitter controversy between Roosevelt and Stalin, who complained sharply about it.†

---

*"In his way," because a few hours later he told him to wait a bit before signing an armistice. Henke, p. 676: Hitler had known about this for months; he sanctioned Wolff's negotiations with the Americans "because he saw in it a good instrument to cause dissensions within the anti-Hitler coalition." About this episode see Allen Dulles, *The Secret Surrender* (NY, 1966); Bradley D. Smith and Elena Agarossi, *Operation Sunrise* (NY, 1979); and especially the memoirs of one of the chief middlemen negotiators, the Swiss Max Waibel, *1945: Kapitulation in Norditalien* (Basel, 1981). The negotiations began as early as February.

†With some reason. Waibel, p. 28: Parilli, the Italian middleman, thought that certain Germans "had hoped eventually to fight together with [the Americans] against the Russians." P. 31: ". . . the thought of dividing the Western Allies from the Russians was the last great hope of the German leadership and ran like a red thread through all of the negotiations." Thus two months before Hitler's suicide, American generals and an SS general sat at the same table in Switzerland. On 15 April, Wolff wrote a letter to Dulles, expressing his condolences on President Roosevelt's death. The next day Himmler—and Hitler—ordered Wolff (repeating the order three times) to Berlin, where he spent more than ten hours with Himmler and Kaltenbrunner before seeing Hitler. Waibel, p. 106: ". . . in this way alone the dividing of the Allies from the Russians could be achieved." And pp. 107–8, citing Hitler to Wolff: In the East and in Italy the German armies may fight for another two months. "During these two decisive months of the war a break . . . between the Russians and the Anglo-Saxons will come, and whichever of the two sides comes to him, he will gladly ally with them against the other."

There were other such military moves in 1944–45 that Hitler permitted. There was the German withdrawal in northern Norway, including the calculated hope that within that subarctic vacuum the Russians advancing from northern Finland would bump into landing British commandos. There was the German withdrawal from Greece, where they left weapons behind to both the Royalist (that is, the pro-British) and the Communist guerrillas, hoping thereby to contribute to a coming civil war. (Hitler thought—wrongly—that Stalin would move through Bulgaria to Thrace and the Aegean.) In April 1945, there arose the increasingly obvious inclination among some German commanders to give up fighting the Americans while their comrades were still bitterly fighting the Russians. This evoked practically no condemnation from Hitler, who was not, of course, informed of all of them. In any event, it was too late to matter.

More significant than these military episodes were the political attempts by leaders of Hitler's Reich in 1944 and 1945 to split the coalition of the Allies. Save for shorter monographic articles and studies, a general survey of German foreign policy of that period does not yet exist; and not much attention has been devoted to it by Hitler's biographers. Yet some of the evidence is interesting. In 1942 and 1943, Ribbentrop and Goebbels (and at least on one occasion Papen in Turkey) had tried to suggest to Hitler the advisability of establishing some contact with one of the Reich's enemies; but we have seen that Hitler rejected that, convinced as he was not only of the futility but of the danger of such a move before some resounding German military success on one front or another. Thus, for example, in 1943 (when for a few months Stalin's dissatisfaction

---

In Patricia Meehan (*The Unnecessary War: Whitehall and the German Resistance to Hitler*, L, 1995, p. 327), there is a telling entry from a dispatch by Dulles to Washington in late 1944, cited from the National Archives (NA. RG. 226. OSS Entry 138, Box 2, Folder 83): "I feel we should prepare quietly and without formality in Switzerland, France and elsewhere certain individual Germans. . . . If we do nothing of this nature, the ready-made Russian-German committee may monopolize the field." Both Allen and his brother John Foster Dulles have at least indirectly contributed to the acceptance of the German two-war theory after the war.

with his Anglo-American allies was appreciable, and when for about three months there was a lull of fighting along almost the entire German-Russian front line), Hitler forbade the further development of a—perhaps—promising contact between German and Russian agents in Stockholm.* (Whether that was a great opportunity missed is debatable. There are indications that Stalin permitted such a—not entirely secretive—contact to impress—that is, blackmail—his Western allies: a tactic not unlike Hitler's "message" to London via Burckhardt in August 1939.)

But in 1944 there was a new development. Heinrich Himmler himself, and officials of the SS, were establishing contacts with Jewish organizations and, through them, indirectly with American ones. Note that by that time Himmler had become the most powerful personage in the hierarchy of the Third Reich. (In the winter of 1944–45 Hitler also appointed him to a high military command.) Yet it was Himmler, the director of the extermination of masses of Jews and others, for whom "Staatsräson" (another German word for Realpolitik) now had risen above the categorical dictates of National Socialist ideology. The negotiations of his agents (including Eichmann) with certain Jewish persons in Budapest had but one aim: to engage in some contact with Americans and make that fact known to Allied intelligence, including that of the Russians. The British knew what this was about. They were unimpressed with some of the Jewish agents whom the SS had permitted to travel to Turkey in June 1944, and arrested them. Yet Himmler was able to arrive at a clandestine agreement with a representative of Roosevelt's Refugee Board in Switzerland in September 1944; and a month later he ordered the ending of the gassings at Auschwitz. Near the end, in April 1945, he himself negotiated with Jewish representatives from Switzerland and Sweden, with a former Swiss president, and with the Swedish prince Bernadotte. On 25 April 1945, he broke with Hitler, offering capitulation to the Western Allies. Of course there

---

*Fest exaggerates this possibility. F, p. 948: "In December 1942 and once more in the summer of 1943 [in reality, the most significant contacts were suggested in September], the Soviet Union through its representation in Stockholm made known its willingness to negotiate with Hitler about a separate peace."

were historical precedents for this. Often it is the head of the secret state police who knows the power of his foreign opponents better than do others in the government. It was thus that Fouché negotiated against Napoleon, whom he betrayed in the end; thus, too, it was Beria who after Stalin's death attempted to arrive at wideranging compromises with Washington.

These and other similar attempts of Himmler and the SS were, in part, arranged behind Hitler's back—but not all of them against his wishes. We know of only one difficult scene, in February 1945, when Hitler ordered Himmler to stop such dealings; but a few days later Himmler resumed them. Except for that single instance, there is no evidence of accusations or criticisms of Himmler because of these attempts—and Himmler had plenty of jealous enemies in the German hierarchy and in Hitler's own circle.* The aim, for Himmler as well as Hitler, was a break in the enemy coalition. That Hitler had fewer hopes about this than Himmler is unquestionable. Yet this was his objective until the end.

While Himmler hoped to achieve some kind of accommodation with the Western Allies, Ribbentrop and Goebbels were partisans of seeking a deal with Stalin. On one occasion Ribbentrop even offered to fly to Moscow. Hitler, probably rightly, rejected the idea, saying that Ribbentrop should not do what Hess, flying to Scotland, had tried in May 1941. Still, in February 1945 he allowed Ribbentrop (who was the most rigid of his followers) to send a memorandum to German diplomatic posts abroad, a "Sprachregelung," permitting German diplomats to seek contact with Western counterparts to remind the latter that a Russian penetration into Germany and to the center of Europe would present the gravest danger to the world. But Hitler no longer believed that such attempts would be successful. He still believed that the unnatural alliance between Americans and Russians would break up—though no longer necessarily

---

*Including the cold and brutal Kaltenbrunner within the SS. (About this see also Fleming, FL, pp. 169–70.) Maser (M/A, p. 349) makes too much of Himmler's conspiracies, suggesting the possibility—in my opinion, wrongly—that Himmler recommended the physician Dr. Stumpfegger to Hitler with the purpose of eventually poisoning the latter.

because of him.* Neither his strategy nor his statesmanship was of much further use. In this respect his face-to-face talk with Speer on 28 March may be telling. He knew that the war was lost. But he grabbed Speer's arm and, with tears in his eyes, implored him: "If you still believe that the war could still be won, if you could at least believe that, all would be well."† Belief still mattered—in fact, it was the only thing that mattered. It could no longer be adjusted to conditions. It was the only condition left. That was no longer the mark of a realistic idealist; it was the admission of the defeat of his determinist idealism.

Eight days before his suicide, when he had decided to stay in a Berlin encircled by the Russians, he said to Jodl: "I should already have made this decision, the most important in my life, in November 1944, and should have never left the headquarters in East Prussia." That could have achieved two things. One: Hitler the *Feldherr* would have died in battle, on the front, at the head of his battered armies, on the eastern frontier of the Reich, breasting the Asiatic flood—an act that might have had incalculable symbolic

---

*Goebbels diaries, citing Hitler, 22 March 1945: "The enemy coalition will break up in any circumstance; the question is only whether it breaks up before we are beaten down, or only after that." 28 March 1945: "Sometimes one had the impression that he [Hitler] lives in the clouds. But so often he has come down to earth like a deus ex machina. He is as convinced as before that the political crisis in the enemy camp is a justification for our greatest hopes." Speer, SP, p. 425: In "February and March 1945, Hitler occasionally hinted that he was contacting the enemy by various means, but he would never go into details."

†Speer's account in SP, p. 453. Irving's account (I/H, p. 785) is predictably condemnatory of Speer. Contrary to Haffner, who thinks that Hitler's Scorched Earth order (to destroy all installations in the German cities and towns before and during the retreat of the army) was not only categorical but unalterable and the definite evidence of Hitler's criminal intent. Speer, SP, p. 456: "I think Hitler realized that he was making some important concessions." Yet the same Hitler still wished to instill faith in his people. Irving (I/H, p. 768) cites Hitler to Kaltenbrunner in late February 1945 (after the architect Giesler had come to show Hitler his model of Linz): "My dear Kaltenbrunner, do you imagine I could talk like this about my plans for the future if I did not believe deep down that we really are going to win this war in the end?" (As often with Irving, no source is given, but perhaps it is not implausible.) Also Hitler to Speer, a fortnight after that 28 March confrontation, at the news of Roosevelt's death (SP, p. 463): "Here . . . who was right? The war isn't lost."

consequences for future German generations. Two: Such an end of the Third Reich, in late 1944, must have meant the flooding of most of Germany by the Americans and the British, a great swirling confusion of Anglo-Saxon and German armies, the former wending their way eastward in the midst of a still largely intact German army and a still largely intact German people, eventually meeting the suspicious Russians somewhere in eastern Germany, Anglo-Saxons as well as Russians attempting, first nervously, then more and more determinedly, to get the Germans on their side during a developing confrontation. Schramm quotes Jodl further: "He should have fallen in battle rather than taking flight in death, it is said. He wanted to, and he would have done so if he had been physically able. As it was, he did not choose the easier death, but the more certain one. He acted as all heroes in history have acted and will always act. He had himself buried in the ruins of his Reich and his hopes. May whoever wish to condemn him for it do so—I cannot."*

With all respect to the forthright quality of Jodl's loyalty: did Hitler really "not choose the easier death"? This is debatable. More important: was he a hero? This is perhaps not a matter left for historians to debate. The moral dimensions of that epithet are more important, greater than that. Let me say only that he was bereft of the nobility that the word *hero* implies, as imply it must. His mind and his willpower were extraordinary: but mind and willpower alone do not a hero make.

---

*Schramm, SCH, pp. 180–81. Also Haffner's discussion of Hitler's last days (HF/AI, p. 234): "We have no proof that Hitler actually continued to believe in final victory up to the very end." A similar duality in Maser (M/A, pp. 426, 428): He no longer believed in victory but "to postpone his own end . . . was an awesome crime." Bullock's judgments are unduly simplistic (BU, p. 397): ". . . and in the last years of his life he was cut off from all human contact and lost in a world of inhuman fantasy"; also BU, pp. 783, 797: "All the grandiloquent talk of dying in Berlin cannot disguise the fact that this petulant [?] decision was a gross dereliction of his duty to the troops still fighting under his command and an action wholly at variance with the most elementary military tradition." And: "His death was anything but a hero's end; by committing suicide he deliberately abandoned his responsibilities and took a way out which in earlier years he had strongly condemned as a coward's." (No: Hitler angrily condemned General Paulus for *not* having committed suicide at the end of Stalingrad.)

Even so, there remained something of a "realpolitical" calculation in Hitler's last testament, whereby he appointed Admiral Doenitz as his successor as Reich president, and Goebbels as Reich chancellor.* Doenitz, who was not a committed National Socialist but a nationalist conservative, would head a new government, very obviously inclined to seek some kind of agreement with the Western Allies; Goebbels, on the other hand, the most radical of Nazis, was believer and spokesman for a deal with Soviet Russia. A statesman-like balance, between West and East, Hitler may have thought. That balance—if that is what it was—is also perceptible in the wording of his testament and in its so-called postscript. In the testament itself, he did not say one word about the war against Russia: he blamed the Jews for having created the war with the West. Yet in his postscript, his last statement to the armed forces, he insisted on the inevitability of the struggle in the East.† On 1 May Goebbels, who had made an attempt to negotiate with the Russian commanding general in the Battle of Berlin, killed himself and his family. Doenitz remained personally intact in the north, ready to contact the Western Allies, while insisting on the necessary continuation of the war against the Russians, for the defense of Germany and "Europe" against "Bolshevism" well after Hitler's death, well after the dissolution of the National Socialist Party. He was the head of an almost powerless but still functioning Reich government, representing the two-war theory until the end, according to which the war against the Western Allies was regrettable, while the war against Russia was both unavoidable and heroic; and it was regrettable, too, that the Western Allies had failed to appreciate that. This was not only a tactic but a conviction of men such as Doenitz; it was believed by many Germans for many years after

---

*Hitler had held these two offices and titles since 1934, but a directive in 1943 ordered that in the customary "Führer and Reich Chancellor" the latter designation be omitted.

†Note the language of Hitler's last Order of the Day to soldiers of the Eastern Front, 16 April 1945. It began: "For the last time the Jewish-Bolshevist mortal enemy masses have begun an attack." Did he really believe in their "Jewish-Bolshevist" character? He did not.

the war;* and it is reasonable to think that it would have been approved by Hitler.

AT THE END OF THIS, the longest chapter of this book, I must attempt to clarify, once more, my view of Hitler the statesman and the strategist. I felt compelled to emphasize that he possessed both political and military talents, which existed together with his often fanatical obsessions; and that, as his reasoning about the decision to invade Russia indicated, we may find method even in what may seem to have been madness. What we must also understand is that this capacity of his was not innate but had evolved through his experiences. Thus, for example, his aim of a German *Lebensraum* in the East gradually ceased to be as primary and unyielding as it had once been—a devolution *not* simply due to his bitter experiences in the war against Russia. A blind fanatic is both unable and unwilling to learn; but Hitler did learn certain things during his career—things that his minions did not, and he understood that.

This brings me, once more, to the intentionalist-functionalist debate that has been coursing among German historians.† Of course it is true that Hitler was not the author of every decision or action of the Reich government; that he was, on many occasions, hesitant; that he did not follow up some of his directives; that in many ways his Third Reich was governed by a complicated and overgrown administrative apparatus on which he had to depend. Yet this is necessarily, and inevitably, true of almost any dictator. Here now is one difference between strategy and politics. A general knows that the course of no battle is entirely foreseeable; that, while

---

*It surfaced, here and there, during the "Historikerstreit"—in two-war suggestions not only by Hillgruber but by Klaus Hildebrandt (HS, p. 90), where this historian blamed both the Allies and Hitler for having subordinated "practicality" to ideology during the war.

†Jäckel is right (JH, p. 32): "Against the functionalist interpretation it should be stressed that internal opposition could at times prevent Hitler from doing certain things, but it could not force an action upon him." According to Jäckel, the Hitler regime was both "monocratic" and "polycratic." A good summary of the (pre-1988) "polycratic" literature is in Schreiber (SCHRB, pp. 284–85).

his orders *must* be carried out obediently and loyally, in the whirl of a battle they *cannot* be expected to be carried out with exactitude. But the outcomes of the principal directives of a dictator are more enforceable; their details may be carried out by committed underlings with an exactitude beyond subtleties and conditions and even possible reservations in the dictator's mind.* Hitler knew that— which is exactly why (and how) he was unquestionably responsible for their most brutal misdeeds.

---

*During the last year of his life there is some (very limited, to be sure) evidence of a kind of comprehension—though not of any kind of appreciation—of the "realpolitical" purposes of some of the people who turned against him. Consider, for instance, the relative—very relative—moderation of the retribution with which Hitler reacted to some of those foreign heads of state, former allies of his, who, for the sake of the survival of their countries, decided to break away from their alliance with Germany in 1944. Among them were Marshal Mannerheim of Finland, Admiral Horthy of Hungary (whose armistice attempt Hitler's minions brutally squashed and who was arrested but then transported to Germany with his family and interned in a castle), and General Antonescu of Romania, whose contacts with the Allies Hitler knew of but did not bring up during their last meeting. About the conspirators of 20 July 1944, too, he expressed his contempt, for their "ineptitude" even more than for their "treachery": Had they succeeded, what did they expect to do afterward? (Heer, HR, p. 452, cited Hitler talking to General Bodenschatz: "I know that Stauffenberg, Goerdeler and Witzleben thought to save the German people through my death . . . but these people had absolutely no clear plan what to do then.") Fest (F, p. 973) wrote that Hitler wanted to watch the film of the execution, but though others in his circle did so, it is not clear whether he did. He did not, however, order or suggest anything to restrain even the most brutal measures of his minions.

6

The Jews:
Tragedy and Mystery

Hitler and the Jews: the evolution of a historiography—
The motives of his obsession—The purposes of his policies—
Levels of his knowledge

IT IS NOT POSSIBLE TO separate a biography of Hitler—or a study of his strategy and statesmanship—from the history of Jews, particularly those within the Reich before 1939 and generally those within Europe and Russia during World War II. He and his regime engaged in many kinds of barbaric cruelties, involving millions of victims who were not Jewish. But we must give at least a thought to whether Hitler's historical reputation would be different had it not been for the mass murder of at least 4.5 million Jews due to his orders, or at least in accordance with his wishes. (The trouble with what is unthinkable is that at times it must be thought about.) He wanted to win a great war for Germany, and he wanted to eliminate Jews from Europe; and these two aims were complementary, indeed inseparable, in his mind. Near the end he was compelled to separate them. In February 1945, he said that he had at least "lanced the Jewish abscess." Yet in this he failed, too: It was because of him that anti-Semitism became unacceptable, if not unthinkable, intellectually as well as politically after the war, and especially in Germany.

The consequences of the mass murder of Jews have been multiple, protean, and perhaps incalculable. (They surely have included the swift international acceptance of the creation of the State of Israel.) The origins of that awful event are not simple either: anti-Semitism existed in many places and among many people, both before and independently of Hitler.* But the decision to proceed to the mass executions cannot be separated from him; and to the evolving historiography of this the present chapter is directed.

The literature of the Holocaust is enormous; but only a relatively small part of it has been addressed to a minute examination of the evidence connecting Hitler with the ordering of it—more precisely: (a) the search for the documentary evidence of this connection, (b) the reconstruction of the exact date that the policy of expulsion, deportation, and "resettlement" (that is, concentration and ghettoization) of Jews changed into a policy of physical extermination. We shall turn to some of this evidence—and to some of its problems—later. But before that, it may be appropriate to make a rapid sketch of the history of the Holocaust.

That the cruelties visited upon the Jews in Europe were due to Hitler was obvious enough both during and after the war, so that no special attention was directed to their causal and effective connection by professional or popular historians for a relatively long time. Of course, documentary materials became available only gradually after 1945 (though more rapidly than after any previous great war), but there was more to this. There seemed to be no general, or popular, interest in the Holocaust for many years—indeed, for about two decades. The very word "Holocaust" did not begin to appear in American (or English) usage until the late 1960s.† For reasons that are not easy to assess, the intensity of preoccupation with the Holocaust began to grow rapidly only after that time, espe-

---

*See LEW, p. 436 *et seq.* for a treatment of the "pathogenesis" and the "etiology" of the sources and symptoms of modern anti-Semitism.

†I found what may have been its first use in an article by Julian Franklyn in *Contemporary Review*, March 1944. (A curious coincidence: An excerpt from an article of the same issue of this, not-very-widely-read, conservative English political periodical was brought to Hitler's attention; but there was no connection between that and the Franklyn article.)

cially among American Jews. Something like this was also true of the works of many historians—with exceptions, of course—which does not mean that they intended to deny its existence or importance.* It was probably the worst of Hitler's crimes, and perhaps there was no need for a detailed reconstruction of his intentions. However, in the 1970s it gradually became apparent that besides our knowledge of the infamous Wannsee Conference of January 1942, there existed problems about the documentary reconstruction of when and how Hitler had decided to proceed to a policy of physical extermination. In the "Bibliographical remarks" of *The Last European War, 1939–1945* (published in 1976, though the manuscript had been completed in 1973), I wrote: "There is not a single paper, not even the [written] record of a verbal instruction that connects [Hitler] with the decision for the physical extermination of the Jews." But this did not mean that my treatment of the history of the Jews of Europe in 1939–41 mitigated or even circumscribed his responsibility for it.†

Entirely different were the interpretations, the "documentation," and the purpose of apologists (more precisely, rehabilitators) of Hitler, especially David Irving, beginning with his massive *Hitler's War* in 1977. (Unusually for an English writer, a German edition of this book, *Hitler und seine Feldherren*, had already been published in 1975 by the reputable Ullstein-Verlag in Berlin; but only after its director, Wolf Jobst Siedler—later publisher of his own firm—insisted on the elimination of Irving's pages in which Hitler had no connection with the extermination orders.)‡ More important than Irving's argument about the absence of any "document" of a Hitler

---

*Among the earliest biographers of Hitler, Görlitz-Quint devoted relatively little attention to it. Bullock (BU, p. 40): "Hitler's anti-Semitism bore no relation to facts, it was pure fantasy. . . ." One significant, and valuable, exception: Karl A. Schleunes (*The Twisted Road to Auschwitz: Nazi Policy Toward the German Jews 1933–1939*, Urbana, Ill., 1970), traced the gradual and, to some extent, pragmatic evolution of that policy very well (perhaps one of the first important works with a functionalist interpretation, though that was not its author's thesis).

†LEW, "Bibliographical remarks," p. 531; "The Problem of the Jews," pp. 429–53.

‡Siedler to Irving, 7 May 1974: "In a publishing house under my direction no book shall appear for which I cannot take political and historical responsibility. Should you be of a different opinion, we will have to go our different ways." Irving accepted this; but thereafter he insisted that he was a victim of censorship and that

order was his insistence that the Holocaust had been arranged behind Hitler's back by Himmler, Heydrich and others, and against Hitler's intentions; indeed, that Hitler wished to "postpone" the "solution" of the Jewish "problem" until after the war.* Thereafter Irving's argumentation and evidence of the "twisting" of his "documentation" were critically examined—and dismissed—by serious German historians† (without much effect on Irving's subsequent publishing career).

During the next twelve years, then, more detailed studies connecting Hitler with the Final Solution appeared, the most valuable of which were Uwe-Dietrich Adam, *Judenpolitik im Dritten Reich* (D, 1979); Gerald Fleming, *Hitler and the Final Solution* (Berkeley, 1982); and the extraordinarily intelligent and relatively small volume by the Swiss Philippe Burrin, *Hitler et les juifs. Genèse d'une génocide* (P, 1989).‡

---

the abridgments and alterations in the Ullstein edition had been made without his consent. (A "full" edition of the same book, with the title *Hitlers Krieg*, was published in Munich in 1983.)

*Examples of Irving's argumentation: During his trial in Jerusalem (1961) Eichmann said that Heydrich had told him that the Führer ordered the physical annihilation of Jews. "This kind of evidence, of course, would not suffice in an English magistrate's court to convict a vagabond of bicycle stealing, let alone assign the responsibility for the mass murder of six million Jews, given the powerful [?] written evidence that Hitler again and again [?] ordered the 'Jewish problem' set aside until the war was won." In 1/w, p. xi: ". . . and who are those emotional historians of the Jewish holocaust . . . Hitler never indicated in his book [*Mein Kampf*] any intention to liquidate these enemies [note this telling word] of his . . . nor was such intention referred to in the various transcripts of the Wannsee Conference . . . the conference was neither convened nor attended by Hitler and I do not think he even knew of it."

†Most telling: Martin Broszat, "Hitler und die Genesis der 'Endlösung.' Aus Anlass der Thesen von David Irving," vfz, October 1977. Also two trenchant articles by Eberhard Jäckel in faz, 25 August 1977 and 22 June 1978, showing the proper context and content of a "document" that Irving had produced jubilantly in support of his thesis. See also Jost Dülffer in gwu, 1979 (pp. 686–90), and Gitta Sereny and Lewis Chester in the London *Sunday Times*, 10 July 1977.

‡On p. 172 Burrin asks what to me is the most telling question: "Had Hitler died in the summer of 1942 [note this late dating], would the Final Solution have taken place?" Burrin says: most probably not. Yes, "the Jews would have gone on suffering in a Europe directed by Goering, Goebbels or Himmler." There would have been ghettoes, camps, perhaps even mass killings. But the mass manufacture of millions of Jewish corpses, no. Burrin is also convincing when he posits the time of Hitler's decision for the Final Solution as probably September 1941.

At the same time different—and sometimes at least implicitly apologetic—interpretations of Hitler's relationship to the Final Solution appeared. I am not referring here to pamphlets or to other small books that explicitly deny the mass murders, attributing them to a "hoax," but to authors published by reputable publishers. Toland, for example, asserted that in the fall of 1944 "Hitler instructed Himmler to prepare the dismantling of all killing camps except Auschwitz"* but gave no convincing source reference for this statement in a book that has many other errors. More lamentable were the theses of Ernst Nolte, who was one of the principal figures in the Historians' Controversy of the 1980s. In several of his books, Nolte insisted that Hitler and National Socialism must be understood as consequences of the murderous practices of Bolshevism— an absurd thesis whose dismissal, however, does not belong to this chapter—and that at least one factor in Hitler's declaration of war against Jews was a reaction to a declaration of war against him by leaders of world Jewry, in September 1939.† He tied together these two theses in a peculiar way. Yet outside the Historians' Contro-

---

*TO, p. 820.

†Examples: HS/W, pp. 42, 44: The "Brown [National Socialist] mass murders cannot be understood without the Red ones . . . a causal connection is probable." HS, p. 32: "Auschwitz was not first of all a result of traditional anti-Semitism and was not essentially a 'genocide' but before everything a reaction born of the anxieties about the previous practices of exterminations by the Russian revolution." HS/W, p. 16: "Seen in the proper historical perspective . . . the extermination of the Jews of Europe . . . cannot be understood but as the second and not the first mass liquidation" (the first was the Bolshevik practice). Nolte did *not* defend Auschwitz ("irrational," "horrible"). But in his article "Between Myth and Revisionism: The Third Reich in the Perspective of the 1980s," in H. W. Koch, ed., *Aspects of the Third Reich* (L, 1985), p. 27 (also HS, p. 142), Nolte made much of a letter by Chaim Weizmann, president of the World Zionist Organization, to Neville Chamberlain on 2 September 1939: "In this hour of supreme crisis . . . the Jews stand by Great Britain and will fight on the side of democracies." Nolte: This was "something like a declaration of war . . . it might justify the consequential thesis that Hitler was allowed to treat the German Jews as prisoners of war and by these means to intern them." Nolte misdated the date of Weizmann's letter to 2 September (that is, the day after Hitler's and before Britain's declaration of war); in reality, the letter was dated 29 August. It may also be significant that Nolte found the reference to this Weizmann statement in Irving (I/W), who got it from one of Hitler's table conversations (Picker ed., 24 July 1942). Moreover, Weizmann was but the president of the World Zionist Organization, not a spokesman of the diverse Jews of Europe

versy relatively little interest was directed at Nolte. Finally there is Zitelmann, who tended—albeit with some reservations—to give Irving considerable credit. In an article in *Die Zeit* (6 October 1989), Zitelmann wrote that Irving had "struck a nerve." In fact, there was no Hitler order for the Final Solution. "Irving must not be ignored. He has weaknesses, [but he is] one of the best knowers of sources . . . [and has] contributed much to research."* And in Zitelmann's own Hitler biography: he wrote that "there is yet no definite explanation of the origins of the so-called 'Final Solution.' "†

This last statement is not incorrect and is at least worth consideration;‡ so is Zitelmann, who, unlike Irving, ought not to be easily dismissed. However, this chapter cannot include yet another survey of the entire literature (including controversies) of the terrible history of the Holocaust, limited as it is to the relationship of Hitler to Jews and, even more, to the historical treatment of that relationship. Like anything and everything in history, that goes on and will never

---

or of the world. And what could Hitler expect from Jews at that late time? There is the ironical French ditty:

| *Cet animal est très méchant* | (Mean indeed is this animal's self |
| *Quand on l'attaque il se défend.* | When he's attacked he defends himself.) |

*In his review of Irving, *Führer und Reichskanzler Adolf Hitler 1939–1945*, Herbig, 1989.

†ZIT/B, pp. 158–59. There was no written order by Hitler, "and there is no evidence that because of secrecy Hitler gave only an oral directive. . . . Irving's thesis . . . led to an agitated controversy among historians. Though Irving's conclusions have been dismissed, even such historians as Martin Broszat and Hans Mommsen suggest . . . that Irving had struck a nerve." (Note this repeated phrase.) "Neither the 'Functionalists' nor the 'Intentionalists' are convincing." Also ZIT/B, p. 124: "The mass murder of the Jews was not foreseeable." Hitler had not planned it from the beginning. Probably true: but (p. 126): "The Nuremberg Laws were meant to put an end to the agitation of the radical anti-Semites of the Party. Hitler expressly forbade further atrocities." This is at least arguable. P. 20: "Anti-Semitism was more widespread in Vienna than in any other European city." Not so: Bucharest? Warsaw? Moscow? "Like other of his contemporaries, Hitler became an anti-Semite. That his anti-Semitism took obviously an especially extreme and sharp form was a result of the character of his personality." This is too simplistic—especially in view of Zitelmann's own words (ZIT/B, pp. 8–9): "The picture of Hitler as described until now is too simple, too simple to be true."

‡Except that: is there a "*definite* explanation of the origins" of anything in history? Of, say, the origins of the American Civil War; or of World War I; or of Hitler's coming to power?

"definitely" end;* but allow me to conclude this introductory subchapter with what I think is a trenchant statement by Haffner:
"After 1933 something like a Führer state would probably have
come into being even without Hitler. [Possibly.] And there probably
would have been another war even without Hitler. [Perhaps.] But
not the murder of millions of Jews."† [Yes.]

THE *MOTIVES* OF HITLER's Judeophobia remain a mystery. More
ascertainable—at least to a considerable extent—are his *purposes*.‡
But before my attempt to make a necessary—and seldom observed—
distinction between motives and purposes, some other distinctions
may be in order.

We must recognize that the Jewish "problem" was Hitler's fundamental obsession—as I suggested in chapter 5, more fundamental
than his obsession with the importance of Lebensraum.** At a certain time of his life, Hitler convinced himself that the presence of
the Jews was a fundamental problem of Germany and of Europe,
and probably of the entire world—the key to history, so to speak. I
write "convinced himself," rather than "became convinced," since
the latter phrase at least partly suggests the result of outside influ-

---

*Schreiber in SCHRB, pp. 286–87: "Obviously there exist a great number of
excellent studies [about the Final Solution] . . . but a comprehensive survey that
considers all the various perspectives and includes all of the most recent single
studies does not yet exist."

A good summary statement by Jäckel (JH, p. 46): "It can be ruled out that a
single killing order was given. The extermination was divided into several phases
and covered a wide variety of methods and victims. We must therefore assume a
correspondingly wide variety of orders extending over a period of several months."

†HF/AI, p. 216.

‡In ZIT/A, pp. 42–43, Zitelmann comes close to suggesting that Hitler's anti-
Semitism served principally propaganda purposes, which is very debatable. He cites
a Hitler speech (27 February 1925): It is "psychologically wrong to establish a
variety of aims for the struggle"; it is right "to select but one enemy that everyone
can recognize: he is the only guilty one." Then: "And this enemy is the Jews."

**This is the very opposite order from that of Zitelmann, who in an interview
with the Swedish historian Alf W. Johansson in November 1992 stated that the creation of a new Lebensraum in the East was Hitler's "central aim" and that it is at
least debatable whether the liquidation of the Jews was his aim, surely not for a
long time.

ences; and while Hitler, like every other human being, was undoubtedly influenced by what he read and by what others may have said,
this conviction was largely a creation of his own mind, sui generis.

As a matter of fact, the term "anti-Semite" does not entirely fit
him. "Anti-Semitism" as a word appeared in the 1870s when—
perhaps especially in Germany—the former, mainly (though never
exclusively) religious discrimination against Jews had grown weaker;
what rose in its stead was a categorization of and a sentiment for
segregating Jews (or even expelling them from the national community) because of their alleged racial characteristics, including even
Christians of recent Jewish ancestry. Thus anti-Semitism was often
directed at assimilated Jews who were successful in occupying important positions in their national societies, confident of their rights
and of their unquestionable acceptance as national citizens. Many
people, in many parts of the world, reacted against such an unques-
tioned assimilation; so had Hitler; but he was no ordinary anti-
Semite. Few anti-Semites regarded—or still regard—the presence
of Jews as not only a problem or a national irritant but as the *principal* problem of their nation. Many anti-Semites also happen to
be racists—indeed, their anti-Semitism is but part of their racism—
whereas Hitler was the opposite. His obsession with Jews was deeper
and more consistent than his racism,* which is why I preferred to
write *Judeophobia*, rather than *anti-Semitism*, at the beginning of this
subchapter. Even in 1919–23, when he became prominent in the
midst of many nationalists, riding a wave of popular anti-Semitism,
it is possible that among all the other National Socialists (except for
marginal fanatics such as Julius Streicher), Hitler was one of the
very few, and perhaps the only one, to whom the Jewish "problem"
was absolutely primary.

---

*Fest, F, p. 780: "The unmistakable difference between his rigorous obsession
with Jews and the lukewarm German anti-Semitism . . ." now (November 1938)
became even more evident. The otherwise so perceptive Haffner is wrong about
this (HF/AN, p. 9): "Hitler's anti-Semitism is an East European plant." (Not really:
Austrian more than German around the turn of the century.) But p. 103: "Nowhere had that Jewish patriotism such fervent, deeply emotional features as in
Germany." Largely true: which is one of the deepest elements of the German
tragedy.

It was a phobia—and, like some other phobias, not at all irrational to his mind. Several times, as early as 1920, he said that the Jewish "problem" must be "solved" not by emotional but by "cool," "rational," "scientific" means. Then and throughout the rest of his life, he kept repeating that Jews were bacilli, viruses, parasitic pests on the bodies of living nations;* and that the time comes in the life of just about every nation when, like a sheepdog, it rises to shake itself and get rid of pests in one big heave. Then, in the very last sentence of his testament, a few hours before his death (when, as we saw, he said nothing about Lebensraum), he dictated: whatever may happen, the German nation must not allow Jews to return in their midst.

The question now arises: when did his Judeophobia crystallize—or congeal—in Hitler's mind?† In *Mein Kampf*, he wrote that his "realization" of what the presence of Jews meant occurred in Vienna, around the twentieth year of his life; that he was no convinced anti-Semite before he had come to Vienna; and that in Vienna his startling, though gradual, realization of the influence of Jews led to "my most difficult mental struggle. Only after months of struggle between reason and feeling, victory began to favor reason. Two years later sentiment had followed reason, and from then on became its most faithful guard and watchman."‡ (It is interesting to note Hitler's own sequence: emotion catching up with reason, not the other way around.) Yet Jäckel and others found no anti-Semitic utterance by Hitler until the thirty-first year of his life, in Munich. In chapter 2, directed to the Vienna-Munich question, we saw that there were perhaps four instances where Hitler, probably consciously, had altered conditions and facts about his early life. We

---

*By a horrible coincidence, the gas used in Auschwitz and in other extermination camps—Zyklon B—had been widely used by exterminators of pests and other insects in the houses and apartments of Central Europe.

†Maser, M/A, p. 263: "Despite all of our knowledge of details, the origin of Hitler's anti-Semitism is not entirely clarifiable."

‡Cited in Maser, M/A, pp. 247–48, also in M/F, p. 100. According to Heer (HR, p. 117), this was not true; Hitler left Linz already imbued with anti-Semitism. (Perhaps, but only partly; see his relationship to Dr. Bloch, pp. 195–196.)

must admit at least the possibility that, in this instance, the alteration may have been unconscious: that Hitler placed and exaggerated the event of the congealing of his Judeophobia to Vienna in retrospect for more reasons than that of propaganda, or to convince his eventual readers. We should not doubt that, at the latest in Vienna, Hitler had come to share some of the routine, run-of-the-mill anti-Semitism of the people of that place and period. But there is no evidence that this had become his basic obsession—in other words, that the mutation of his anti-Semitism into his Judeophobia occurred in Vienna and not later in Munich.* There is not much room for doubt that his experiences with the Munich leftist and then Soviet-like "regime," including its many Jewish leaders, were decisive. Still the sudden eruption of his anti-Semitism into his principal obsession remains a mystery.†

There remains one possible consideration of the motive force of his Judeophobia—a consideration which cannot and does not amount to an explanation and which is no more than a hypothesis. It involves Hitler's relationship with his father. We have seen (in chapter 2) that in *Mein Kampf* he described his father, as well as his relationship to his father, in terms that did not at all correspond to what he would sometimes reveal to others. Everything indicates that his version in *Mein Kampf* was a conscious choice, and that it went well beyond the properly expectable few phrases of a public figure about his respectable relationship with his sire. Everything we know also points to the strong probability (at times expressed by Hitler

---

*In addition to a lack of evidence of extant anti-Semitic expressions of his before 1919, there are such facts as his friendship (or at least friendly acquaintance) with a Jewish man in the Vienna men's hostel who helped him and on occasion lent him his overcoat (many such details in Hamann, summed up also above, chapter 2, p. 59); the fact that Hitler's Iron Cross decoration was awarded him on the recommendation of a Jewish reserve officer, Gutmann (whom, however, Hitler did not respect); that a number of Viennese Jewish people had bought paintings and watercolors by him in the years 1910–1913. He gave one of his earliest watercolors to Dr. Bloch.

†Schramm, SCH, p. 51: ". . . in the end, all attempts to explain the unprecedented and immeasurable intensity of Hitler's anti-Semitism finally founder on the inexplicable."

himself) that he feared and disliked and perhaps even hated his father. Throughout his career, attempts were made to connect Hitler with some kind of partly Jewish parentage, foremost among them the possibility that his father had been the illegitimate son of a Jewish man in Graz. Of course no one can fix the fact of fatherhood with absolute certainty; but the researches of some historians are sufficient in establishing that the Frankenthaler-Schicklgruber relationship was insubstantial speculation, nothing else. Yet we may consider the mere possibility—and I emphasize "mere possibility"—that Hitler may have *thought* that his father was half Jewish (perhaps also that during this childhood and adolescence there were people, young or old, who made taunting remarks about his father, true or not). It is interesting that in *Mein Kampf* he described his father as "liberal" and "cosmopolitan," which the latter was not, and that he heard the word "Jew" only in conversations in his fourteenth or fifteenth year—that is, after the sudden death of his father—which, again, is unlikely. Among his biographers, Deuerlein was one of the few who left the question open: ". . . throughout, the possibility exists that the question of the paternity of Hitler's father can never be clarified," to which add Marlis Steinert's perspicacious argument: "Everything that he hates in himself, the Führer projects on the Jew; everything that causes his and Germany's suffering is the fault of the Jews."* This is more convincing than Professor Binion's psychoanalytic suppression theory, according to which Hitler hated the Jewish doctor who had treated (or mistreated) his beloved mother; that he suppressed that hatred; and that hatred then burst forth in 1918 when Germania took the place of his martyred mother. Men often hate (and fear) in others what they hate (and fear) in themselves; and Adolf Hitler, surely after the age of thirty, was moved by a most powerful kind of hatred.†

---

*D, p. 12; ST, p. 195.

†About his exaltation of the power of hatred, see chapter 2. Also Schreiber, SCHRB, citing a book by Irene Harand, *Sein Kampf. Antwort an Hitler* (Vienna, 1935): "There is no Hitler without [his] hatred of Jews." And Edgar Alexander (pseud.: Alexander Emmerich, a Catholic priest), *Der Mythus Hitler* (z, 1937, repr. M, 1980): "Hate in National Socialism became a system." (SCHRB, p. 124, note 233)

"MOVED BY HATRED"—WE HAVE enough evidence of this, including Hitler's own words. But such a general statement is no more than the observation of a psychic tendency. Allow me to repeat: The true motives—or, in other words, the real sources—of Hitler's Judeophobia are not ascertainable. What is more—and legitimately—ascertainable is the evidence of his expressed purposes. There is a difference between legal and historical evidence, but for both the great commonsense maxim of Samuel Johnson properly applies: "Intentions must be gathered from acts." Truth is a slippery fish, and law is often a coarse net: but even law, or at least English law, admits "motive" as evidence only when it refers to an intention expressed. The historian's search for and admission of evidence is not constrained by the categories of legal procedure. Potentially all is grist to his mill—which makes his work both easier and more difficult than that of the lawyer or judge. But he, too, must be aware of the difference between motives and purposes; he must eschew the categorical, and often false, attribution of psychic motives—a pestilential intellectual habit of this century—while his task includes looking for evidence of his subject's expressed purposes.* In other words, the psychic sources of Hitler's motives are one thing, while expressions of his intentions are another—and the historian's principal task is the attempt to comprehend and describe the latter, not the former, including the evolution of when and how those intentions resulted in acts.

There was an evolution in Hitler's Jewish policies—its stages corresponding, by and large, to turning points of his life and career. His original policy was expulsion: to force all Jews to leave Germany. Then came the first change, in the winter of 1938–39, forcefully expressed in his speech of 30 January 1939: He saw the coming of a war; if so, the Jews will have made it and they would have to pay for it. From this time on, his intentions involved more than the Jews of Germany and Austria—they involved all the Jews of Europe. In his mind the war and Jews were inseparably connected. It was only

---

*Cf. HC, chapter 4, "Motives and Purposes."

decades later that historians recognized the great significance of the key sentences in that speech, which otherwise were but yet another example of his anti-Jewish diatribes.* Also significant is the fact that Hitler kept referring to this "warning" in his wartime speeches again and again. Significantly, too, he, perhaps consciously, misdated the date of his warning, referring to the date of his speech as 1 September 1939, the moment the war began—obviously wishing to impress people with the categorical and inescapable connection of Jews and the war that had been forced upon him. For about two more years, emigration—that is, expulsion—of Jews from the Greater German Reich still went on, together with the first drafts of plans to expel Jews from all of Europe, perhaps to Madagascar; and then, in the summer of 1941, came another change.† The invasion of Russia—and the American entry into the war—involved new problems: the presence of more millions of Eastern European Jews in the territories overrun and occupied by Germany, and the closing off of the last possibilities of expulsion overseas. Some time in August–September 1941, Hitler either ordered or approved a Final Solution. The first mass executions of Jews took place during the summer and autumn of 1941 in Eastern Europe, while the Final Solution (meaning the collection and extermination of most Jews throughout Europe) was being planned and drafted and finally set down on paper by some of Hitler's minions at the Wannsee Conference on 20 January 1942.‡ Most of the Jews who were murdered

---

*"Today I will once more be a prophet. If the international Jewish financiers *inside and outside Europe* should again succeed in plunging the nations into a world war, the result will not be the bolshevization of the earth and the victory of Jewry, but the *annihilation* of the Jewish race *throughout Europe*" (my italics).

†Haffner in HF/AN, p. 84: The Jews "had to be removed not like a piece of furniture that is taken away to be put elsewhere, but like a stain that is removed by wiping it out." Yes, but only after 1941.

‡That conference was first set to meet on 8 December 1941. Its postponement may have had something to do with the American entry into the war. Hitler's knowledge of its decisions is at least indicated by his table conversation of 27 January 1942, recorded by Heim (HM, p. 239): "The Jew must disappear from Europe! *At best they go to Russia.* I have no compassion for Jews. They will always remain an element inciting peoples against each other. They do this in the lives of nations as they do it in private life. *They must be extracted from Switzerland and Sweden.* [My italics.] Where there are few of them they are the most dangerous. Five thousand Jews

during World War II were killed between the summer of 1942 and the fall of 1944. In October 1944, Himmler ordered the termination of the gassing—probably not against Hitler's intentions or behind his back. Still, Hitler insisted on—and, from all existing evidence, believed in—the inseparable and principal responsibility of Jews for the war, whence his exhortation to the German people in his last-minute testament.

This summary of a sequence of events will, I think, be accepted by most serious historians without reservations. But to this we must add some details that may suggest the complicated character of Hitler's intentions.* To begin with, categorical and unyielding as his condemnation of Jews was, allowing for no exceptions, on several occasions in the 1930s he did permit or order the exemption of men and women of Jewish ancestry in individual cases.† Yet there was not the least semblance of such mitigations in his speeches and public expressions. What is at work here is not a clearly Machiavellian

---

briefly in all kinds of Swedish positions. That much easier to extract them! We have reasons enough for that. . . ." My italics should suggest the duality within Hitler. On the one hand, Hitler refers to the deportation of Jews to Siberia (about which he talked on other occasions, too), not about their physical extermination. At the same time, his intention to comb through Europe to extract all Jews from every where is entirely in accord with the expressed intentions of the protocol of the Wannsee Conference.

*Carr, c, p. 93: "Just as one must pay due regard to 'alternative' foreign policies which to some extent modified Hitler's own concepts, so, too, in studying the Holocaust we must allow the possibility that there were other 'final solutions' before the gas chambers."

†Between the two crucial elections of September 1930 and March 1933, he did not strongly emphasize anti-Semitism in his speeches. On one occasion he said that "well-meaning Jews" may stay in Germany, "once they demonstrate their proper behavior [*Wohlverhalten*]." Heiden (HD, p. 347) cites a Hitler remark about the comic actor Felix Bressart: "Pity that this Bressart is a Jew!" Görlitz-Quint (GQ, pp. 362–63) mention that on 27 January 1933 Papen supported and Hitler agreed to a cabinet post for the nationalist Theodor Düsterberg, who had a Jewish grandfather. On several occasions, he (as late as 1940) ordered the reactivation of half-Jewish officers in the armed services (examples of this in Admiral Raeder's memoirs, Erich Raeder, *My Life*, Annapolis, Md., 1960, pp. 263–64). Also, when it came to the Nuremberg laws, he did not approve the plans of the Party to equate half-Jews with Jews. Schleunes in *The Twisted Road to Auschwitz*, p. 131: "Hitler's hand appeared occasionally at crucial moments, but it was usually a vacillating and indecisive one. He did not delegate responsibility for Jewish policy, nor did he keep a close check on it."

discrepancy between his public statements and his private beliefs. Many things—and witnesses—indicate that he not only wanted people to believe what he said, but that he himself believed everything that he said *while he said it.**

However, there were some differences between his intentions and those of some of his minions. There is evidence that it was not he but Goebbels and others who organized the "Kristallnacht" pogroms of 9–10 November 1938, and that Hitler ordered their cessation—not, of course, to protect its victims but to protect the reputation of his regime and of Germany.† (At that time, he also rejected Heydrich's proposal to require German Jews to wear a yellow star; he agreed to more restrictions for Jews, but not to all of them.) Yet there is no evidence of the slightest discrepancy between his own convictions and his public statements attributing all of the blame for the coming war to Jewish influences (meaning the decisions of the British and French governments, and of President Roosevelt, to resist him).

We have seen that in the spring of 1941 Hitler was preparing himself, his army, his people, and his propaganda, for a new kind of war—an unrestricted and brutal war, against Russia; that he found it useful to employ the category and the argument describing the enemy as "Jewish-Bolshevism"—but that he did not entirely, or really, believe in the truth of that category. And soon after the beginning of the Russian campaign came the change: the passage from expulsion to extermination, the so-called Final Solution.‡ Evidence that Hitler ordered that, or at least consented to it, is strong—

---

*In his *Germany 1866–1945* (NY, 1980), Gordon A. Craig puts this well: One of Hitler's psychological principles was "that arguments are weakened by qualifications or concessions to the other side, so that the uncompromising and categorical style tends to be the most convincing." Craig wrote this about Hitler's speeches in the early 1930s, but it is also true of statements made to his circle, including his wartime table conversations.

†Speer (SP, p. 111) recalls a few words of "Hitler's to the effect that he had not wanted these excesses." Other sources confirm this.

‡We must consider that it is only in retrospect—and principally because of the employment of this term at the Wannsee Conference—that we equate "Final Solution" with extermination. Among the frequent instances of the employment of this term (see Lukacs DL, p. 131, note), on 24 June 1940 *re* the plan to deport all Jews of Europe to Madagascar, Heydrich's memorandum to Ribbentrop: The Jewish

in spite of the previously mentioned condition that he left no written directive to that effect.* Important decisions could be—and sometimes were—made without Hitler's knowledge. But no important decisions could be—or were—made against his wishes.

There are many indications that this turning point occurred in August (or early September) of 1941. It had much to do with the war against Russia,† but we must now add the—often ignored— American connection; for not only the invasion of Russia but the then seemingly unavoidable American entry into the war was a factor. There is a significant passage in the Koeppen notes of 20 September 1941: "The Führer has not yet made a decision about reprisals against *German* [my italics] Jews. . . . As Minister von

---

problem "can no longer be solved by emigration. A territorial final solution *Endlösung* becomes therefore necessary." To the best of my knowledge, this is the first time that the ominous phrase appears in German documents—not in 1941, as is generally believed. To this add that Hitler talked of the Madagascar plan on 20 June and as late as 2 February 1941: "The question is only how to get them there. He has now other ideas, too, not very kind ones, to be sure [Er dachte über manches jetzt anders, nicht gerade freundlicher]." The significance of the date and of the language of this statement is considerable.

*Jäckel, JH, p. 46: "We must ask not simply whether Hitler ordered the Holocaust but whether the Holocaust was improvised or premeditated. The clarifications should prove illuminating but will have to be subjected to further scrutiny, since the improvisations may have been premeditated."

†According to Jäckel (JH, pp. 52–53), this was preceded by an order to kill Russian Jews, but it is also likely that while "Hitler had not issued a formal order . . . in May 1941 he expressed the desire to proceed to the final solution in the foreseeable future." Yet Hitler did not openly admit that a Final Solution actually meant extermination. JH, p. 53: "According to Frank, Hitler declared outright on June 19, three days before the Russian campaign began, that the Jews would be removed from [Poland] in the foreseeable future, and that [Poland] should become a transit camp only. This statement can be interpreted as a cynical metaphor for transit to death, and indeed the killing centers were sometimes called transit camps. It can also be taken literally. On July 21 Hitler dropped a hint that the Jews could be sent to Siberia. . . ." (He also mentioned this on several occasions later.) Also JH, p. 113: In August and September 1941, he still hesitated about the deportation of the remaining Jews in Germany. (Goebbels and Heydrich were trying to push him in that direction.) Uwe-Dietrich Adam in *Judenpolitik im Dritten Reich* (D, 1972), p. 357: ". . . it is very possible that the mass extermination was not Hitler's a priori aim that he tried to achieve." He dates the decision sometime between September and December 1941. See also Hans-Heinrich Wilhelm, "*Offene Fragen der Holocaust-Forschung*," in Uwe Backes, Eckhard Jesse, Rainer Zitelmann, eds., *Die Schatten der Vergangenheit. Impulse zur Historisierung des Nationalsozialismus*, B, 1990.

Steengracht told me, the Führer considers to hold this measure for an eventual entry of America in the war."*

In any event: the reason Hitler gave no written directive ought to be obvious. He knew what these measures meant,† and he also knew how their evidence would shock people throughout the world—including Germany. Like other decisions throughout his career, the Final Solution had to be (and to remain) a state secret. There is plenty of evidence of directives to that effect.‡

To this we may now add something else. The mass extermination

---

*Koeppen notes in IFZ, 20 September 1941, p. 21. It corresponds with Goebbels's diary, 19 August 1941: "We also talk about the Jewish problem. The Führer is convinced that his former prophecy in the Reichstag had come true, that if Jewry were to succeed to provoke a world war again, he would end that with the extermination [*Vernichtung*] of the Jews. . . . In the East the Jews must pay the bill; in Germany they have already partly paid it, and in the future they will have to pay more. Their last refuge is North America; and there too they will have to pay sooner or later. . . . In any case the Jews will have no reason to laugh in the future. . . . And will not rest until we too have taken the final measures against Jewry." On that day, Hitler allowed Goebbels and Heydrich to order the compulsory wearing of yellow stars for the remaining Jews in Germany.

Broszat (in VFZ, October 1977, p. 761) considers that Hitler's unwillingness to proceed to a wholesale deportation of Jews from Berlin in November 1941 *may* have had something to do with the presence of remaining American journalists in Berlin. Haffner (HF/AN, p. 142) dates Hitler's decision to proceed to extermination only in early December 1941, "[after] he abandoned all hope of a negotiated peace with Britain (and the associated hope of preventing America from joining the war)"—and he had to face the end of the German offensive before Moscow. I think this is too late. (There is one symbolic coincidence: the first gassing of Polish Jews took place in Chelno on 8 December 1941.)

†In his speech to officers on 26 May 1944: He had to eliminate [*entfernen*] the Jews. "One could of course ask me: Well, could you not have done this more simply—not simply; for anything else would have been more complicated—or more humanely?" Cited also by Broszat, p. 759.

‡Görlitz-Quint, GQ, pp. 552–53: His original plan was ghettoization, but then he consciously went along with the gassing plans as "head of the state . . . this dark side of [his war leadership] was even more strictly kept as a state secret than was the euthanasia program." (For that a written Hitler order did exist—if only because it was necessary to free German physicians from their oath to preserve life.) Fleming, FL, p. 20: "Already at the beginning of the euthanasia program," Hitler ordered that "the Führer's Chancellery must under no circumstances be seen to be active in this matter." FL, p. 22, quoting Jodl at Nuremberg: "the 'Final Solution' of the Jewish

of Jews was a state secret of the Reich, not to be admitted to the outside world or even to the German people at large. But it was also Hitler's own secret—a secret at least to the extent that he pushed that knowledge away from himself. He surely did not want to know anything about its details. There are three kinds of evidence for this. One consists of his repeated statements that the Jewish "problem" must be looked at and dealt with in "cool, scientific" ways.* Another was his refusal to admit—not only to foreign visitors whom he accused of not being severe enough with their Jews but also to people close to him—that the aim of the concentration of the Jews into camps in the east was something other than deportation, and their being forced to work.† Finally, and most significantly, there

---

question was a 'masterpiece of concealment.' " (FL, p. 61, calls it "Hitler's Cunning," perhaps not the best term.) Deuerlein, D, p. 152: "Hitler did not talk about everything . . . including the so-called Final Solution. . . . He was not a murderer in the sense of criminal justice; he did not murder or kill anyone; but he was still the author and the cause of all of the murders committed by members of the German people." Finally, there was Bormann's confidential instruction from the chancellery on 11 July 1943: The words "Final Solution" must not be mentioned, not even the term "Special Treatment" [*Sonderbehandlung*]; only references to Jews sent to work are allowed.

*As late as in his speech of 30 January 1944: He hopes that "other nations too will become acquainted with the elements of a scientific understanding and objective solution of the [Jewish] question." (Also in 1944, cited by Heer, HR, pp. 446–47: "England too may shake herself and get rid of the Jewish bacteria in the last minute.")

†Throughout the war, Hitler kept speaking of Jews being deported eastward to work. On 17 July 1941 to the Croat Kvaternik: "where the Jews are sent, to Siberia or Madagascar, is the same for him." As late as July 1942, he still talked to his circle about Madagascar—and about Siberia too. When he berated the Hungarian Regent Horthy in April 1943 for not being tough about Hungarian Jews, Horthy responded, plaintively, that he could not simply beat them to death—whereupon Hitler said something about Jews being "bacilli," while Ribbentrop declared that they "would either have to be annihilated or put into concentration camps: there were no other alternatives." Goebbels in his diary of 27 March 1942 wrote of "a fairly barbaric procedure that cannot be precisely described: how many Jews will be left over. Roughly speaking about 60 percent liquidated, 40 percent in labor detachments." In 1944, Hitler asked Horthy for 100,000 Jews to work in German factories. Speer confirmed to Fleming (in a letter in 1981, FL, p. 161, note 12) that Hitler wanted Speer to gather Hungarian Jews for the construction of large underground

was his evident unwillingness to read or hear or see reports of what was really done to Jews in the east. This unwillingness accorded with his unwillingness to visit or even to look at photographs of severely bombed German cities, or at pictures of the German refugees trekking westward in the brutal winter of 1944–45, pictures that he, at least on one occasion, pushed aside (and perhaps even with his unwillingness to look at photographs of the July 1944 conspirators' executions).* Here we are faced, again, with a duality in his character. Generally speaking, not wanting to know something means preferring not to think about it at all. Within Hitler's person we may recognize an element of weakness in a man who otherwise could not be described as a coward; or, at best, a sensitive (and, in a way, feminine) element in the character of a man whose brutal ideas and brutal expressions were the very opposite of sensitive. Hitler was not a sadist. He took no sensual pleasure in the sufferings of his enemies or victims. Sadism is a sin of the flesh; Hitler's sins were those of the spirit. There is no evidence that his often-stated beliefs—that by persecuting the Jews he was acting as an instrument of God, and that the war had been forced on him by Jews—were meant for public consumption only.†

---

factories in Germany. In March 1943, Dr. Korherr, a statistician working for the SS, was ordered by Himmler to prepare an exact statistical account of the number of Jews remaining in the East; this was then summarized and typed on a special typewriter for Hitler to read. According to Eichmann (FL, p. 138), Hitler saw it and then ordered it to be destroyed.

See also the article by Dieter Pohl ("Die Holocaust-Forschung und Goldhagens Thesen") in VFZ, January 1997, p. 11: "... it is still not wholly clear whether economic motives, meaning the preservation of Jews for work, did not have a considerable influence on the sequence of the mass murders."

*Maser (M/A, p. 255) makes an interesting remark about Hitler's unwillingness to confront one of his last cooks, Frau Manzialy, who was of (partly) Jewish origin: "... this also suggests that even in connection with the killing of Jews he was 'only' inhuman as long as he did not have to face his victims."

†To this we may add another possible connection of the Final Solution with his private knowledge that the war could no longer be won: He knew not only that he would lose his war but also that the Jews of the world knew this. The perceptive Burrin (his concluding paragraph), p. 169: "Around the middle of September 1941, when he decided to kill the Jews, he certainly did not think defeat was inevitable. But he must have assuredly felt that it would take a great deal of luck in the future

THERE WERE, as we have seen, a few exceptions to Hitler's categorical condemnation of Jews. There were his exemptions of certain individuals. There is the statement by his apologist, the architect Giesler,* who saw Hitler reading, in October 1944, the great biography of Emperor Frederick II by the fine German Jewish medievalist Ernst Kantorowicz. In one of Hitler's table conversations (11 December 1941), he asked the rhetorical question: Were there, are there, any decent Jews? Hardly any. Otto Weininger, perhaps, "who took his own life as he realized that the Jew lives by the decomposition of other nations and peoples!"† But on other occasions Hitler mentioned the "Edeljude," the "noble Jew," Dr. Bloch.

Dr. Bloch, as we have seen (in chapter 2), was the Jewish physician

---

for him to win; and he saw clearly the price he would have to pay to avoid defeat. The extermination of the Jews, then, was at once a propitiatory act and an act of vengeance. By putting to death those he thought of as his archetypal enemies— little did it matter to his obsessed mind that these were powerless and unarmed civilians—he was demonstrating his will to fight to the end. By means of the somehow sacrificial death of the Jews, he was fanatically steeling himself to achieve victory, to fight on to annihilation. At the same time, and above all, he was expiating spilled German blood, and avenging beforehand a possible defeat. He would conduct this exercise of vengeance, as it turned out, with mounting determination as the situation worsened, and as he advanced toward an apocalyptic end."

*Giesler, p. 520; about him see chapter 7.

†In *Hitlers Tischgespräche im Führerhauptquartier*, ed. H. Picker-A. Hillgruber (M: 1968), p. 36, Dietrich Eckart, Hitler's early mentor, had told Hitler about this *only* decent Jew. Lukacs, LEW, pp. 452–53: "Weininger in 1902 wrote an extraordinary book entitled *Geschlecht und Charakter* (*Sex and Character*) about women and men, Jews and Christians, the problem of whose relationship consumed his fiery mind. [He . . .] was probably right in foreseeing the rise of a tremendous movement of anti-Semitism. He was wrong in believing that this would be the result of a new, and rising, Christianity: 'Against this new Jewry a new Christianity comes to light: Humanity thirsts for the founder of a new religion, and the struggle moves toward a decision as in the Year One. Between Jewry and Christianity, between commerce and culture, between woman and man, between earthbound life and a higher life, between nothingness and Godhead, mankind will again have to choose. These are the two opposite kingdoms: *There is no Third Reich.*' There *was* to be a Third Reich, a Third Reich that was to be ruled not by the religion of Christianity but by the religion of the folk."

in Linz who treated Hitler's mother during her last, painful illness. In March 1938, the old Dr. Eduard Bloch saw Hitler's triumphant entry into Linz from the window of his apartment in a house on the main street. Thereafter he and his family were treated with circumspection by the National Socialist authorities, who assisted his emigration to the United States. On 16 November 1938, before his departure, Bloch sent a letter to a Renato Bleibtreu, the director of the Viennese office of the NSDAP Central Archives, enclosing Bloch's medical record book of 1907, to be transmitted to the Führer. This was a remarkable letter, sentimental, memory-laden, and deeply melancholy, and yet not a groveling one. It included a long description of the young Hitler at the time of his mother's death, who left a long and searing impression on this physician's memory: "In my almost forty-year-long practice I have never seen a young man who was so struck by pain and sorrow as the young Adolf Hitler! I had the impression that here stands a man before you of whose very being, of whose heart, a piece had been torn out! . . . I have the conviction that he has not forgotten his mother's doctor, whose practice has been governed not by material but ethical considerations; but I am also convinced that the same principles govern thousands of my coreligionists whose many spiritual sufferings are the same as mine."*

There is a humility in Dr. Bloch's letter that I find deeply moving. I write "humility"—which is of course different from cowardice, just as confidence differs from arrogance. The great historian Jakob Burckhardt once wrote that humility is something of which the ancient world was not capable; it was a virtue brought into our world by Christianity. Was Hitler capable of humility? Hardly: except on that occasion on Christmas Eve in 1907, when before this modest Jewish doctor he bowed deep, thanking him for what he had done for his mother.

---

*To this were added another two pages, dated 7 November 1938: "Recollections of the Führer and of his [departed] mother." These are reproduced in Schenck, PH, p. 520ff. In these pages Schenck demolished Binion's thesis about Bloch's medical errors and his medical—and financial—irresponsibility. (See also Dr. Bloch's article about Hitler in *Collier's*, 15 and 22 March 1941.)

7

The Germans:
Chapter or Episode?

Hitler in the history of the German people—
The problem of "public opinion"—Hitler and the history of the
Third Reich—Conservatives—Working
class—Resistance

THE HISTORY OF GERMANY—and of the German people—includes Hitler. This is a statement of the obvious; yet, perhaps understandably, there were and are many Germans who shy away from it. I remember having read somewhere the statement of a German refugee scholar in the United States that Hitler does not belong in German history, which struck me (and presumably also other non-Germans) as an absurdity. Much more understandable—and excusable—is the inclination of many Germans to regard the Hitler years as an unnatural episode in the history of their country and of their people: an episode, rather than a chapter, suggesting something exceptional and discontinuous. These are popular inclinations and habits of thought, as are those of non-German people (perhaps especially Englishmen and Englishwomen) to the effect that Germans are Germans, and that Hitlerism was but another German thing, and that World War II was but the Second War, a continuation of the First German War, the 1914–18 one. What we face here are either simplistic or exaggerated applications of a perennial question: Is history marked principally by continuity or by change? Applied to any period or place in history, the answers are not easy; and they are perhaps especially difficult when we are confronted with Hitler and his rule. And it is to the credit of German historians that they have tried to grapple with this problem for many years now, some of them having had the courage to admit that this problem is, has been, and will remain their own.

"For all those interested in German history, and perhaps not for them alone, the seminal question of the twentieth century is: How could Hitler have come to power? The question has been raised many times and has received as many answers," wrote Eberhard Jäckel.* The question of why (and how) Hitler came to power, wrote Ernst Deuerlein in a moving passage, "is unquestionably germane to the generations who supported Hitler, who rallied to him, or who had to endure and suffer under him. Beyond that it is addressed, too, to forthcoming generations, for whom Hitler is a historical phenomenon. . . . Undiminished and unchanging is the validity of the truth that Reinhold Schneider, a very serious German Catholic writer and thinker, stated in 1946: 'Our confrontation with Adolf Hitler is not yet ended and cannot be ended; in a way we are connected with him forever. In a most serious examination of our consciences we must try to become free—which means an acceptance of the burden of responsibility for those whose heart is strong enough to carry that burden.' . . . The German people, no matter how grotesque such a list might seem, are the people of Martin Luther, of Karl Marx and of Friedrich Engels and also of Adolf Hitler. . . . With Hitler, too, as Reinhold Schneider rightfully said, we are 'connected forever.' "†

This accords with the judgment of another German-speaking Catholic, the Austrian Friedrich Heer, who cites Schramm: "The confrontation with this strange, sinister [*unheimlich*] man is a political duty of the first order."‡ Heer continues: "After the collapse of

---

*These are the first two sentences of JH, p. 1.

†D, p. 158. Also D, p. 159: "Long-lasting developments of German history became actualized through events during and after the First World War, creating situations of mass psychology that not only made the rise of Hitler possible but helped to evoke it."

‡HR, p. 11.

his rule, after his death, after the triumph of the Allies, in German lands, especially in Christian and conservative circles, [people] were willing to regard Hitler as a daemon, an anti-Christ, as a phenomenon beyond understanding, disappearing [thus] into metaphysical clouds. This retreat into a . . . metaphysical hell . . . served, first of all, as a kind of relief: one did not want to admit that one was also responsible for the rise, for the assumption of power, for the Europe-wide destructive achievements of this man."

In his massive biography Fest is sometimes, at least implicitly, ambiguous about such an assumption of a unique German responsibility. Yes, Germany was a special place. There evidently existed "national characteristics that had made National Socialism different from the Fascistic movements of other countries, but then Hitler had found obedient followers everywhere." And: "Even though every nation carries in itself the responsibility for its history," it is wrong "to deny the recognition that in [Hitler] culminated the powerful tendency of a time that marked the entire first half of the century."* This may be too Hegelian, with its implication of Zeitgeist, but there is truth in Fest's conclusion: "In the end it is also certain that he could not have destroyed Europe without [a] concurrence from the latter." In sum: "He was much less a great contradiction than the reflection [*Spiegelbild*—literally "mirror image"] of his times." The young Zitelmann, in his early commentary on "Hitler-research,"† which contains interesting and insightful commentaries and criticisms of Hitler's various biographers, distinguishes the external circumstances that allowed Hitler to assume power and to accomplish his extraordinary success from what Zitelmann—in my opinion employing the wrong term—calls the "subjective" factor; that is, the characteristics of Hitler's personality.

In 1985 Martin Broszat summed up the problem: "Extraordinary in our situation is the necessity, as well as the difficulty, of fitting National Socialism properly into German history."‡ Haffner asked

---

*F, pp. 516–17; F, p. 1024.

†"Hitlers Erfolge—Erklärungsversuche in der Hitler-Forschung," in *Neue Politische Literatur* (hereafter: NPL), 1982, p. 22.

‡In *Merkur*, 8 May 1985.

the concordant question: "Did the Third Reich represent continuity in the history of Germany, or did it depart from the beaten path? The simple answer is that it contained elements of both continuity and discontinuity, and that continuity predominated."* This is significant because Haffner was a conservative—but also someone deeply aware of what Armin Mohler and others had called "The Conservative Revolution" among important German thinkers and writers in the 1920s who thought that Germany must represent something new, breaking out from an antiquated liberalism and parliamentarianism, in the direction of a stronger, brighter, sun-laden future.†

However, it was *not* inevitable—as some Germanophobes during and after the war, including the American journalist William Shirer, wrote—that German history unavoidably and necessarily culminated in Hitler. That is, too, why the debate among German (and sometimes English) historians about a Special German Path in modern history ("Sonderweg"), meaning a departure from Western democratic development, going back to the failure of a German democratic revolution in 1848 and even earlier, may be exaggerated. Not only Germany but the majority of the present nations of Europe refused to follow or adopt the French, the British, the American, the Swiss, the Scandinavian, or other Western models in the 1920s and 1930s. Still, some of the statements of serious German historians during the "Sonderweg" discussion are worth

---

*HF/AI, p. 211.

†Haffner cites, in some detail, the poet Stefan George in 1921, who prophesied the coming of an age which "Brings forth the one who helps, the Man / He bursts the chains, restores on fields of rubble / His order; scourges those who've gone astray / Back to eternal justice, where the great / Is great again, and master once more master / Obedience reigns, and on the people's banner / Pins the true sign and through wild storm and terror / Of the red dawn he leads his faithful band / To the day's deed—the New Reich's planting." George was (as were some others) a prophet of *a* Third Reich; but he disliked Hitler, and left Germany in 1933 for Switzerland, where he died. One of his last close followers was the hero Count Stauffenberg, who attempted to kill Hitler in 1944. "The chapter of German intellectual history entitled 'George-Hitler-Stauffenberg' still remains to be written." (These quotes from the American edition of *The Meaning of Hitler*.)

considering.* The historian Thomas Nipperdey warned against the unquestioning acceptance of the "Sonderweg" as a cliché. On the other hand, the sociologist Kurt Sontheimer: ". . . eliminating the thesis of the German 'Sonderweg' means breaking the back of the German political consensus after 1945 . . . if historians, albeit with the best of scholarly intentions, incline to deny it, they must at least know that, willingly or unwillingly, they contribute to those political forces that tend to oppose our new political and moral order after 1945." The thoughtful historian Karl Dietrich Bracher distinguished between a particular German mentality ("Sonderbewusstsein")† and the "Sonderweg." "The German 'Sonderweg' should be limited to the era of [the Third Reich] but the strength of the particular German mentality [*Sonderbewusstsein*] that had arisen already with its opposition to the French Revolution and grew stronger after 1870 and 1918 must be emphasized. Out of its exaggerated perspectives [and, I would add, rhetoric] it became a power in politics, out of a myth reality. The road from democracy to dictatorship was not a particular German case, but the radical nature of the National Socialist dictatorship corresponded to the power of a German ideology that in 1933–1945 became a political and totalitarian reality."‡

From a very broad historical perspective it may be said that the two world wars of the twentieth century represented, among other things, the last attempt of a state to dominate most of Europe. Spain was the great European power in the sixteenth century, France in the seventeenth and eighteenth centuries, Britain was the largest world power (and an important factor in the European balance of power) during the nineteenth century, and in the twentieth century it was Germany's turn, in both the First and the Second World Wars. Yes, there was a connection between the two world wars, and it is imaginable—indeed probable—that sometime in the late 1930s Germany might have risen to be the dominant power in Europe without Hitler. Yet in more than one important sense there were fundamental differences between the two world wars. I am not only thinking of the terrible conduct of World War II, when many of the previous distinctions between armies and civilians disappeared. What we must consider is Hitler's ability to engage an entire people (or at least the overwhelming majority of a people) in a war for his aims. There is a crucial statement in *Mein Kampf*: "Either Germany will become a World Power or she will not exist." (That most Germans thought that the war was forced upon them by their enemies is another question; that was not altogether different from their thinking about World War I.) German nationalism and German national unity had been powerful forces during World War I, too. Deeply ingrained national habits of obedience and discipline carried through into World War II. But the psychic (and the social) structure of the achievements of the German people in World War II had changed, and that was both the condition and the result of Hitler. *Without* Hitler the Germans could not have achieved what they did; and Hitler could not have achieved what he did *without* the German people—more precisely, without his overwhelming acceptance by most of them.

Still, the subject of this chapter is not a history of the German people during the Third Reich; it is that of Hitler's relationship to the German people. And in this respect there is a duality—perhaps a divergence—of German tendencies still extant. On the one hand there is the previously mentioned tendency to blame everything on Hitler—even among some historians who have been engaged in a cautious revision of their perception of some of the realities of the Third Reich (evident, among other things, in the Historians' Controversy). On the other hand, there is the inclination of men and women of a now disappearing German generation to think better of Hitler than of the National Socialist hierarchy, often expressed in such exclamations as: "If only the Führer knew!" ("Wenn das der Führer wusste!") As Bracher stated in 1977: "It was not with Himmler, Bormann, and Heydrich, also not with the National Socialist Party, but with Hitler that the German people identified itself enthusiastically. In this there exists an essential problem, especially for German historians. . . . To identify the sources of this fateful mistake of the past and to research it without minimizing it ["bagatellisieren"] remains a task of German historical scholarship. Ignoring it means the loss of its commitment to truth.*

There remains the other side of this question, which is Hitler's affection for the German people. A quarter century ago, I wrote that "the fundamental source of Hitler's strength was hatred. Compared to the power of his hatreds, even his love for his people—the living purpose of a great national leader—amounted to little. In this he was quite unlike Napoleon."† Perhaps "little" is not the right word, for in any case, love is a matter of quality, not of quantity. And—as also in other instances—ambiguities in Hitler's thinking are discernible in such a complex matter.‡ Many German historians—again, understandably—have made much of some of Hitler's remarks, especially toward the end of the war, about Germans being a people who deserved to perish if they proved to have been too weak. Yet at the same time (on 2 April 1945, for instance), he spoke of his "unbreakable faith in the future of the German people."** In

---

*In VFZ, October 1977, p. 745. Also Gisevius, GI, p. 7: ". . . especially we Germans must see clearly that this man has never been apart from us. We have not only endured the phenomenon of Hitler—we had contributed to its formation ["mitgestaltet"].

†In LEW, p. 166.

‡On one side there is Hans Frank: "Volk and Führer, Führer and Volk were betrothed. Each searched and desired the other, each trusted the other." On the other side Haffner: "Did he love the Germans? . . . It was only as an instrument of power that he was ever genuinely interested in them. He had great ambitions for Germany, and in that he found himself at one with the Germans of his generation." (HF/AN, p. 164) "During the final years, he increasingly despised them." (No.) " . . . He no longer sought contact with them." (Yes.) (HF/AN, p. 141)

**The evidence is contradictory. Schramm (SCH, p. 4) cites Hitler at one of his table conversations, 5 July 1942: ". . . in the struggle of peoples those with the better average quality will always be the victors . . . the natural order of things would be disrupted if the inferior should master the superior." Schramm also cites (p. 176) the report of General Carl Hilpert, dictated to his war diaries, on 18 April 1945: "Hitler leaned back and began a long lecture on the struggle of the German people. It culminated with the words: 'If the German people loses the war, it will have proved itself not worthy of me' " ["meiner nicht würdig"]. Yet on the same page: "The more people have to endure, the more magnificent would be the ultimate rebirth of eternal Germany."

March 1945, Speer was deeply shocked when Hitler ordered the destruction of all factories, plants, bridges, and the like before the retreating German lines in the west. But Speer also recorded his impression that by the end of March Hitler no longer seemed to insist on that. What he insisted on, till the very end, was that the Allies wanted to destroy the German people.*

IN A MOST TRENCHANT (though, alas, seldom sufficiently contemplated) short chapter—"Some Characteristics of Historians in Democratic Times"—in the second volume of *Democracy in America* Tocqueville made some very important statements about the problems of history in the then coming mass democratic age. Among other matters, he suggested that, contrary to expectations at first sight, a proper reconstruction of the history of peoples will be a more difficult task than the reconstruction of history at the time of aristocratic societies. Despite the increasing openness of all kinds of archives during the last one hundred years, this has proved true. Of course, it is a mistake to believe that the phenomenon—as we shall soon see, imprecisely so named—of public opinion became a factor not only during the last century or two. It has played a role from the beginning of history. As Pascal wrote in his *Pensées*: "Opinion" is after all "the queen of the world." But it is also true that the evolution of modern history toward democracy (and by this I do not only mean the evolution of universal education but the evolution of consciousness), what may be called "the structure of events" has undergone changes, by which I mean an increasing intrusion of mind into matter. Contrary not only to Marx but also to Adam Smith and, indeed, to all materialist philosophies, it is at least

---

*An interesting observation by Klaus-Dietmar Henke, *Die amerikanische Besetzung Deutschlands*, M, 1995, p. 308. Allied propaganda was directed against Nazism and militarism, not against the German people. "It is remarkable that Hitler was personally and accurately concerned with this, and that he wanted to falsify the expressed intentions of the Allies. In February 1945 he looked over the text of a speech by Hermann Esser which he changed only in one way. Each time Esser wrote that in Yalta 'the destruction of National Socialism' had been decided, [Hitler] changed the wording into 'destruction of the German people.' "

arguable that what matters principally—not only within private lives but in the events of the world at large—is what people think and believe; and that the very material organization of the world is but the consequence of that. And this is as applicable to the Hitler era as, for example, to "market" or "consumer research"—because of Hitler's dependence on the German people, a dependence of which he was wholly aware, and which was different in both kind and degree from—perhaps both deeper and greater than—that kind of dependence in the cases of Cromwell or Napoleon or perhaps even of Mussolini and Stalin.

But there are peculiar problems here which the historian has to deal with. The modern "sampling techniques" of "public opinion research" are relatively new (Gallup's Institute was established in the United States in 1935)—and we shall soon turn to its inevitable and, alas, seldom considered limitations. Add to this the academic trend away from political to social history, which began to affect German historians after 1965–1970. Analyses and, what is perhaps more important, descriptions of the sentiments and the opinions of German people during the Third Reich, particularly involving their relationship to Hitler, of course existed earlier, sometimes in insightful passages in the memoirs of contemporaries and other participant observers; but systematic studies of that relationship appeared only during the last twenty or twenty-five years.* All of the authors have been aware of the complexities of their subject. Still, many of the most valuable of these works dealt with how Hitler had come to power,† few of them with his relationship to people thereafter and during the war.

---

*A few examples. Thomas Childers, *The Nazi Voter* (Chapel Hill, N.C., 1983); Jürgen W. Falter, *Hitlers Wähler* (M, 1991); the serious and methodically valuable Ian Kershaw, KER/HM, and his pioneer study, *Popular Opinion and Political Dissent in the Third Reich, Bavaria 1933–1945* (Oxford, 1983) (hereafter: KER PO/PD); the especially insightful J. P. Stern, *Hitler: Der Führer und das Volk* (B, 1975); and the important Steinert, ST/HK/D; there are many others.

†In addition to many of the excellent and now standard works about the end of the Weimar Republic (Bracher, for example), reconstructions of popular opinions and attitudes may be found in *1933: Wie die Deutschen Hitler zur Macht verhalfen*, Brodersen, Humann, v. Paczensky, eds. (Hamburg, 1983); also Josef Becker, ed., *1933: Fünfzig Jahre danach* (M, 1983).

Complicated and difficult as the subject of German popular opinion may be, materials for its study do exist—in addition to a myriad of personal papers, recollections, police reports, memoirs, and recorded observations of foreign observers. For more than thirty years, we have been aware of the "opinion" summaries gathered by Himmler's Security Office (Sicherheitsdienst), under the title *Meldungen aus dem Reich*, first edited and published by Heinz Boberach in 1966 (with seventeen volumes now in print), and files and files of them have been at the disposal of researchers. Their value is, of course, limited by the character of the organization that attempted to collect, evaluate, and summarize such random expressions of the population; they are *reported* opinion, and reported by men thoroughly committed to the regime; but they are useful and significant in more than one way. (There is also evidence that Hitler read some of them.) During the last twenty-five years or so, there emerged other "sources": for example, the very interesting and thoughtful 1933–40 summaries of SOPADE, the Social Democrats' exile organization;* and there are other reports that deal with popular opinion and popular morale by other authorities of the Third Reich (especially by the so-called *Regierungspräsidenten*, particularly in Bavaria).

"The concept of public opinion," wrote Marlis Steinert in her thoughtful introduction to ST/HK/D, remains (especially in Germany, now as well as in the past) unclear and debatable; its scientific definition is more or less like a "squaring of the circle."† This is not only applicable to Germany or to the history of the Hitler era. That kind of "research" is only in its infancy. This is not the place to discuss or even to sum up the problems of this vast and complicated subject; but allow me to state a few—I think necessary, and overdue—distinctions that I made more than thirty years ago,‡ only because they may be relevant to our subject here. There is a differ-

---

*Kershaw, PO/PD, p. 9: ". . . a most nuanced assessment of the patterns of popular opinion in the Third Reich." In an article by Bernd Stöver, "Loyalität statt Widerstand. Die sozialistische Exilberichte und ihr Bild von III. Reich," in VFZ, July 1995, p. 470: These reports "are not so much sources [proving] the resistance of any group in the population as documentations of the existing loyalty to the regime."

†ST/HK/D, p. 23.

‡In Lukacs, HC, pp. 69–92.

ence between public opinion and popular sentiment. (Kershaw, above, prefers to use the term "popular opinion.") What is "public" is not necessarily "popular"; and "opinion" is not identical with "sentiment." (The subtitle of Marlis Steinert's study suggests this: It is "Stimmung und Haltung der deutschen Bevölkerung im Zweiten Weltkrieg"—and note that the German "Stimmung" means sentiment rather than opinion; in other words, an inclination rather than an actuality—while "Haltung" suggests something like character, attitude, or behavior.) To this we ought to add the inadequacy of quantitative formulations of "public opinion." Such numerical affirmations are useful, and even close to being precise when it comes to electoral predictions—that is, to questions involving *choices*. But choice is not necessarily identical with opinion (especially when it involves a choice of predetermined and fixed alternatives, as in the case of electoral procedures). While each vote amounts to one vote and to nothing else, both the intensity and the influence of opinions vary. Moreover, history is full of examples of "hard minorities" and "soft majorities"—with the influence of the former often being larger than its numbers might indicate. This applies to the German people in the Hitler era, too.* If, on the basis of nearly discovered and reliable evidence, someone should convincingly prove that at a certain time "only" 20 percent of Germans were opposed to Hitler, this does not mean that 80 percent of the rest were convinced Hitlerites; conversely, a convincing study indicating that at a certain time "only 20 percent" were unquestioning followers of Hitler does not mean that

---

*HC, pp. 92–93, quoting the eminent Dutch historian Pieter Geyl in an essay about the American Civil War: "Did the majority of the Netherlands people will the complete rupture with Philip II and with the Roman Church? . . . No. Did the majority of the English people will the overthrow of the monarchy and the execution of Charles I? . . . No. Did the French people will the Republic and the execution of Louis XVI? . . . No. Did the majority of the German people in 1933 want Hitler, did they will war? No." The very election of 1860, in which Lincoln polled less than 40 percent of the votes, proves that the majority of the American people had not deliberately willed the Civil War; but Geyl rightly asks: "Does this prove that the war might therefore have been avoided? Is it not rather one more proof of the general truth that the course of history is not governed by the conscious will of the majority?"

80 percent were his committed opponents.* (Also, belief in Hitler and belief in National Socialism were not always the same thing.) Furthermore, it is not always, and not necessarily, true that a mass is more than the sum of its individual components. In many ways a collective is *less* than that, since its members are men and women, Catholics and Protestants and atheists, former monarchists and former Socialists, and so forth; and the interesting question is *how* a German Catholic or a former Socialist voter became either a partially or fully committed believer in Hitler. A further difficulty presents itself with the German terms "Volksgefühl," "Volksstimmung," and "Volksmeinung" (especially employed by Zitelmann), which are only imprecisely translatable into English ("popular" or "national feeling," "sentiment," "opinion"), and are undefinable and overlapping. This touches on yet another particular problem, which is that of the categories and tendencies of German rhetoric—already evident in the tone of German public statements and publications during World War I, when, for example, French or British nationalism was often as sharp or even brutal as the German; but somehow the *rhetoric* of the Germans was different. Here we must recognize that, Freud notwithstanding, speech is not only an expression of thought, but that habits and patterns of speech have an evident, and often ascertainable, effect on habits and patterns of thought.†

Closely connected with this is another necessary recognition: that

---

*Kershaw in PO/PD, p. vii, is very good about this: His book "is about the muddled majority, neither full-hearted Nazis nor outright opponents, whose attitudes at one and the same time betray signs of Nazi ideological penetration and yet show the clear limits of propaganda manipulation. The picture painted is not a simple, straightforward, and clear-cut one."

†Some of this is ascertainable in the memoirs of German generals and other high officials of the Third Reich. A careful study of the gradual (though rapid) adjustment of the German press to the era of the Third Reich in 1933 is, as yet, missing. About "adjustment"—great writers such as Tocqueville and Fontane gave us incomparable portraits of what happened in 1848 in Paris or in Berlin, but such portraits about 1933 hardly exist, partly because, as I attempted to express earlier, "the structure of events" and the mental habits of large numbers of people were not what they were a century before.

of the difference between mentality and ideology. For Hitler expected more of the mentality*—of the mental habits and the predictable mental reactions—of the German people than of their wholesale acceptance of the National Socialist ideology. As he wrote in *Mein Kampf*: "To lead means to be able to move the masses."

BUT ENOUGH OF THESE methodological—or, more properly, epistemological—considerations. Our subject is Hitler's popularity, and its variations.† To begin with, there are serious reasons to question the widely accepted thesis, according to which the 1930–33 Depression not only contributed to but made it possible for Hitler to acquire power. We know that a most important step—literally a breakthrough—in his fortunes was the September 1930 Reichstag election, when the National Socialists received nearly seven times more votes than they did two years before—from less than 3 to almost 19 percent of all votes cast. Yet historians have devoted relatively little attention to the already rapid increase of National Socialist votes in the summer of 1929 and in early 1930 in the municipal and state elections (in Saxony, Mecklenburg, Baden, for instance), rising at times to 13 or 14 percent. This happened *before* the worldwide Depression and the tide of unemployment in Weimar Germany. Some historians have remarked that during his crucial ascent from 1930 to 1933, which coincided with the worst years of the Depression, Hitler had no definite economic program—in other words, his appeal was *not* primarily, and perhaps

---

*"Mentality," here, is not altogether identical with the now fashionable use of *mentalités* among historians. This is a greatly overdue recognition (especially among French academics) of the fatal shortcomings of a materialist philosophy and reconstruction of history. Admittedly a difficult task, calling for sensitive minds and perspectives, it must mean more than particular references to the "mental climate" of a certain place and time.

†Steinert, in ST/HK/D, p. 336, makes the convincing argument against those who have claimed that Hitler's success was due to his radio speeches and that he would have been greatly handicapped by his television image. As Goebbels proved, pictorial materials were more easily manipulated and on occasion falsified than was voice or text.

scarcely at all, economic. What came to the fore in 1930 and after was a tremendous surge of German nationalism*—among all classes, and significantly among those who were worst affected by unemployment and other economic woes. "The workingmen have no country," Marx wrote. He could not have been more wrong— something that was already evident in 1914, and even more in the 1930s. Haffner is especially commendable for having recognized this. German nationalism "now suddenly became part of every-day political discourse. Even the Communists began to speak in nationalistic tones. . . ."† And what happened in Germany in 1933 and after proves again the superior quality of Proudhon's insight

---

*A very telling description of a significant episode in Heiden, HD, pp. 231–32. In April 1928 Stresemann spoke in the Bürgerbraukeller in Munich, a good speech. A group of young National Socialists entered, shouting, and then began to sing "Deutschland, Deutschland über alles!"—and the chairman of the meeting stood up and sang with them. Stresemann was white with fury at the cowardice of this man. That night he had a kidney attack; a year later he died. "The meeting was destroyed—thanks to the cowardice of its organizers. . . . When Stresemann confronted them later, one of them answered: 'Herr Minister, one had to show these boys that we are just as good Germans as they!' Instead of having shown them the door. Afraid not to look sufficiently 'national' to a ruffian, they abandoned their dignity. What more remains to be said? Thus would Hitler come to power."

†HF/AI, pp. 169–70. As late as *17 May 1933* there were still some Social Democratic deputies sitting in the Reichstag who applauded Hitler's foreign-policy speech, about greatness coming to Germany—probably sincerely, and not because of mere opportunism.

In a thoughtful article P. Stadler, in HZ, 1988, p. 25: Germany was different from other countries; Hitler rose to power by largely democratic means. "Historical research, in masterful analyses—as in Bracher's seminal work—worked out and reconstructed the events leading to January 1933, illuminating the responsibility of people [around Hindenburg] and thus contributing essentially to [the historical recognition] of important factors. . . . On the other hand it did not emphasize that the main responsibility is not to be found among the Papens, etc., but with the average German voter."

To this let me add: To what extent are people responsible for their regimes? In 1792–93, in France, the Jacobins were not a majority. In 1917, the Bolsheviks in Russia were not. In 1922, the Fascists in Italy were not. But Hitler had a large plurality, a near-majority, behind him in 1933—as a matter of fact, the July 1932 elections should have made him chancellor then, except for Hindenburg's temporary reluctance.

over that of Marx—that people respond not to social contracts but to realities of power.*

Hitler understood that thoroughly. Kershaw noted: "Only one of the four general plebiscites to take place during the Third Reich did not follow a major foreign-policy triumph. Externally, the Western powers had not merely missed an opportunity of halting German expansion: they had to witness the enormous popularity boost which [the Rhineland occupation] had given Hitler."† One cannot, and should not, blame the German people for being impressed with how foreign statesmen treated and praised Hitler in the 1930s. At the same time their mute acceptance—indeed, their approval—of Hitler's brutal mass executions in June 1934 shocks us in retrospect. As Haffner put it, "if one can speak of the collective guilt of the German people, then perhaps this is where it all began."

"What kind of state was Germany during that time? Contrary to widely held beliefs, it was not a one-party state, unlike the German Democratic Republic or the Soviet Union, dominated by a highly structured political party. The National Socialist Party had no Central Committee, no Politburo, and Hitler never convened executive committee meetings. . . . It was not the party that dominated the state but Hitler who dominated everything, including the party . . .

Again Haffner, HF/AI, pp. 185–86: "The Germans in the Thirties became a politically unified nation. It is a process that is still not fully understood, probably because people like to forget that in the spring and early summer of 1933 something like a national coming together was indeed taking place, not necessarily behind the National Socialist Party, but behind Adolf Hitler, behind the Führer, as he was beginning to be called." Also M. Broszat, *Nach Hitler*. Der schwierige Umgang mit unserer Geschichte (M, 1986), p. 164: "The . . . populist attraction of National Socialism was more important than its ideological indoctrination of the masses."

*Or consider that Ferdinand Lassalle, the founder of German Socialism, told Bismarck in 1863: "a secret . . . that the working class has an instinctive inclination to accept dictatorship." In Reinhold Schneider, *Der Balkon* (Frankfurt, 1959), p. 120: "an insight of immense significance, that of the guilt and shame of twelve years. . . ." Or Julius Fröbel, a German Liberal, in 1848: "The German nation had enough of principles and doctrines, of literary reputations and a life devoted to theory. What it wants is power, power, power; and who gives it power will be revered, more than it dreams of."

†KER, p. 105. This was already so well before 1936: Hitler's rejection of the League of Nations, or the Saar plebiscite, for example.

Hitler's Third Reich was not a party state, it was a Führer state. . . . A colossal achievement to have united virtually the entire nation behind him [by 1938]—and accomplished in less than ten years! Accomplished, moreover, on the whole not by demagogy but by achievement. . . ." Thus wrote Sebastian Haffner, a liberal conservative with an unimpeachable intellectual reputation. And Hans Frank, in the shadow of the gibbet: the Party Congress in 1938 was Hitler's "wedding with the German people. . . . Above everything smiled the great magician Hitler, blessing, bewitching, touching their hearts. . . ."* These are emotional images in the memory of a desperate man. Yet we ought not to ignore other such evidence of national confidence, such as the fantastically high German marriage and birthrates in 1938–39, together with the extraordinary drop in the number of suicides, and so forth.

We have seen that in 1939 the German people, after so many years of anti-Communist propaganda, reacted to Hitler's pact with Stalin without a murmur, indeed with sentiments of admiration—by which Hitler himself was surprised, and relieved. Thereafter, during the war German opinion and sentiment sometimes lagged behind Hitler,† and sometimes it ran ahead of him—as in the summer of 1940, when all of the surveys reported an impatience among the people about the expected invasion of England: "Wann geht es los?" "What are we waiting for?"

"The Germans," wrote Jäckel, "loved him rather than feared him." (This was not true of Russians under Stalin.) "Under Hitler the Germans never doubted, despaired, or revolted as they might have under a tyrant. Forces from abroad had to take him away from them, and only then was the spell that had bound them to [him] for over twelve years broken. . . ."‡ As late as September 1944, a call for volunteers of the year 1928 (fifteen- and sixteen-year-olds) in the Catholic "Westmark" (the Saar and the Palatinate) resulted in 96 percent volunteering. Kettenacker cites a British survey of German

---

*HF/AN, p. 34; HF/AI, p. 194; Frank, FR, p. 264.

†Steinert, ST/HK/D, p. 91, agrees with Helmut Krausnick, who wrote that in September 1939 the majority followed Hitler into the war with a "reluctant loyalty [widerwillige Loyalität]."

‡JH, pp. 89–90. "And broken immediately." This may be put too simply.

prisoners of war near the end of the war: Not more than 9 percent were convinced anti-Nazis, 15 percent were passive anti-Nazis.* We must of course consider the cohesion of soldiers in camps run by an enemy; and there is much evidence that within Germany, after mid-January 1945, the belief in National Socialism was eroding. Then, and only then, began the erosion of trust in Hitler, too. But even then it was not an overall development.

The mass of the German people admired, and perhaps even loved, Hitler, while they did not necessarily admire or love National Socialism and the party. We must, perhaps for the last time, observe this distinction—keeping in mind, too, the limitations of such a categorical statement, for there were overlappings and split-mindedness at work, too. The German people believed in Hitler. Or: they put their faith in him. This may not be excusable. But it was understandable. It had much to do not only with his startling successes, with his elevation of German prestige in the world, but with the national prosperity he achieved soon after his assumption of power. "Hitler," wrote Hans Frank from prison, "had become the leading principle of all the nation's deeds and hopes. . . . [But] about the party, the bureaucracy, the ss and many other things the people had many reservations [Sehr ablehnend] . . . 'Der Führer,' 'der Hitler,' was the exception. Quite popular were such expressions as: 'The Führer does not know about that!' or: 'The Führer will get into this!' Or: 'The good Führer, how he is being misused!' "† Written shortly before his execution—note Frank's title, "Within Sight of the Gallows"—he saw in this the very obverse of a poverty in the national imagination; rather, it was a sentimental German kind of faith, and, indeed, touched by a primitive loyalty. His pages,

---

*Lothar Kettenacker, "Sozialpsychologische Aspekte der Führerherrschaft," in *Der Führerstaat: Mythos und Realität*, s, 1981, p. 107. Henke, p. 806: At the end of 1944, 40 percent of German prisoners of war still believed in a German victory; in the first months of 1945, 44 percent, but in early March only 11 percent. (Yet a belief in a German victory was not necessarily identical to loyalty to National Socialism or even to Hitler.)

†Frank, pp. 260–61. Another high official, Otto Dietrich, Hitler's press secretary, in *Hitler* (Chicago, 1955), "The majority of the German people had put their trust in a single man, had revered him like a saint and loved him as a father. This man then led them into the greatest catastrophe of their history."

written in nerve-racked haste, have all the marks of feverish sentimentality and exaggeration. They were not really meant to rehabilitate Hitler but to insist on the sources and the elements of that kind of faith (implicitly, of course, also his own), and they cannot be entirely ignored.

Thirty-five or forty years later, historians of another German generation attempted to comprehend this phenomenon. Their approach was perhaps the opposite of Frank's, since they did not attempt to revise the portrait of Hitler, though they did attempt to alter some of the accepted views of the Third Reich. This was mostly what the Historians' Controversy was about. An early example of their argumentation was a statement by Klaus Hildebrand in 1981: "One must not speak of National Socialism but of Hitlerism."* This is too simplistic. In his crisp and terse summary of the Historians' Controversy, Gerhard Schreiber wrote in 1988: "The 'Historikerstreit' involved, first of all, two assertions. One suggested that the genocide of the Jews was, in its way, a reaction of fear [Angstreaktion] to the Bolshevik class war with its mass murders, while the other aimed to suggest that the attack on the Soviet Union in 1941 may have been a preventive war. In the end both suggestions, whether consciously or not, lead to a relativization of the National Socialist era. . . . Both controversies are emotionalized and politicized to a high degree. . . ."†
Jürgen Habermas, whose article started the controversy, asserted that Michael Stürmer had raised the question: "How far was the war Hitler's war and how far a war of the Germans?" Here I am inclined to repeat my observation of the German inclination to a two-war theory: that the war against the Soviet Union may have been inevitable, while the war against the West was regrettable, and that the latter was, after all, still a war waged within traditional limits, a "normal European war" [europäisches Normalkrieg]. But was it? Were Hitler's treatment of the Polish people, his invasion of Denmark and Norway, his occupation and rule of France, his bombing of

---

*In *Der Führerstaat: Mythos und Realität*, s, 1981, p. 75. (This was the volume in which the English historian Tim Mason first produced the "functionalist" adjective.)

†In SCHRB, preface to the 1988 edition.

Rotterdam, Coventry, Belgrade, his treatment of the Jews before 1941, categorizable within the confines of a "Normalkrieg"? As Horst Möller wrote: "Judgment about the National Socialist dictatorship is a key to the historical-political consciousness of the [West German] republic. Mutations in the assessment of that era of German history are often seen as being seismographic for our political culture."* There are reasons to believe that (as, among others, Zitelmann's example suggests) a revision of the history of the Third Reich is going on and will continue to go on, among historians. This is inevitable and not necessarily regrettable. What matters are the purposes and, consequently, the quality of such a revisionism: for revision may suggest or even lead to rehabilitation—and a certain kind of revisionism may, in the end, lead to a rehabilitation not only of some of the character and achievements of the Third Reich but eventually, though implicitly, of Hitler.

"War alles falsch?" "Was everything wrong?" That was the question that many Germans asked when it came to a retrospective view of Wilhelmine Imperial Germany during the Weimar Republic (much later, in 1951, it was the title of a book by Joachim Kürenberg, appraising and defending the character of Kaiser William II). That book (a moderate publishing success) appealed to the memories of an older German generation. That phrase, "War alles falsch?," "Was everything wrong?," when applied to the Third Reich (and implicitly even to Hitler) involves not only the memories of the now dwindling German survivors of the 1930s and 1940s but also the sensitivities, perspectives, and inclinations of generations of Germans yet to come.

THE RESPONSIBILITY FOR HITLER of an older German generation, and especially of German nationalist conservatives, did exist. This generalization allows for many significant individual exceptions and requires certain qualifications about German "conservatism." Yet generalizations, like brooms, should sweep and not stand in a corner.

---

*HS, p. 323. Christian Meier quoted a leader of the Christian Democratic Party in 1983: Germans should finally "step out of the shadow of Hitler." (IIS, p. 51)

As some German historians, as well as Bullock, put it: Hitler was appointed to power not through a popular revolutionary movement but through the intrigues of conservatives such as Papen.* Perhaps for "not" I would put "less," but generally speaking, the statement is valid.† As Walter Euchner wrote during the Historians' Controversy: "Contrary to the Bolsheviks, the National Socialists . . . could accomplish their political aims with the voluntary support of a considerable part of the traditional elites."‡ And by March 1933 many of the latter responded to the desiderata of a Third Reich. This strange man, Hitler, was no longer only an inevitable element for a conservative and nationalist revival, a "faute de mieux," in place of something better, but someone who had become eminently respectable.** Thereafter Hitler's power contributed to his respectability

---

*Bullock's paragraph in BU, pp. 254–55, is a fair summary, and unexceptionable: ". . . the heaviest responsibility of all rests on the German Right, who not only failed to combine with the other parties in defence of the Republic but made Hitler their partner in a coalition government. The old ruling class of Imperial Germany had never reconciled itself to the loss of the war or to the overthrow of the monarchy in 1918. They were remarkably well treated by the Republican regime which followed. Many of them were left in positions of power and influence. . . . All this won neither their gratitude nor their loyalty. Whatever may be said of individuals, as a class they remained irreconcilable, contemptuous and hostile to the regime they continued to exploit. The word 'Nationalist,' which was the pride of the biggest Party of the Right, became synonymous with disloyalty to the Republic." In BU, p. 120, Bullock also makes a trenchant statement about the considerate treatment Hitler received at his 1924 trial: "Such were the penalties of high treason in a state where disloyalty to the regime was the surest recommendation to mercy."

†To this, however, we must add the stunning evidence from the Goebbels diaries—from 1930 and, in a way, even earlier—of Hitler's absolute conviction that he would be assuming power, sooner or later.

‡HS, p. 357. Fest noted that already in the summer of 1932, "conservatives" such as Papen, von Braun, and Schwerin von Krosigk doubted whether a government without Hitler could exist for long.

**One example: The old monarchist Field Marshal Mackensen was much impressed with Hitler at Potsdam in March 1933. He was somewhat critical of Hitler's mustache and hair but said "he won my heart as a statesman, soldier, and man." Even though men such as Mackensen had no political influence or following, Hitler understood them well. He awarded a large estate to Mackensen. In December 1939 he visited the aged martinet on his ninetieth birthday. In 1941, he allowed him to travel to the kaiser's funeral in Holland on a special train.

(perhaps especially among the people at large); but the converse was also true: His respectability contributed to his power (perhaps especially among the conservative elements of German society)—or at least to the feebleness of resistance against him. As Heer concluded: "Neither in German Catholicism nor in the Vatican did Hitler meet an opponent who was worthy of him [der ihm gewachsen war]."* Among all of the institutions, including the churches, of the Hitler era, the record of the Catholic Church—of some of the bishops and priests as well as some of the Catholic population—was, relatively speaking, the least compromised and was sometimes even inspiring. The historical literature devoted to that complicated subject is extensive. At the same time, some of the responses to Hitler by otherwise non-Nazi or even anti-Nazi members of the hierarchy are less than inspiring, especially in retrospect.†

---

*HR, p. 471.

†A few random examples. Cardinal Faulhaber, archbishop of Munich, to Hitler at the signing of the 1933 Concordat: "What the old parliaments and parties had not been able to accomplish in sixty years, your far-seeing statesmanship achieved in six months on a world-historical level . . . a great deed of immeasurable blessing." In 1936, Faulhaber visited Hitler at the Berghof. He was much impressed, agreeing entirely with Hitler about the necessary worldwide fight against Bolshevism. "The Führer also demonstrated social and diplomatic manners worthy of a born sovereign. . . ." HR, pp. 282, 316: "Evidently the Austrian charm of the Führer had impressed the Cardinal." Faulhaber's strong pastoral letter against Communism (on 27 December 1936) was made at Hitler's request. In 1936 even the principled and anti-Nazi Cardinal Preysing of Berlin remarked: "National Socialism in Berlin has undoubtedly eliminated the very dangerous agitations of Socialism and Communism as well as many phenomena of smut and dirt [Schmutz und Schund] so very dangerous to religion and morality." In Joachim Kuropka, ed., *Clemens August Graf von Galen. Neue Forschungen zum Leben und Wirken des Bischofs von Münster* (Münster, 1992), p. 211. The weak Cardinal Bertram of Breslau, then president of the Catholic Bishops' Conference, sent fulsome congratulatory telegrams to Hitler on the latter's birthdays. (In 1939 he said: "I told the children: Heil Hitler—this is valid for this world; Praised be Jesus Christ—that is the tie between earth and heaven." No neater formula can be imagined. Lukacs, LEW, p. 465.)

Public respectability for many German hierarchs was inseparable from expressions of nationalism. Bishop Berning in a letter to Göring in March 1942: "The entire nation must stand united, to accomplish the final [!] victory over its enemies." Kuropka, p. 357. About Bishop, later Cardinal, Galen's praise of the German invasion of Russia in 1941, in the same sermon in which he attacked the

There were elements of resistance to Hitler in institutions such as the church and the army—and Hitler knew that very well—but their activation was compromised not only by Hitler's undoubted powers but also by the respectability he had achieved as head of the state (as well as by at least some of his popular and accepted ideas). At the same time we *must* understand that in Germany (as elsewhere in Europe) the main and many of the most principled opponents of Hitler *were* traditionalists—believers in the patriotic, often religious, and above all moral and noble standards of an older and better world. In more than one way, surely, during the crucial phase of World War II (in 1940 and 1941) the struggle was less between Left and Right than between two Rights. This was as true of Stauffenberg and his circle in 1944,* as it was of Churchill and de Gaulle in 1940, and of untold examples of patriotic and religious men and women throughout Germany and Austria.

This is why Jäckel's otherwise convincing thesis (in *Hitlers Herrschaft*), which is a completion of his earlier *Hitlers Weltanschauung* about the long-range sources of Hitler's appeal and power, must be qualified. His survey of the long division in Germany between "Monarchists" and "Democrats"—or in other, perhaps less precise terms, between the German Right and Left—remains valuable and useful, as Jäckel traces convincingly and fairly accurately the contributions of the former Monarchists and of the Right to Hitler's assumption of power. But he writes hardly more than a page

---

National Socialist euthanasia policies (to which Hitler reacted by ordering the discontinuation of the large-scale euthanasia program). But consider, too, Galen's first sermon in April 1945, after Münster was liberated from Hitler by the British army: "My heart bleeds at the sight of the troops of our enemies [!] passing through." A particularly repellent—though atypical—episode: At the bishops' yearly conference in 1942, anxieties were raised when some priests reported that there were people in their church who refused to take communion together with Jewish Catholics, whose yellow stars were affixed to their clothes. Some priests were thus reluctant to distribute the Eucharist to Catholics of Jewish origin; others suggested special services for them. This did not come about, save for a few isolated instances, but also because by 1942 only a handful of such Catholics of Jewish origin remained.

*But then the brave Georg Elser, who tried to kill Hitler in November 1939, was a workingman.

about the, perhaps even more startling, passivity of the German working class and the millions of former Socialist and Communist voters, or about the unions, who, in 1933, "watched rather passively [Hitler's] assumption of power and then tried to adjust themselves to the new regime."* It would be wrong, I think, to attribute Jäckel's argumentation to the Social Democratic sympathies of this otherwise thoughtful historian. But in his intention to emphasize the responsibility of the German traditional classes for the inclination (whether actively or passively) to support Hitler, he overlooks something that many historians, and not only Marxists, have overlooked for more than a century: the inclination of the working classes, too, toward respectability—something that on many levels, and in many cases, has been inseparable from their nationalism. Added to this was Hitler's unquestionable ability not only to declare but actually to elevate the German industrial working class to newer and higher situations within the structure of German society (and in the armed forces). In chapter 3 we saw his consistently high estimation of the "working class" and his often expressed contempt for the "Bürgertum." During the last thirty years many studies have revised the earlier general opinion according to which Hitler's main support had come from the middle and lower-middle classes. In reality, the former boundaries between lower middle class and working class had begun to melt away during the Hitler era. More than that, there is ample evidence that among the workers support of Hitler and belief in him not only remained strong but endured to the very end. There are many accounts of this, from many sources.†

---

*JHH, pp. 49–50.

†Not only in Goebbels's diaries, where some of the significant items record workers' reactions to Hitler, even close to the end of the war. Also a report by the Reichspropaganda Ministry in December 1944, cited by Henke, p. 572: "The worker is the most reliable follower of the Führer and willing to shoulder any kind of burden." Steinert in ST/HK/D, p. 526, gives many examples of a "radical commitment to the war" among armament workers as late as the spring of 1945. This impressed Speer decisively, deterring him when he first began to think of the need to do away with Hitler. Kershaw is right in KER, p. 181: "Hitler's popularity among the German people, greatly reduced though it was since the heyday of 1940, was, given the conditions of the last war years, remarkable."

THERE *WAS* RESISTANCE to Hitler in Germany—a German resistance that was perhaps more admirable (and not only because of its obvious and often terrible risks) than the resistance of men and women in other nations that had been subjugated or were unwillingly allied with Hitler. It was limited to solitary persons, families, and small groups, and one varied and changing small minority conventicle within the only institution, the General Staff of the Army, that could have been effective (though that, too, was unlikely). This does not mean that, as I suggested earlier, a resistance to Hitler did not exist within the majorities, sometimes within the split minds of individual men and women. In any event, "resistance" meant a mental or actual reaction of opposition to Hitler (and we ought not to forget that, after all, the very word "resistance" suggests something that is *reactionary*). We must also consider that the anti-Jewish brutalities in Germany evoked *less* support among the German people* than among some Eastern peoples (examples: Romania, Latvia, Ukraine). This is not merely a tentative general statement about popular attitudes; it is evident from many of the recorded expressions of the time, and in the acts of many Germans who tried and dared to help Jews in the most difficult times. On the other hand, there were the brutal expressions and evident acts of a hard National Socialist minority, and the mute obedience and respect of the majority—less for National Socialism than for Hitler.

THE GENERALLY HELD VIEW, according to which respect for Hitler vanished within an instant of his death, also requires some qualifica-

---

*According to Haffner (HF/AI, pp. 208–09): ". . . Hitler's anti-Semitism was the line that separated the loyal followers of the Führer—the majority of the people— and the not insignificant minority of Antis, people who in the privacy of their homes railed against Hitler and his party, and who were convinced that this proved their adherence to traditional values even if they no longer dared to speak out, let alone act. There always existed a substantial number of Antis who later, after Hitler's fall, tried to describe themselves as the 'inner emigration,' or even as the 'resistance.' I believe that both these labels should be used with great caution." (I would say: with a mixture of respect and caution.)

tion. The majority of the German people, in the midst of their greatest dangers and shocks and tribulations, were stunned. Many of their remaining officials were unwilling and unable to come to terms with the phenomenon of their departed leader. After all, as late as March 1945 his successor, Admiral Doenitz, had addressed his commanders: "Let us place our trust unconditionally in Adolf Hitler's leadership. Believe me, in my two years as Navy Commander-in-Chief I have found that his strategic views always turned out right." During the days between Hitler's death and the final capitulation of Germany, Doenitz and most of his government continued to be respectful of Hitler. (Doenitz did not announce the dissolution of the party, nor did he remove the swastika flag or pictures of Hitler from government offices at Flensburg.) He announced on 2 May: Hitler's "struggle against the Bolshevists was made in behalf of Europe and the entire civilized world. . . . The Anglo-Americans are therefore no longer continuing the war in the interest of their peoples but only in order to promote the spread of Bolshevism in Europe."* His diary on the day after the capitulation, 9 May 1945: "The fundament for the continued existence of the German people is the national community created by National Socialism."†

That giving up the struggle against the West was preferable to giving up the struggle against the East was obvious by then. It was also obvious that for Germany, National Socialism was preferable to Bolshevism—among other things, because of the living standards of the German people. For a long time after the war, this notion that National Socialism was, after all, better than Bolshevism remained a strong article of belief, surely in West Germany (and also among some Americans in the anti-Communist 1950s). There were many reasons for such a belief: not only the prosperity that Hitler had

---

*Doenitz in Nuremberg, IMT, XIII, p. 33, cited by Maser: [Hitler] was "a tremendous personality . . . with extraordinary intelligence and willpower, with a truly universal culture [*Bildung*], with a powerfully impressive character and with an enormously suggestive power."

†This is perhaps the only instance where I must express my disagreement with the otherwise unexceptionable Schramm, SCH, p. 180: "That Admiral Doenitz, who unexpectedly succeeded to power, immediately initiated the surrender, remains a service for which he deserves no less recognition than General Weygand in France five years earlier." This estimation of Weygand is questionable.

brought to his people but the fact that Stalin had ordered the imprisoning and the killing of many more millions of his own people than had Hitler. Yet somehow all such comparisons are amiss. They lack moral substance. There are moral—and historical—reasons to ask whether National Socialism and Communism, and the misdeeds of Hitler and Stalin, should be compared at all.

In his contribution to the Historians' Controversy, Fest—defending Hillgruber and Nolte—advanced the disingenuous argument that making Germany particularly responsible for the totalitarian misdeeds of the Third Reich—that is, *more* responsible than Russia during Stalin's rule, because of the educational and cultural qualifications of the German people—amounts to an assumption of the *Herrenvolk* (Master Race) idea. A cogent answer to this was given by Christian Meier: "Is one a proponent of the ideology of 'Herrenvolk' when one states that through the long history of Germany one may presume civilizational and ethical developments other than those, say, of Russia or Turkey or Indochina?" Such a presumption involves not "privileges . . . but duties. . . . Should we not measure ourselves against these standards?"* I began this chapter by stating that the history of Germany—and of the German people—includes Hitler. But his place in that history was more extraordinary than Stalin's in the history of Russia. There was no Ivan the Terrible (whose rule, in many ways, resembled Stalin's) in the history of Germany. Stalin fits more into the pattern of Russian history than Hitler fits into that of Germany. Yet included in it he must be, alas.

---

*HS, p. 211.

8

Admirers and Defenders, Open and Hidden

Main arguments for Hitler's rehabilitation—
The relative hierarchy of its proponents—Their argumentation

W E HAVE NOW SEEN THAT more than fifty years after his death significant questions regarding Hitler remain. That condition is not unusual. History is not a physical science. *Biography* is not *biology*. Everything we know we know through retrospect, and retrospect is likely to change. There is another, unavoidable limitation of the human condition. While perspective is not identical with reality, it is an inevitable component of it. In his memoirs Kaiser William II wrote that "Historical truth is no less sacred than religion." Sacred, yes, but not pure,* for what is given to us is not the pure truth but the pursuit of truth; and that pursuit is inseparable from the purposes of the pursuers. This does not mean that truth is relative—that is, so variable as to be largely meaningless—and not the opposite of untruth. The "relativization" of Hitler and of National Socialism may not be the most fortunate of terms—except when it refers to the purposes of the "relativizers."

---

*Religion is not pure, either, because of the inevitable human alloy; but then without that alloy faith, like gold, is unusable.

When their purpose is his rehabilitation, that should be detectable from the relativizers' selection of their "facts" and of their own words. This is true of many of Hitler's admirers or defenders, whether they admit or realize their purposes or not. Some historians (Zitelmann, for example) evoke a now outdated (and originally Cartesian) physical vocabulary, suggesting that "subjective" prejudices have clouded an "objective" historical representation of Hitler. On the other hand, Maser refers to Hitler's unabashed admirer Hans Severus Ziegler's* "very subjectively composed book"—as if "subjective" were sufficiently explanatory.

Throughout this book we have met some of the arguments that professional and amateur historians and others have produced for the purpose of revising important elements in the history of Hitler; and this may be the place to sum up the main ones, as briefly as possible. Fifty years after his death, it is—or should be—uncontestable that Hitler was a more complicated—and also more secretive—man than has long been assumed; and that his powers of intelligence were considerable. At the same time, his apologists tend to emphasize the sensitive, the artistic, the surprisingly human side of his personality—often one-sidedly so. One-sided, too, is their portrait of the happiness and the prosperity that Hitler brought to the majority of the German people in the 1930s—without mentioning, let alone emphasizing, the darker elements in that overall picture. Then, among extreme apologists as well as among cautious rehabilitators, there is the tendency to exonerate Hitler—at least partially—from the responsibility of having started World War II. This is done by emphasizing the warlike purposes of his enemies, and their rigid unwillingness to compromise, particularly the Poles and the British.†

---

*In M/A, p. 283. Ziegler's *Wer war Hitler?* (Tübingen, 1970)—an extreme apologist and admirer.

†This tendency appears even in serious works. Two examples: Oswald Hauser, *England und das Dritte Reich. Eine dokumentierte Geschichte der englisch-deutschen Beziehungen von 1933 to 1939 auf Grund unveröffenlichen Akten aus dem britischen Staatsarchiv*, I-II (Göttingen and Z, 1982). A long commentary in SCHRB, p. 56. Schreiber: Hauser's tendency is "to exonerate Hitler, in part even to assert his innocence [teilweise sogar zu verharmlosen], while accusing the British side." To a much lesser extent, this is also applicable to Dietrich Aigner, *Das Ringen um England* (M, 1969).

In addition, there has been an increasing tendency to absolve Hitler, at least partly, for his most fateful step in the war, his decision to attack Russia in 1941, by arguing—on the basis of very questionable documentation—that Stalin was about to attack Germany in 1941.*
In preceding chapters I have frequently drawn attention to the two-war thesis, according to which the war against the Soviet Union was both understandable and excusable, since it amounted to a defense not only of Germany but of Europe and of Western civilization, Germany serving as a bulwark against Bolshevism. A consequent variant of this argument accuses the Allies, especially Churchill, of having been blind to the dangers of Communism, and thus having contributed to the collapse of Europe because of their hatred of Germany.†

Another instance of this kind of "relativization" is the minimization of the merits of the German resistance—of which the more extreme examples consist of blackening the characters of the July 1944 conspirators (as, indeed, of most of Hitler's opponents). We have, finally, seen Irving claim that Hitler was not responsible for the extermination of the Jews of Europe, that it was decided and perpetrated by others, and that places such as Auschwitz were work camps rather than death camps. Consequent to this are the argu-

---

*See, for example, Günter Gillessen in the respectable FAZ, 2 August 1995; other articles by this writer have blamed the horrors of the air war principally on the British.

†Example: the military historian Karl Klee, in his introduction to his study of Hitler's plans for the invasion of England, *Dokumente zum Unternehmen 'Seelöwe,'* I–II (Göttingen, 1959), I, p. 25: "The tragedy of what was to come is that the British, who concentrated only on the struggle against their immediate opponent, were ready to accept any partner—that means, also the Soviet Union—in that war. [The British] did not foresee that their policy would only lead to the replacement of a strong Germany by the overwhelming power of Russia." Lukacs, DL, pp. 214–15: "This argument—amounting, in essence, to a kind of selective indignation—appeals to some people even now, and not only in Germany. I am compelled to correct it here. It was not that only without that 'partner' the British could not expect to win. That 'partner' was forced into an alliance with Britain by Germany himself. It is also that Churchill saw the choice clearly: either all of Europe dominated by Germany; or—at worst—the eastern half of Europe dominated by Russia for a while; and half of Europe was better than none." There were Spanish newspapers that, as late as the 1960s, wrote on the anniversary of Hitler's death that "he had fallen at the head of his army in the struggle against Bolshevism."

ments in books and pamphlets by others to the effect that the accepted views of the extent of the Holocaust have been falsified by propagandists determined to obscure the "objective truth."

What is common in all of these works is their inordinate exaggeration. There *is* a grain of truth (or should we call it reality?) in almost all of them, but it is neither quantitatively nor qualitatively sufficient to command serious consideration. At the same time we must distinguish among these works and their authors. While eschewing a survey of pamphlets and books on the fringes of this kind of literature, we may distinguish a relative order among such "rehabilitators"—a relative hierarchy according to the ascending importance of the seriousness of their scholarship. We shall proceed from open admirers of Hitler (often those of an earlier generation of people who knew him) to such rehabilitators as Irving (and, at least partially, Toland), and then to some of the arguments of respected German writers and professional historians appearing during the Historians' Controversy and after.

WE MAY ESCHEW A DISCUSSION, or even a partial list, of the most extreme apologists for two reasons at least. One is the limited circle of their readership: Their books are published by small, sectarian, and seldom reputable firms; they are preaching to the convinced, or to those who are ready and willing to be convinced. The other is that oddly, or perhaps not so oddly, the authors of most of these extreme books and booklets are "not yet ready for Hitler." In most of their denials of the exterminations of Jews, and in their rehabilitations and apologias and, indeed, praise of such Third Reich institutions as the SS, for example, there is scarcely a direct mention of Hitler. It is as if he were a "subject" still too big and too dangerous to handle—even though it is evident that they admire him. More important, for the purposes of this book, are the reminiscences of those men and women who were personally acquainted with, employed by, or otherwise close to Hitler,* or have been (few of them are still alive fifty years after his demise) unwilling to condemn him or at least

---

*Examples: his pilot Hans Baur, his chauffeur Erich Kempka, his secretary Christa Schroeder.

compromise their loyalty to him in retrospect.* Their written or oral reminiscences were eagerly searched and scooped up by amateur historians, often with purposes of their own (as, for example, Irving or Toland)—yet, with all their limitations, it is perhaps regrettable that at least some of them, by and large, have been ignored by professional historians (as, for example, the memoirs of Hitler's secretary Christa Schroeder, a difficult and quarrelsome woman, meticulously annotated by the exemplary Anton Joachimsthaler).†

Widening this circle, we arrive at the memoirs and reminiscences of more important persons who were also close to Hitler, and whose aim *has been* explicit: to rehabilitate him.‡ Their books, too, have customarily been published by small extremist houses, without much of an echo in the wider sphere of readers. But some of them call for our attention, especially the unabashed apologist Hermann Giesler, the very title of whose book is telling: *Ein anderer Hitler*** (Another Hitler). Giesler was an architect, a young admirer and acquaintance of Oswald Spengler, and then of Adolf Hitler, who was impressed by Giesler's talents and by his loyalty. Among his favorite architects Giesler was second only to Speer. While Speer's achievements included a large and detailed model of a future monumental construction of central Berlin, presented to Hitler in 1940, Giesler's included the monumental model of a future Linz that he presented to Hitler in February 1945, when he had been encouraged by Bormann, who told Giesler that Hitler needed that kind of

---

*Examples: Friedrich Grimm, Lothar Rendulic, Hans Rudel, Annelise Ribbentrop, Otto Skorzeny, W. von Asenbach, Erich Kern.

I am excluding the, often valuable, memoirs and reminiscences of such secretarial or military aides of Hitler whose purposes did *not* include, even implicitly, a rehabilitation of his historical portrait (examples: Hanfstaengl, Engel, von Below, Puttkamer, Wiedemann, and others). Allow me to emphasize, again, that this book is not a biography of Hitler.

†*Er war mein Chef*, M, 1987.

‡I am not including the previously mentioned—and sometimes cited—Hans Frank, whose writing, before his hanging, was intended not so much to rehabilitate as to counter then current misimpressions of Hitler.

**Leoni am Starnberger See, 1978. Subtitle: *Erlebnisse—Gespräche—Reflexionen*. I must, however, qualify the above statement about a small circle of readers: Giesler's book had five or six reprintings. (He had previously failed to secure a contract from a more reputable German publisher.)

relaxation from his awesome burdens.* Indeed, Hitler and Giesler contemplated and discussed that architectural model of Linz during that morbid February evening for many hours, late into the night. Giesler's portrait of Hitler is a very positive one. It must be treated with caution, and only because of the purposes of its author. His reconstructions of many of Hitler's expressions are not only devoid of references; some of them are not plausible or provable. A significant—and perhaps prototypical—Appendix in Giesler's book is a letter by the sculptor Arno Breker to the author. Breker was a young, attractive, and talented sculptor whom Hitler liked, and whose book, *Paris, Hitler et moi*, was published—in Paris—eight years before Giesler's. (Breker had lived in Paris many years before the war; he had many friends and acquaintances there, including Cocteau, Maillol, and others, whom he then cultivated—and who, aware of his close relationship with Hitler, cultivated him—during the German occupation.) That book was not an apologia for Hitler but an apologia *pro vita sua*, hastily written, with few interesting details about Hitler,† and full of respect for Albert Speer. But in this letter to Giesler, dated 29 November 1977,‡ Breker turns violently against Speer—because of Speer's portrait of Hitler.

---

*GR, p. 437: Hitler: "Now talk to me about Linz." This "relaxation" [*Entspannung*] the night after the terrible destruction of Dresden.

†However, elements of Breker's admiration for Hitler were extant in his book—for example, p. 180: "If he had not provoked the war Hitler would have entered history as one of the greatest builders: the scope of his projected works for Berlin, Munich, etc. is sufficient to prove this." Interesting, too, is Breker's insistence (p. 129) that Bormann knew more about Hitler than did anyone else, and thus it is regrettable that Bormann's papers were "destroyed—they, and they alone, would have furnished the complete [?] documentation of the phenomenon of Adolf Hitler."

‡A few passages from that letter (GR, p. 523): "Your book has brought for me many things to light that I did not know; above all, the extent of how Hitler was betrayed. Until now one did not know what had stood behind that. . . . Far back in history there was nothing comparable [to him] . . . a solitary and great personality, determining his times. I am convinced that the press is speechless [*ratlos*] before this phenomenon. Thanks to your comprehensive documentation historiography stands before a new task. . . . Hitler's primitive and blinded opponents did not know that here stood a man who wanted to create a new—and also architectonic—age. . . . The world is still blind. . . . Your book will either declench an avalanche of commentaries or it will be silenced to death."

What bursts forth in this book and in this letter is Giesler's and Breker's admiration for Hitler and their conviction of his place in history: the insistence of these artists on the historical greatness as well as the artistic sensitivities of a genius. Much of this was, of course, due to their fortunate and opportune association with Hitler. Should we attribute their persistent convictions merely to that? I cannot answer this. At the same time I dare to say that their violent hostility to Speer raises the allied question: was Speer's "conversion" nothing more than the choice of an opportunist? I do not think so; indeed, I am inclined to think that Speer's purpose was the expression and the detailed illustration of his, admittedly late-coming, convictions, and thus more than opportunism—which is also why Speer's reminiscences of Hitler are immensely more valuable and more telling than those of Giesler or Breker, even though some of the latter's reminiscences cannot be entirely ignored.

Now I come to the amateur historian David Irving, whom we have met several times in this book. We have seen (in chapter 1) his evolution from a young sympathizer of Germany and things German to a "rehabilitator" of Hitler and then to his indubitable admirer and partisan. More than thirty years after his first publications, Irving arrived at a stage of his career where publishers in Britain and the United States seemed reluctant to publish him. But it would be wrong to underestimate his influence, for at least two reasons. One is the not inconsiderable extent of his readership. The other—more significant, for our purposes—is that certain professional and, by and large, respected historians have relied on some of Irving's researches and then given him qualified praise.* This is regrettable, but not merely because of the often lamentable and, in many cases, unsavory character of Irving's opinions. Few reviewers and critics of Irving's books, including professional historians, have bothered to examine them carefully enough. Had they done so, they

---

*Examples: Nolte, Zitelmann, and the English Charmley; the latter's favorable references to Irving are buried in some of his dense footnotes. Also see John Keegan, p. 27n.

would have found that many of Irving's references and quotations are not verifiable. In his *Hitler's War*, for example, there are many errata in names and dates; more important, unverifiable and unconvincing assertions abound.

These two matters are connected, since there is a clue to Irving's method that appears from his use of the language. One of the rhetorical habits of ideological advocates is their emphatic use of adverbs and adjectives, which they employ not as qualifiers but to carry the main thrust of their statements. They become rhetorical substitutes for evidence. Thus Hitler, in Irving's breathless prose, "*evidently* made some promise about the Jews" (there is no evidence); General Schörner in April 1945 fought "a *convincing* victory" (it was not a victory, and it convinced no one); in 1939 the Polish army was "*optimistically* assembled at Posen" (a queer adverb for an English writer, but then the Polish army was not assembled at Posen, nor was it optimistic); in 1941 Stalin had "*obviously* laid immense plans for an offensive into Europe" (to the contrary, Stalin was so fearful of Hitler that he ordered the Soviet military not to proceed with defensive measures, let alone "offensive" ones, since they might irritate Hitler). This last assertion, for example, appears on page 285 of *Hitler's War*. As far as evidence for the assertion goes, there is nothing that could be considered even remotely substantial, including Irving's own referential endnotes. Another Irving (Washington) told his readers in *Tales of a Traveller*: "I am always at a loss to know how much to believe my own stories." This sense of loss, for David Irving, is not apparent.*

---

*Examples in 1/H, p. 6. The invasion of Poland: ". . . these were fields long steeped in German blood; ancient German land was coming under German rule again." "Apparently convinced that the German tanks were only tinplate dummies, the Polish cavalry attacked with lances couched." (A legend, long disproved by military historians.) P. 28, Warsaw, October 1939: ". . . when [Hitler] saw the banquet that the army had prepared at the airfield, either his stomach rebelled or his instinct for bad publicity warned him not to sit at the vast, horseshoe-shaped table with spotless white linen and sumptuous food at a time when hundreds of thousands of Warsaw's inhabitants were starving." (No source.) P. 61: "There was clear evidence of a Russian military buildup that could be unleashed against Germany." (In October 1939! Not one shred of such evidence.) P. 156: Early in August 1940

In his Introduction to *Hitler's War*, Irving: "I saw myself as a stone-cleaner—less concerned with a wordy and subjective architectural appraisal than with scrubbing years of grime and discoloration from the façade of a silent and forbidding monument. . . . I believe that that drubbing had disclosed a picture of the man that nobody until now has suspected. . . ." All credit—and honor—is due to those, mostly German, historians who have seen it as their duty to research—literally: re-search—and thereby refute Irving's

---

at the Berghof, among close friends, Hitler "often thought out loud. . . . He would build great autobahns far into the east, he would build new cities; on Victory Day the people of Berlin would dance in the Wilhelmsplatz, and then the rebuilding of Berlin was to begin. He would be gracious and magnanimous to the vanquished enemy heads of state—even to Churchill, to whom he would 'give leave to paint and write his memoirs.' " (No source for this.) P. 348: "How Hitler must have cursed the General Staff for having foisted its Moscow campaign on him." P. 391: "It seemed no coincidence that the Jews were at the bottom of the spreading partisan movement everywhere." About Hitler's speech of 30 September 1943, pp. 428–29: He "spoke to the German people for the first time in many months, he apologized, as he had less time for speechmaking than a prime minister who could cruise for weeks around the world in a white silk blouse and floppy sombrero or some other ludicrous garb." (Hitler did not say that.) About the end at Stalingrad, p. 453: "The blame for the disaster was diverted onto Hitler. In later years memoirs were fudged by field marshals, fake diaries were concocted, guilty sentences were expunged from the OKW's war diary, and 'contemporary' judgments on Hitler's leadership were slotted in." About the July 1944 conspirators, pp. 704–05: "A champagne orgy lasting far into the night had been their reaction to the news of Hitler's 'death.' " There are many statements praising Hitler and blackening his generals. (One odd example: a solicitous Hitler prefers to lunch with his stenographers, letting his hungry generals wait.) Others: in 1941 and 1942 the rigidity of some of the generals thwarted Hitler's rational plans for a victory in Russia; Hitler predicted where the Russians would attack at Stalingrad and Voronezh, where his generals failed; on occasion Hitler was not inclined to talk forcefully to his commanders, especially to those with aristocratic backgrounds. Another instance: Irving about the meeting of the Hungarian Arrow Cross leader Szálasi with Hitler in December 1944. According to Irving the former was supposed to agree to the bitter defense (and potential destruction) of Budapest, as long as Hitler would not attempt to deal with Stalin—whereas the contrary was the case: Szálasi hoped for a last-minute deal between Hitler and Stalin. I/H has many references to "Hungarian archives in Budapest" without dates, places, or file or page numbers.

This is a very random sampling of Irving's "methods."

"documents" and arguments, not only by concentrating on Irving's morally questionable theses but by pointing out carefully misinterpretations of his "sources."*

The work of the American journalist John Toland is hardly comparable to Irving's portraiture of Hitler. Yet Toland's admiration for Hitler seeps through in many of his pages, and his documentation, too, is inadequate.†

IN HIS ASSESSMENT AND SUMMARY of the Historians' Controversy, the English historian Richard J. Evans wrote:‡ "The whole debate ultimately has little to offer anyone with a serious scholarly interest in the German past. It brings no new facts to light; it embodies no new research; it makes no new contribution to historical understanding; it poses no new questions that might stimu-

---

*Even Hitler's former secretary Christa Schroeder, whom Irving cited often and to whom she had given information and papers, wrote, p. 26ff: ". . . even the 'serious' and 'honest reputed' David Irving is not immune . . . against inaccuracies . . . so I must say that David Irving, too, has disappointed me."

†See chapter 1. Examples in TO, p. 262: In 1932, "amid the confusion of the nation [Hitler] seemed to stand like a rock, insisting only on what was best for Germany." P. 226: "Many a hand-kiss insured lifelong devotion from women; men were reassured by his firm handshake, his down-to-earth, man-to-man approach." About 1938, quoting Schwerin-Krosigk, p. 470: ". . . we can only win by waiting. And that is why the Communists, Jews, and Czechs are making such frantic efforts to push us into a war now." This from his letter to Toland, p. 973. On Hitler's 23 May 1939 conference: "This was not the irrational ranting of a man possessed by the will to conquer but an admission that Germany could not continue as a great nation without war." About August 1939, p. 568: "The Poles never for a moment considered accepting the German proposals." P. 524: "Hitler's charge that political possibilities of a peaceful settlement with Poland have been exhausted was not without foundation." P. 619: In the summer of 1940, Hitler to France was "magnanimous." P. 621: Hitler's 19 July speech "began with a derisive attack on Churchill" and then went on with a peace offering to Britain. The sequence of that speech was the exact opposite. Many similar misattributions, including citing Pope Pius XII on pp. 674–75: He made it clear that he backed the Nazi fight against Bolshevism, describing it as "high-minded gallantry in defence of the foundations of Christian culture." There was no such statement by the Pope.

‡"The New Nationalism and the Old History—Perspective on the West German Historikerstreit," JMH, December 1987, p. 785.

late future work. It is scarcely surprising that some commentators on the discussion have wanted to stop the whole affair and get historians back to writing real history." (Whatever *that* is.) "But the debate is more than a diversion. It has obvious implications for the way in which history is written." This is both too vague and too broad. The "Historikerstreit" had nothing to do with methods of historical writing. Its "obvious implications" were (and remain) that respectable German professional historians had come to find it proper to reconsider the place of the Third Reich—and, at least indirectly, of Hitler—in the history of Germany and of Europe in the twentieth century.*

Ernst Nolte, whose contribution sparked the Historians' Controversy, has presented in multiple books† and writings a very dubious explanation of the Third Reich (and, again indirectly, of Hitler): that National Socialism and its misdeeds were a consequence of the Russian Communist revolution and its terror. "Did not the 'Gulag Archipelago' precede Auschwitz?" "The extermination of the Russian bourgeoisie" and that of the "Kulaks" preceded Hitler's extermination of the Jews; the latter was not only equivalent but a consequence of the former. "National Socialism . . . was the radical reaction to the victory of the Bolshevik ideology in 1917 in Russia."

This kind of argument—more than that, this kind of a historical perspective—requires attention, if only because it largely accorded (and still accords) with that of many "conservatives" and "neoconservatives" not only in Germany but also elsewhere. This includes

---

*An odd footnote. Evans, in the same article (December 1987): German "reunification is simply not a realistic possibility, and to talk about it or to advance historical arguments in its favor is to indulge in political fantasizing." It was to occur less than two years later, and it was not entirely unforeseeable in 1987.

†He developed and repeated this thesis in various later books: *Der europäische Bürgerkrieg* (1987), *Geschichtsdenken im 20. Jahrhundert* (1991), *Streitpunkte. Heutige und künftige Kontroversen um den Nationalsozialismus* (1994, in which: "the greatness and tragedy of National Socialism . . . it was an extraordinary response . . . we must acknowledge its greatness." Earlier, Nolte also found it proper to make favorable references to David Irving and David Hoggan (a forerunner of Irving), whose contributions were "useful" (HS, pp. 19, 25), and later even to the American engineer Fred Leuchter, who "proved" that there could not have been any gassings at Auschwitz.

the United States, where during the "cold war," and even now, many people saw the Communist revolution in Russia as the greatest turning point in the history of the twentieth century, leading to the worldwide struggle between Communism and "Freedom," during which World War II and Hitler were but an aberrant episode. (This was, at first, James Burnham's and William F. Buckley's thesis: "In 1917 history changed gears"—whatever *that* means.) This view of history not only gained many adherents (including many ex-Trotskyist "neoconservatives" in the 1970s) but it remained an important element in forming the basic ideology of the Republican Party after 1948, eventually propelling men like Ronald Reagan into power. It is nonsense, and, departing from the main subject of this chapter, I am here compelled to sum up why: (1) The main events of the century were the two world wars—of which the Communist revolution in Russia in 1917 and the establishment of Communist regimes in Eastern Europe after 1945 were but the consequences. (2) Even in 1917, the greatest (meaning: the most consequential) event was not the Russian Revolution—which meant Russia's withdrawal from the war—but the American entry into it, in both the short and the long run. In the short run, it was not Russia's falling out but America's falling in that decided the outcome of World War I; and in the long run that meant a break with the long American tradition of not getting involved in the struggles of the Old World. (3) If anything, the history of this century has shown the Americanization, not the Communization or the Russianization, of the world. (4) The failure of Communism after 1917 and before 1945 to establish itself anywhere outside Russia (very much unlike the French or the American revolutions), and the collapse of the Russian empire after 1989 were proofs enough of the feebleness of its appeal, especially in Europe.

Within Germany it was perhaps regrettable that in 1986 Chancellor Kohl invited Nolte to join the "Kuratorium" (Board of Directors) of a new "Haus der Geschichte." Nolte was also defended in the FAZ (3 March 1988) as "one of the most original thinkers of present Germany"—and, on occasion, also by Joachim Fest. In 1994, in an interview with Rudolf Augstein (publisher of *Der Spiegel*), Nolte said: "Hitler was not only an ideologue but . . . the Second

World War was also a war virtually for European unification . . .
Germany could be conceived as the Piedmont of Europe."*

One of Nolte's defenders in the "Historikerstreit," Klaus Hildebrand, wrote: "Much work is left for historiography to research and
present the history of the Third Reich in connection with German,
European, and universal history."† Such an attempt in the "Historikerstreit" was made by Andreas Hillgruber. His advocacy of
what I called the two-war theory in 1986 contributed to the sudden
outbreak of the Historians' Controversy. In *Zweierlei Untergang*
(1986) he praised the desperate defense of the Eastern Front in
1944–45 "for the protection of the integrity of the great power
status of the German Reich which, according to the will of the
Allies, had to be destroyed." Anti-Prussianism "was the basis of
the British war policy against Germany."‡ According to Hillgruber,
respect and admiration are also due to leading National Socialist
officials and to the SS units (including the volunteer Flemish,
Dutch, and other SS units) in that struggle. Like Nolte, Hillgruber
spoke of the "European conception" of the SS. A second—and to
me more disturbing—matter was Hillgruber's reluctance to com-
mend the patriotism of the July 1944 conspirators against Hitler.
(This is significant because of the accepted consensus of the West
German Republic, officially identifying itself with the patriotism of

---

*Piedmont: the state from which the unification of Italy had proceeded—its role
comparable to the thirteen colonies in the history of the United States. We have
also (see above p. 180n) seen Nolte's misdating and misconception of a letter by
Chaim Weizmann to Neville Chamberlain in 1939. (He had found this in Irving,
who, in turn, had gathered it from one of Hitler's table conversations.) Another
example: Nolte's repeated references to the Rat's Cage (*Rattenkäfig*), a Bolshevik
practice of forcing a victim's head into a cage inhabited by a raging rat. Hitler was
supposed to have spoken of this in one of his table conversations. Yet it had been
mentioned earlier by an excellent anti-Bolshevik historian of the Russian Revolution (Melgunov) and then described by George Orwell in *1984*—of these Nolte
seems to have been ignorant. "[Hitler's] horror of the rat's cage was but an outstanding expression of a general and genuine experience of the earlier postwar
period. I think that here we may find the deepest roots of Hitler's most extreme
impulses of action." Nolte in HS, p. 226. The Rat root?

†HS, p. 292.

‡HS, p. 341. HS/W, p. 48. Hillgruber accused Germany's enemies of having
brought about not only a German catastrophe but "a destroyed center of Europe."

the 1944 opponents, resisters, and martyrs.) Hillgruber expressed his sympathy for the commanders on the Eastern Front who had failed to support the 1944 plot. His distinction between two German terms, cobbled together by himself (Hillgruber was a rather poor stylist) was suggestive. Men like Stauffenberg were "Gesinnungsethiker" (convinced or sentimental moralists; "Gesinnung" in German may mean both), whereas the last-ditch fighters in the East were "Verantwortungsethiker" (responsible moralists)—hardly translatable into English, but the essential meaning is obvious: Stauffenberg and the plotters against Hitler may have been moralists; but the others acted as morally responsible men. Last, and also least, is the small but perhaps indicative evidence of how, on occasion, Hillgruber aligns himself with Nolte's extraordinary thesis and that on other occasions he gave cautious recognition to Irving.*

In Nolte's and Hillgruber's defense it must be said, in all fairness, that while elements of a rehabilitation of Hitler may be implicit in some of their writing, that does not seem to have been their purpose. They were moved by a passionate bitterness against what to them seemed an unfortunately broad—yet inadequate—and antinationalist consensus among German historians. They wanted not to rehabilitate but to explain. Yet many of their explanations amounted to a kind of relativization that ought to be dismissed. Nolte and Hillgruber, as well as most of their supporters and followers, are not admirers of Hitler but defenders of Germany and of the history of the German people during the Third Reich. But since the history of the Third Reich is inseparable from that of Adolf Hitler, they inevitably find themselves (at times at least) defending Hitler, too.

THE CASE OF RAINER ZITELMANN is somewhat different. It is significant that Zitelmann—an entire generation younger than Nolte

---

*Hillgruber in *Rheinischer Merkur*, 31 October 1986: The mass murder of the Jews "cannot qualitatively be judged different" from Stalin's mass deportations and murders of Ukrainian peasants. In FAZ, 18 June 1979, Hillgruber published a critical and judicious review of one of Irving's books; however, Irving's collection of papers "amounts to an indubitable and in no way small merit of Irving." It may be significant that no such qualifications can be found in Hillgruber's violent attacks against Habermas, Wehler, Jäckel, and others during the "Historikerstreit."

and Hillgruber, and who had not been part of the Historians' Controversy—began the second edition of his important ZIT/A with a strident preface denouncing those historians who had criticized Nolte and Hillgruber in the "Historikerstreit."* This, as well as Zitelmann's subsequent career, revealed the ideological and political inclinations of this talented young historian, who abandoned his (potentially very promising) professional academic prospects for a career in public journalism and politics. This, in itself, is not necessarily regrettable; we have seen that some of the most valuable contributions to our understanding of Hitler have been written by men who were not professional academic historians. However, we have also seen, throughout this book, that many of Zitelmann's statements indicate not only his serious and commendable effort to present and sustain a portrait of Hitler that is more varied and complex than has generally been assumed, but that sometimes there is no real distinction between his "revision" and a kind of rehabilitation. This is suggested by some of his—questionable and erroneous—statements on Hitler's foreign policy,† as well (as was true of Hillgruber) as his reservations about the July 1944 conspirators against Hitler. Their motives, according to Zitelmann, were mixed: "religious and ethical-moral motives and the concern about the future of Germany played a role as well as their antipathy [*Widerwillen*] to Hitler's Socialism"—an unfair summation by a nationalist "neoconservative" of the purposes of those noble and patriotic conservatives of a former generation.

More than a quarter century before the "Historikerstreit" erupted, the Swiss journalist F. Allemann wrote a thoughtful book with the

---

*Zitelmann had completed his manuscript in early 1985. The "Historikerstreit" occurred in 1986. The first edition of ZIT/A was published in April 1987. This preface was written for the second edition, in October 1988.

†Examples, in ZIT/B: P. 108: in March 1939 "forces became stronger in England that were spokesmen of a hard policy against Germany." P. 109: Hitler's proposals to Poland in August 1939 were "more generous and moderate than was the entire Polish policy of Weimar diplomacy." P. 113: "Hitler did not want war, was forced [?] to make an alliance with the Soviet Union." In the summer of 1940, "in view of the ruling war psychosis in Germany it was not at all easy for Hitler to make such a peace offer to England." P. 146: "England showed its unwillingness for an alliance" with Germany. P. 141: "Hitler's thesis that England was pursuing a policy of selling out its Empire, allowing it to be inherited by the United States, fell on eager ears in [English] conservative circles." Not so.

title *Bonn ist nicht Weimar* (Bonn is not Weimar). His aim was to emphasize the stability of the West German political and social structure. He pointed out multiple evidences of how much more solid and healthy those conditions and institutions were, compared with those during the Weimar Republic, and that the Bonn Republic was thus unlikely to succumb to extremisms. Allemann's book was not simply a political pamphlet, nor was it Pollyannaish; indeed, many of his comparisons remain valid even now, nearly forty years after its publication, for a considerably different and now reunited German state. There is, however, one important exception to Allemann's general thesis. *Culturally* speaking, there have been similarities between Bonn and Weimar. Of course, in one sense or, rather, on one level, this has been a worldwide phenomenon. The cult—and the often excessive admiration of the art and literature of "modernism" of the 1920s—has persisted during the last decades (perhaps especially in the 1960s, which were not much more than excessive exemplifications and applications of the ideas, forms, and fashions prevalent in the 1920s). From this general cultural tendency West Germany could hardly have been exempt. But what had been peculiar to Weimar Germany was the existence of an all-but-unbridgeable gap—not only politically and socially but also intellectually and culturally—between the then conservative-nationalist and radical-liberal and cosmopolitan camps. And what the Historians' Controversy in the 1980s revealed was the reappearance of a division among German historians and political thinkers and publicists and commentators, with the compositions of their camps being not identical, but also not entirely dissimilar, to those of the 1920s; and the course of the controversy revealed— regrettably—that such a gap may still be unbridgeable. The bitterness of the controversy was evidence enough of this.* Unlike the 1920s, the historians whose writings provoked the controversy

---

*Consider the language. Examples: Hillgruber: "A scientific scandal." (HS, p. 233.) "Character assassinations" (Rufmordkampagne). Stürmer: "A proscription-list," "A show trial." (HS/W p. 92, *et seq.*) Fest: "Ritual conforming against 'the freedom of raising questions.'" (HS/W, p. 127.) The vehemence of the other side was not less. An extreme example by the eager publicist Elie Wiesel, branding Nolte, Hillgruber, Hildebrand, and Stürmer "the four bandits" (Viererbände).

(Nolte, Hillgruber), their supporters (Hildebrand, Fest, Stürmer), and their successors (Zitelmann) complained that German universities and German professional historianship continued to be dominated by a Left-leaning and antinational intelligentsia who had done their best (or rather, worst) to denigrate their opponents and, at least indirectly, the history of their country. Detectable behind such agitated statements were suggestions of a conspiracy*—and a conspiracy of not only an academic but an antinational character.

In his interview with the Swedish historian Alf W. Johansson in November 1992, Zitelmann said that the Historians' Controversy ended with a triumph of the "Left-liberal" forces. "Politically, this means that the conservatives are rather defensive and not united." But "that has more to do with academic conditions than with the intellectual situation in Germany where now, naturally a few years after the Historians' Controversy, there is in reality a certain change, since the Leftist intellectual circles are no longer on the offensive but, to the contrary, they find themselves in [increasing] difficulties." Yet many (if not most) of Nolte's and Hillgruber's critics were not leftists or radicals. But Zitelmann is probably correct about there being a change in the political and intellectual climate—with potential echoes and effects among younger generations and even among future historians. This is evident, among other things, in Fest's 1995 introduction to a new edition of his Hitler biography, where he speaks against the acceptance and observance of "taboos" about Hitler.† What we may probably face are more revisions of Hitler's portrait, at best, and more widespread attempts at his rehabilitation, at worst.

---

*"A monopoly of [public] opinion [*Meinungsmonopol*] exists in Germany." Zitelmann, cited in *Die Woche*, 15 June 1995.

†Reprinted in FAZ, 7 October 1995. (See also Preface of the present work, pp. xi–xii.) The term "taboos" was employed by Zitelmann in *Die Welt*, 18 December 1993.

9

The Historical
Problem

*Pieter Geyl's question in 1944—The comparison with Napoleon—
The semantic question of "greatness"—Catastrophic results of Hitler—
Enduring consequences—His place in the history of the twentieth
century and at the end of the Modern Age*

O N 14 October 1944 the Dutch historian Pieter Geyl
concluded the preface of a book, the subject of which had
preoccupied him for more than four years. Those were
dramatic years indeed in his life. In May 1940 his country was suddenly and brutally invaded and conquered by Hitler's Germany.
Geyl had written an essay about Napoleon, which in September
1940 he used for some lectures in the Rotterdam School of Economics. A month later he was arrested and sent to Germany, where
he had occasion to repeat those lectures "in very different surround-
ings and for a very different public, namely in the Buchenwald concentration camp for my fellow hostages." The subject was Napoleon;
but it was "the parallel [between Napoleon and Hitler] that roused
the keenest interest and amusement." A few months later, Geyl was
returned from Buchenwald to Holland, where he spent another
three years of internment. In February 1944, he was freed on medical grounds, and then he began to write his book on Napoleon.* It

---

*All of the following quotes from Geyl are from the preface of his *Napoleon: For
and Against*, New Haven and London, 1949, pp. 7–11.

was completed eight months later in a small room, in the cold and the darkness of a still subjugated Holland, under the shadow of the Gestapo. Seven months still had to pass until Holland was liberated. The book—*Napoleon: For and Against*—was published in 1947, the first English and American editions in 1949.

As the title shows, the subject of this fine and most readable work by probably the second-greatest historian of Dutch origin in this century (the other being Johan Huizinga) was Napoleon, not Hitler. As a matter of fact, Hitler's name does not appear in the text at all, except for a tiny footnote on page 278. But it appears throughout the preface. After all, as Geyl admitted at the very beginning of the preface: "This book is a by-product of our recent experiences." But this was not to be a book of Parallel Lives.* Listen closely to what Geyl wrote in that preface: "Let me state, in fairness to my own word, that I found a good deal more than the parallel to attract me. Napoleon had his own fascination, and French historiography a charm of its own. Not even the article of 1940 had been in the first instance suggested to me by the problem of the resemblance or contrast between Napoleon and Hitler, *but by the historiographical problem, the problem of the endless variety of interpretations of Napoleon, his career, his aims, and his achievements.* [The italics are mine: Isn't this what the present book on Hitler is about?] Yet—how could it be otherwise? I had been struck by the parallel no less than had my readers or hearers, and in this book, too, it has undeniably remained an element, even though I have alluded to it only very occasionally and have nowhere worked it out."

The rest of Geyl's preface, then, *does* compare Napoleon with Hitler; I will return to some of his trenchant statements in a moment. But there is a paragraph in this otherwise brief preface that struck me

---

*His original essay about Napoleon was to be printed in a Dutch monthly review in June 1940. "After the capitulation, in May, the manuscript was returned to me, still marked with an instruction to the printer to be quick, and without a word of explanation. No explanation was needed for me to understand that, although I had not written a single word in it about Hitler and National Socialism, the parallel with our own times had seemed to the editor a little too pointed in the new circumstances." During the above-mentioned lectures in Rotterdam, "occasional bursts of laughter showed the audience to be equally alive to the parallel "

when I first read Geyl's book, almost a half century ago—and which may have sparked my decision to write this one. Geyl wrote that he did not wish to give the impression "that it was written for the parallel and owed to the parallel, in my opinion, its principal interest." But "There [is] a point to which it is difficult not to fear that the parallel may extend—it is only a later generation that will know for certain."

> When one sees the French licking the hand that had chastised them; when one notices how the errors and crimes of the Hero, the trials of the people, the disasters and losses of the State, were forgotten in the glamour of military achievement, of power, unsound and transitory though it was; when one notices the explanations and constructions, ingenious, imaginative, grandiose, that were put up as much as a century later by historians—and such excellent historians!— then one seems already to discern among later generations of Germans* the apologists and admirers of the man who was our oppressor and who led them to their ruin.

Pieter Geyl wrote this in October 1944—exactly fifty years (to the month) before I began to plan and write the present book. I would

---

*But not only Germans. "One can see"—and the spectacle is not a pretty one— Frenchmen "licking the hand that had chastised them": a hand that not only chastised but subjugated and sometimes tortured them, a hand not one of their own but of their national enemy, who had little more than contempt for them. One of their brilliant intellectuals, Robert Brasillach, dared to put it in one phrase during his trial in 1945: "We slept with the Germans; and we liked some of it." (Was it due to this phrase that General de Gaulle, despite the requests of many intellectuals, refused to commute Brasillach's death sentence? Perhaps.) One positive consequence of World War II was the disappearance of Franco-German enmity, indeed, the subsequent reconciliation and alliance of the two nations and states. But there has been a less edifying consequence: a French sense of inferiority—not merely a political but also a cultural sense of inferiority—to things German. This includes their—sometimes outspoken—admiration for the Third Reich and for some of its representatives. The phenomenon of Le Pen and his millions of followers is something that was foreseen by the French "collaborationists" such as Brasillach and others, who were collaborationists not only with Germany but with Hitlerism. To this we may add the cult of Ernst Jünger, Carl Schmitt, Martin Heidegger, and others—not Nazis but believers in German superiority. In no other country have they become respected and admired by intellectuals as they now are in France.

not name it *Hitler: For and Against.* Yet readers who have followed my book until now will know that a pro-Hitler literature by "apologists and admirers" does exist, and will continue to exist, and not only among "a later generation of Germans." There *are*, as we have seen, admirers and rehabilitators of Hitler, hidden and open. Their influence is limited, and perhaps their significance, too. But the future is still ahead of us.

In any event, the subject of this book is both like and unlike Pieter Geyl's. It is not the history of a man but the history of his history; but then its chapters are not divided among his historian opponents and his historian admirers. And this last chapter is—inevitably—historical rather than historiographical (though of course history and historiography overlap): a putative answer to the question of where and how Hitler's place may be, in the history of the twentieth century, at least. And that question does involve a comparison with Napoleon.

THE PARALLELS—OR, MORE PRECISELY, the similarities—between Napoleon's and Hitler's careers (their careers, rather than their lives) should be apparent even to general readers who do not possess detailed historical knowledge. We may sum them up in the briefest possible manner. Both rose—unexpectedly—as national leaders. They incarnated—even more than they represented—a new element in the politics and history of their countries. Their popularity was—for a long time—extreme and indubitable. Their conquests abroad were astonishing. They wished to rule—and for a time did rule—most of Europe. The main obstacle to the acceptance of their conquests was England, which they were not able to invade. Having convinced themselves that England's last continental hope was Russia—after having first made a surprising treaty with Russia—they decided to invade Russia, where they met with disaster, whereafter they could no longer conquer and were defeated utterly. All of this is well known, and some of the coincidences are spectacular: for example, the very beginning of their invasions of Russia, Napoleon's starting on 24 June, almost on the same day (22 June) as Hitler's.

But the differences are even more substantial than the similarities.* I can hardly improve on what Geyl wrote in his preface in October 1944—which I feel now compelled to cite in detail:

> "I always hate to compare Hitler with Napoleon," so, listening to the BBC the other day, I heard that Winston Churchill had been telling the House of Commons, only to continue with a "but" and to enter upon the comparison all the same. So it is with all of us, and so it is with me. It is simply impossible not to do so. The resemblances are too striking. No doubt—and I want to state this with unmistakable emphasis—the differences, the contrasts, are such that, even when as in my case one had hated the dictator in Napoleon long before the evil presence of Hitler began darkening our lives, one almost feels as if one should ask the pardon of his shade for mentioning his name in one breath with that of the other. . . . I do not want to say that French civilization was made of so much finer stuff than German: the difference is that under Napoleon French civilization, albeit stifled and narrowed by him, still accompanied the conquest, while the character of the conquest that it has been the lot of our civilization to undergo is not compatible with any civilization at all. Lastly, the personality of Napoleon—indeed, when I think of elaborating the comparison on that score, I suddenly feel a surge of revolt against [his] "detractors" with whom generally (as will be seen) I am on quite friendly terms.

There follows now a paragraph summing up Napoleon's tyranny and his atrocities. And yet:

> Methods of compulsion and atrocities? The worst that our generation had to witness . . . had no parallel in Napoleon's

---

*Let us recall, for example, that Napoleon entered Moscow and Hitler did not; also that the former arrived there a mere ten weeks after having crossed the Russian frontier; getting to the outskirts of Moscow took Hitler's mechanized armies five months. But then, Hitler survived his first winter in Russia, after which his armies began to advance again into its depths, whereas Napoleon suffered a catastrophe and withdrew from Russia in less than three months.

system. Indeed that system remained true, from first to last, to conceptions of civil equality and human rights with which the oppression or extermination of a group, not on account of acts or even of opinions, but of birth and blood, would have been utterly incompatible. And yet methods of compulsion and atrocities are inseparable from the character of the dictator and conqueror, and we shall see that Napoleon incurred bitter reproaches, at home and abroad, for some of his acts. Nevertheless this is one of the points where the comparison is bound to do good for his reputation. What is the proscription of "the general staff of the Jacobins" beside the annihilation of all opposition parties in jails or concentration camps such as has taken place in the Third Reich? What is the murder of the Duke of Enghien beside those of Dollfuss, of General Schleicher and his wife, and of so many others on June 30th 1934? What are the executions of Palm, of Hofer, what are even the severities with which so many villages and towns in Germany and Spain were visited, beside what in our time all occupied territories have had to suffer from Hitler's armies? The French police were hated and feared in the occupied and annexed territories, but when one reads about their conduct with a mind full of present experiences, one cannot help feeling astonished at the restraints and resistances they still met within the stubborn notions of law and in the mild manners of a humane age.

Written in October 1944, this still rings true. But now allow me to continue this comparison a little further. It may be of some interest to note that throughout his life, Hitler made very few references to Napoleon.* In June 1940, during his fast and almost furtive

---

*A strange coincidence not noted by other historians: It was in Hitler's birthplace, Braunau, that in 1810 Napoleon's new bride, the Archduchess Marie Louise, was festively transferred from her Austrian to her French entourage. During his campaigns against Austria in 1805 and again in 1809, Napoleon spent the night in that frontier town—in the same Haus Schüdl (and presumably in the same second-story rooms) where seventy years later Hitler's father came to live. (It is a well-proportioned building on the south side of the large market square.)

visit to Paris at dawn, he spent a few moments contemplating Napoleon's tomb in the Invalides; and in December 1940 he ordered that the coffin of Napoleon's son be brought from Vienna to a wintry Paris, to be deposited next to that of his father—a gesture that evoked little reaction among the French people. To this we may add that a contemptuous dislike for France and the French marked Hitler's thinking from his earliest years.*

There were grave differences between Napoleon's and Hitler's personalities and temperaments. Unscrupulous cruelty—of a calculating Machiavellian and Mediterranean kind—marked what was probably the worst element in the mental habits of the former; hatred—and the cultivation of unbridled hatreds—was perhaps the worst element in the latter. It is at least arguable that Napoleon, that supreme egoist, was more confident—and often more optimistic— than was Hitler.† Another difference between the two lies in their attitudes toward the past. In that sense Napoleon was much less revolutionary than was Hitler. One attractive—and surprisingly human— facet of Napoleon's personality was his hereditary and family feeling, his 1810 inclination to settle down with a family, for his affection for Marie Louise and his love for his son amounted to more than the calculated purpose of consolidating his power through a grand

---

*A book remains to be written about Hitler's expressed views of other nations and nationalities, which were in many instances varied or changing rather than constant and uniform. There is, for example, place for a serious study of his attitude toward Britain and the British people, which was more complicated than the sometimes overused cliché of a love-hate relationship. However, what is striking is the evidence of Hitler's hatefulness toward people who dared to oppose or defy him. Thus his occasional expressions of respect or even admiration for the people disappeared and gave way to expressions of a contemptuous hatred as the war went on and neared its end. Not dissimilar was his treatment of Poland and the Poles, about whom he uttered few disparaging remarks before 1939 but whose defiance— leading to the outbreak of the war in 1939—made him impose cruelties on them unparalleled anywhere except in his treatment of Jews. We find nothing similar in the reactions of Napoleon or even Stalin, who on occasion showed some respect for the bravery of his opponents.

†Fest in F, p. 309, is convincing that Hitler's "entire intellectual and emotional system" seemed to have been dominated by a fundamental element of "Angst" [Angsterlebnis]. This, among other matters, also differentiates Hitler from the young Mussolini, who resembled the early Bonaparte rather than Hitler.

dynastic marriage. There was a bourgeois (in the best sense of that often maligned word) side of Napoleon that was missing in Hitler. At his most grandiose, Napoleon saw himself as a new Charlemagne at his coronation in 1804; he chose Roman emperors as models; Hitler had none (except perhaps Frederick the Great, at the end).* There is, too, the contrast between Napoleon, who said that his marshals were bloodhounds straining at the leash, so that he had to hold them back, whereas Hitler said that it was he who had to incite and drive his generals forward.

More significantly, Napoleon saw his place in history as that of a third force between Revolution and Reaction. He said, before his downfall: "After me, the Revolution—or, rather, the ideas which formed it—will resume its course. It will be like a book from which the marker is removed, and one starts again at the page where one left off."† Hitler's vision was entirely different. After his disappearance there would be no return, only darkness; and then, perhaps after fifty or a hundred years, a revival of his own revolutionary ideas.

Again, I must insist (for the last time) that I am not writing a biography of Hitler; but I am preoccupied with the problem of his place in history. And it is in this respect that a comparison with the ups and downs of Napoleon's historical interpretation may be proper. Most of the substantial biographies and histories of Napoleon were written and published forty or fifty years after his death, whereas we have seen that substantial scholarly biographies of Hitler began to appear within a decade of his death. During his lifetime, many of the great artists and thinkers of Europe admired or respected Napoleon (Beethoven and Goethe, for instance, if only for a time); this does not apply to Hitler (though cases such as Knut Hamsun or Ezra Pound ought not to be ignored). There were prominent Englishmen who respected Napoleon; with Hitler the

---

*On one occasion in 1940 Hitler was supposed to have said that he would impose his victorious peace treaty at Münster in Westphalia, thus putting an end to the European state system that had been established there in 1648.

†Cited by Mathieu Molé in 1842, receiving Tocqueville in the Académie Française; also by François Furet, *Revolutionary France 1770–1880*, Oxford, 1988, pp. 260–70.

only substantial exception was Lloyd George (who thought Hitler the greatest figure in Europe since Napoleon). There were great French writers and poets (Stendhal, Beranger) whose unstinting admiration for Napoleon remained constant;* about Hitler we find no German writers of comparable caliber. Last but not least—and especially for the purposes of this book—the biographers and historians of Napoleon may be divided into For and Against categories (which Geyl has so impressively done); but—at least during the first fifty years after his death—such an equal or near-equal balance among Hitler's biographers and historians does not exist. There are, as we have seen—besides a few outright but questionable admirers—more cautious and circumspect historians who are inclined to revise the commonly accepted portrait of Hitler, but, unlike some of Napoleon's French biographers, they are not his outright defenders.†

In any event, Hitler, unlike Napoleon, was not loved or revered across Europe.‡ Among his own people, yes; but even there we must consider that the phenomena of the "public" and of the "people" were different one hundred and thirty years before Hitler. But while history does not repeat itself, there exist a few startling similarities: the sunny prosperity of the Third Reich in the 1930s and what many French historians have called "the golden spring of the Consulate"; Napoleon's and Hitler's Concordats (and such things as the pro-Consulate and pro-imperial inclinations of the subsequent Papal nuncio to France, Cardinal Caprera; and those of the nuncio

---

*Stendhal, *Vie de Napoléon*, p. 1837: "The greatest man the world has ever seen since Caesar." And: "The more becomes known of the truth, the greater Napoleon will be" (a belief often repeated by Hitler's admirers).

†One tendency that they have in common with Napoleon's more circumspect— or partial—defenders is their attribution to the British of cruel designs against their country. (Jacques Bainville, for example, in the case of the former; Andreas Hillgruber in the case of the latter.)

‡Chateaubriand in *Memoirs d'outre-tombe*, cited by Geyl: "For there is no gainsaying the fáct that this subjugator has remained popular with a nation which once made it a point of honor to raise altars to independence and equality. . . . The miracles wrought by his arms have bewitched our youth and have taught it to worship brute force. . . ." To this add Aulard's recognition of the loyalty of the Parisian working class to Napoleon—not unlike the loyalty of most German industrial workers to Hitler.

to Berlin under Hitler, the accommodating Monsignor Orsenigo).*
There was Napoleon's explanation to Caulaincourt that his Eastern
and Russian policy was not due to his excessive ambitions but to his
aim to deprive England of hope and compel her to make peace—we
have seen that this was Hitler's explanation too. There remains, in
the history of both, the obvious evidence of the profound limitations of the importance of "economics." After all, it was the Marxist
Georges Lefebvre who proved that in 1801 and 1802 bread was
even more expensive in France than it had been in the crucial year
of 1789, and yet it was in 1801 and 1802 that Napoleon's popularity
was at its highest, in the "Golden Spring of the Consulate." (But
Tocqueville had noted that, too, in his unfinished second book
about the Revolution, about Bonaparte's taxes.)†

Last but not least, there is one profound difference between the
two men. It involves the secret practices of statesmanship. Like Hitler
("It is the Führer's wish"), Napoleon intentionally left no written
instructions of some of his most brutal orders. But, unlike Hitler,
Napoleon made it clear that he wanted to be dissociated from them.‡

---

*Consider a comparison between the way Napoleon and Hitler respectively
treated the Pope. The latter was more circumspect than the former. (But this had
much to do with the fact that popes had greater prestige—and influence—in the
mid-twentieth century than at the beginning of the nineteenth.) Napoleon learned,
too late, that *Qui mange du Pape en meurt*; Hitler knew that only too well. One interesting detail: When Napoleon's envoy to Rome asked the Emperor how to treat the
Pope, Napoleon said, "Treat him as if he had two hundred thousand men." (Albert
Vandal, cited by Geyl, p. 230.) That is the origin of the witticism wrongly attributed
to Stalin in 1935: "How many divisions has the Pope?" (A canard.)

†Also Lefebvre, cited in Geyl, p. 424: "There has remained in [Napoleon] something of the uprooted person. Also of the man torn from his class: he is not entirely a
nobleman nor entirely of the people." The first sentence is applicable to Hitler, even
though we have noted their different personal characteristics and temperaments.

‡Lanfrey—a critic, not a eulogist of Napoleon, ranked among the "Against" by
Geyl, p. 104: "noted that Napoleon's order, in spite of its severity, remains general
and leaves something to the initiative of his subordinates. He has no doubt that this
was intentional, and indeed, did not the Emperor wash his hands of the whole business afterwards?" That Hitler didn't do. Napoleon, at least, chose to cover up in
writing. In a letter to Cambacérès, quoted by Lanfrey, he goes even further: " 'The
Pope was removed from Rome without my orders and against my wishes.' It is surprising, if that is the case, that he acquiesced in the accomplished fact. But indeed it

Hitler's most brutal instructions may have been secret or oral or even too general to pin down; but he never disavowed them or their results; nor did he attribute them to others, in order to exempt himself for the sake of the historical record—another example of the difference between his and Napoleon's sense of history.*

In 1901, the French positivist historian Alphonse Aulard wrote in his *Histoire politique de la revolution française*: his aim was to study and appraise in an objective, scientific way, "historically and not politically." Eighty years later German historians expressed the desideratum of Hitler's "historicization" [*Historisierung*] in similar terms. Yet "objective" and "scientific"† are outdated Cartesian categories (as are their symmetrical antonyms: "subjective" and "artistic"). Like all human knowledge, historical knowledge is both personal and participant‡ (and, its expressions are less motive-bound than purpose-oriented). Or, to repeat: Perspective is an inevitable component of reality—to which I must now add that no perspective is ever devoid of the element of retrospect. And it is in the retrospective perspective of a century that we must consider Hitler's place in it. If the two world wars were the two mountain ranges dominating the historical landscape of the twentieth century, in the shadows of which we were living until 1989, in Europe and America and Germany and Russia

---

is a flagrant untruth. It is all part of the system. In the Enghien affair he sheltered behind the alleged overhasty action of Savary. In the case of Spain it was Murat. And now it was Miollis, the Governor of Rome, who had to bear the discredit of a deed which Napoleon had undoubtedly wished done." To this Geyl adds a telling footnote: "One could make a comparison here with Queen Elizabeth, who was also very ready to saddle her servants with the blame in difficult situations. The best known, but certainly not the only example, is that of her rage against Davison, on the pretext that he had given the order for the execution of Mary Queen of Scots without her authority."

*Consider, too, Napoleon's recorded musings—his "pièces justificatives"—at St. Helena, where, among other things, he predicted the rise of the United States and Russia and the necessity for France of friendship with England. Nothing like this with Hitler. *Avec et après moi le déluge:* improperly attributed to a French monarch but appropriate, in spirit, to Hitler.

†However, we must keep in mind that the German words for "science" and "scientific"—*Wissenschaft* and *wissenschaftlich*—are broader than our contemporary English usage of them. They include both "science" and "knowledge."

‡Veronica Wedgwood's *bon mot*: "History is an art—like all the other sciences."

alike, wherefore World War II was the culmination of these world wars, and with results lasting longer than those of World War I, then it follows that the peak figure of the century was Hitler*— which brings us to the unscientific question of historical greatness.

THE QUESTION OF HISTORICAL "GREATNESS" is hardly more than semantic. (Of the nearly ten thousand words under the entry "great" in the *Oxford English Dictionary*, among its twenty-two definitions, historical greatness, as such, does not figure.)† The history of mankind is the history of the evolution of its consciousness, which includes—indeed, it is inseparable from—the history of words. And there has been such an evolution lately. The last three monarchs to whom the epithet "Great" was applied were all of the eighteenth century: Peter, Frederick, and Catherine (when it had something to do not only with quality but with magnitude). This attribution has declined, if not altogether vanished, since. It is perhaps significant that Napoleon has not acquired the epithet "Great," except for the indirect and sarcastic suggestion that his nephew Napoleon III should be called "Napoleon the Little."

And so, for the last time, a comparison of Napoleon with Hitler. Many things that Napoleon had made or brought about have proved enduring, many of his institutions, laws, reforms, buildings, including an architectural and decorative style (that, to be precise, actually began during the late years of Louis XVI and then continued to develop during the Directory, but still . . .), and some of his sayings, crisp expressions of an extraordinary mind. Hitler, who had an occasional sense of the comic but not much wit and hardly any sense of humor, left few sayings worth remembering (except for a few trenchant observations). What remained and ought to be remembered are his automobile highways and a mostly destroyed

---

*Was Napoleon the peak figure of the nineteenth century? No—he was the unexpected culmination of the eighteenth.

†"Of persons" only "d. 'The Great,' following a proper name [as] merely an honourable epithet, appended as a title to the names of certain historical persons, chiefly monarchs, implying . . . that the person so designated . . . ranks among the great men of history."

array of neoclassical buildings, most of whose designs are attributable to his architects, whose designs he may have approved but whose style was not entirely in accord with his own.*

Konrad Heiden, Hitler's first serious biographer, chose a passage from Goethe for the motto of his book, about the "daemonic" quality of certain people—not necessarily statesmen: "All moral powers are helpless against them; in vain are enlightened minds [der hellere Teil der Menschen] against . . . the mass will be attracted to them." I wrote before about Hitler's extraordinary talent for adjusting circumstances to his ideas—to which I also added that as the war proceeded he was forced to adjust some of his ideas to circumstances over which he had no control—and that the guilt (or, rather, the want of civic responsibility) of most Germans was that they found it easy to adjust their ideas to circumstances—as indeed many people are inclined to do.

The old Germanomaniac and Wagnerite Houston Stewart Chamberlain praised Hitler in 1923: "the great simplifier of all problems." But sixty years before that, Jakob Burckhardt had written: The time of "the terrible simplifiers" will come. In 1981 Vappu Tallgren, a Finnish historian, made a significant contribution in his study of Hitler's "creed of heroism." Through the "cult of heroism in National Socialist Germany, Hitler wanted to prepare a new religion." The creed of heroism, for Hitler, was "a principle, not a rhetoric—which is why he believed that with that he expressed the

---

*An example was Speer's monumental model of a future central Berlin (1940), in which he included Hitler's own 1925 design of a triumphal arch. It was fitted within the proportions of that monumental design but otherwise its style was unfitting, very different from Speer's modern neoclassicism, and utterly inferior both to the Arc de Triomphe and to the Arc du Carrousel.

Haffner, HF/AN, p. 45: Unlike Napoleon, "Hitler did not create any state edifice, and his achievements, which for ten years overwhelmed the Germans and made the world hold its breath, have proved ephemeral and have left no trace, not only because they ended in disaster but because they were never designed for endurance." (Not quite: Hitler often insisted to Speer and others that his buildings must be constructed of granite, "lasting four hundred years.") "As a star performer, Hitler probably ranks even higher than Napoleon. But one thing he never was—a statesman." (Arguable.)

most essential element of his ideology."* That may be largely true. Yet, as I tried to state earlier, Hitler's mind and willpower may have been extraordinary, but mind and willpower alone do not a hero make. Nor does hero worship. The cult of heroism and being a hero are not the same thing.†

There was no nobility in Hitler's makeup—or in his actions. But an easy dismissal of Hitler by ridiculing him is arrant nonsense.‡ The list of people—thinkers, writers, artists—who said and wrote that Hitler was a genius is long. They include such otherwise unexceptional antitotalitarians as Jules Romains in 1934 and André Gide in 1940. An unpleasant but symptomatic case is that of the English writer and thinker Wyndham Lewis, an anti-Left modernist and radical, who—and this was true of many others—despised the tawdry commercialism and decadent intellectualism of the 1920s (he also abhorred Chaplin). In 1931, he wrote an admiring book entitled *Hitler*—about whom he changed his mind in 1939, writing *The Hitler Cult*. But then another fifteen years later, in his novel *Self-Condemned*, the hero is an English historian who loses his position and is forced to live in exile in a frozen Canada in part because of his

---

*Vappu Tallgren, *Hitler und die Helden. Heroismus und Weltanschauung*, Helsinki, 1981, p. 258 (much praised by Zitelmann). Tallgren—in my opinion, convincingly—emphasizes the influence of Karl May's German-Indian "westerns" on Hitler (see p. 155).

†Schramm, SCH, p. 183: "The difficulty is that language offers no negative equivalents to 'hero' and 'genius.' Whoever is concerned that we may be possibly giving Hitler more than his due by seeking adequate terms for him misses the point."

‡It is not only that *The Great Dictator* is one of Chaplin's worst films. (Bullock, BU, p. 805: "Chaplin's brilliant [?] caricature in *The Great Dictator*.") See also Chaplin, *My Autobiography* (L: 1964), p. 316: Hitler: "a baggy-pants comic. . . . The face was obscenely comic—a bad imitation of me[!] with its absurd moustache . . . and disgusting, thin little mouth. I could not take Hitler seriously . . . his hands claw-like haranguing the crowd . . . one up and another down, like a cricketer about to bowl . . . [or] hands clenched in front of him as though lifting an imaginary dumb-bell. The salute with the hand thrown back over the shoulder, the palm upwards, made me want to put a tray of dirty dishes on it. 'This is a nut,' I thought. . . ." (Another famous personage who underestimated and dismissed Hitler was Einstein.)

unorthodox opinions of what Hitler represents in the modern history of Europe.*

Still, it is with this question of "greatness" that many of Hitler's biographers have been struggling.† Haffner, for example: "Of course one hesitates, and justly so, to call him 'a great man.'‡ 'Those who are only vigorous destroyers are not great at all,' says Jakob Burckhardt, and Hitler certainly proved himself a vigorous wrecker. But beyond any doubt he also proved himself a star achiever of high calibre, and not only in wrecking. Admittedly, without his decidedly exceptional vigor the disaster which he accomplished would have turned out less enormous, but one should not lose sight of the fact that his road to the abyss led across high

---

*Examples from Lewis's 1931 book (reprinted in New York, 1972, not easily available in most libraries): "the Communists help the police to beat and shoot the Nazis" (p. 16). The Nazis are "clean and law-abiding" (p. 19). "Whereas the Communist is invariably armed, the Nazi has only his fists or sticks to defend himself with, owing to the discrimination of the Republican police authorities" (p. 28). Hitler: "An asceticism not without nobility" (p. 31). "In setting about to expound the doctrine of Hitlerism, it rapidly becomes apparent that it is rather *a person* than *a doctrine* with which we are dealing." England "is married to Jews," but (p. 42): "still allow a little *Blutgefühl* to have its way (a blood-feeling toward this other mind and body like your own)—in favor of this brave and unhappy impoverished kinsman." "I do not think that if Hitler had his way he would bring the fire and the sword across otherwise peaceful frontiers" (p. 49). "Hitler *is* a very different person from Mussolini, Pilsudski, or Primo da Rivera" (p. 51). In 1939 Lewis wrote *The Hitler Cult*—now very critical of Hitler, with some insights: "He disdains democracy and all its works. Yet he himself, as a demagogue, hanging upon the emotional suffrage of the masses, is a typical democratic statesman—and this in spite of the fact that the agreeable laissez-faire of Western democracy had passed over, with him, into a demagogic despotism."

†The title of Lothar Burchardt's *Hitler und die historische Grösse* (Konstanz, 1979) is promising, but the book does not really deal with the idea or with qualifications of "greatness."

‡Irving, of course, has no such hesitations; in his foreword to I/H, p. xxiii, he suggests the epithet "Hitler the Great," citing Jodl in Nuremberg: "I blame his humble origins, but then I remember how many peasants' sons have been blessed by History with the name 'Great.' " Jodl, too, IMT XV, p. 602, cited by M/A, p. 195: Hitler was "no charlatan, but a gigantic personality, at the end acquiring an infernal kind of greatness, but greatness he possessed undoubtedly. . . ." Doenitz, also at Nuremberg: "Hitler was a great military leader: despite the defeat at Carthage the people admired Hannibal. . . . And despite our German defeat the people still admire Hitler. . . ."

peaks."* Fest wrestles with the semantic question: "All known history shows no phenomenon such as he; should one then call him 'great'?" He says yes and no; "still one is reluctant to call him 'great.' " But then he cites Burckhardt in the opposite sense from Haffner, since Burckhardt "spoke about a remarkable dispensation of the common laws of morality" when it came to the consciousness of "great" individuals.† Perhaps the question of "greatness" is best managed by Schramm. "In terms of sheer magnitude of what he wrought during his twelve years and three months in power he was one of the 'great' men in history. But his perverse greatness was informed less by creative energy than by some malevolent genius, so that even his most positive intentions and deeds acquired a dubious and ultimately sinister character."‡

"By virtue of his personality, his ideas, and the fact that he misled millions, Hitler poses an historical problem of the first magni-

---

*HF/AN, p. 40. See also another unexceptionable anti-Hitlerian, Golo Mann, cited in Scholdt, SCHO, p. 18: Hitler "changed everything . . . Hitler alone could achieve what he had planned, to build a popular movement and then keep it under his control. He proved himself far superior [turmhoch] to all of his rivals, opponents within the Party on occasion, as well as to the conservative holders of his stirrup [Steigbügelhalter]. Hatred of Jews was *his* passion; the war was *his* enterprise from the beginning, from 1933 to 1945. The will to prove that Germany could have won the war of 1914 if he had commanded it then, if he had waged that war with the right means to the right ends, this remains the source of his entire, unbelievable, disastrous adventure. 'Then it was the Kaiser, now it is I.' In the modern history of Europe I find no one who had affected events so decisively and so destructively, even more than had Napoleon."

†F, pp. 17, 189. Karl-Dietrich Erdmann "solves" the problem (or, rather, unsolves it) by a dual adjective: "the impenetrable darkness of his person . . . his diabolical world-historical greatness" (in Gebhardt, ed., *Handbuch der Geschichte. Die Zeit der Weltkriege*, vol. 2, S, 1976). Bullock's conclusion is somewhat better (BU, p. 806): "The fact that his career ended in failure, and that his defeat was preeminently due to his own mistakes, does not by itself detract from Hitler's claim to greatness. The flaw lies deeper. For those remarkable powers were combined with an ugly and strident egotism, a moral and intellectual cretinism. [*Not a mot juste.*] The passions which ruled Hitler's mind were ignoble: hatred, resentment, the lust to dominate, and, where he could not dominate, to destroy."

‡SCH, p. 12. "By comparison, the autocracy of previous despots seems almost timorous and halting." Görlitz-Quint in GQ, p. 234: "In any case there is no leading figure in German history comparable to him." Also p. 628. "We consciously avoid the word 'great' because 'great' suggests a connection to ethical value."

tude."* This is well put. Great and profound is the problem of Hitler's place in history—not whether he deserves or not the sentimental, imprecise, and perhaps antiquated adjective "great."

In November 1936 (after his long discussion with Cardinal Faulhaber), Hitler sat with Speer at the large window of the Berghof, looking out at the mountain twilight. After a long silence he said, "For me there are two possibilities: to succeed with my plans entirely, or to fail. If I succeed, I will be one of the greatest men in history—if I fail, I will be condemned, rejected, and damned."† When, on 1 May 1945, his great opponent heard the news of his death on the radio, Churchill said at the dinner table: "Well, I must say I think he was perfectly right to die like that."‡

> He left the name at which the world grew pale
> To point a moral or adorn a tale.**

The first line is applicable to Hitler; the second is not.

---

*sch, p. 123. In this respect Schramm's view accords with that of the otherwise different Heer. sch, pp. 182–83: "Anyone who speaks of him as satanic or infernal is, in effect, making a theological statement. Whoever calls him a 'demon' is ultimately reserving judgment about the nature of his acts."

†On 6 April 1938 in Salzburg he said: "I think that the times in which I lead Germany are historical times of German greatness . . . I believe that the future and German history will confirm that in the times of my leadership I achieved the highest benefits for the German people." (Deuerlein, D, p. 133.)

‡It saved Churchill from a difficult and perhaps embarrassing problem. "At any time in the last few months of the war he could have flown to England and surrendered himself, saying: 'Do what you will with me, but spare my misguided people.' " (Churchill, *The Second World War*, vol. 6, *Triumph and Tragedy*, p. 673.) Would that embarrassment have been due to Hitler's "greatness"? No: it would have been merely political. (Churchill respected Napoleon but not Hitler.) That embarrassment—together with thoughtlessness—among the Allies also marked the fate of Mussolini in 1943, when they (or the Italian royal government) made no effort to deliver Mussolini to the Allies or even to take him south with the royal government. He remained on the Gran Sasso for nine days after the signing of the Italian surrender, four days after its public announcement and the flight of the king and the government from Rome to the south. No provision was made in the armistice instrument for the surrender of Mussolini.

**Samuel Johnson about Charles XII of Sweden, in *The Vanity of Human Wishes*. Fest, in his conclusion, p. 1029: "In a variation on a phrase of Schopenhauer whom he [Hitler] in his way respected it may be said that he taught something to the world that the world shall never again forget."

"THERE IS NO ARGUMENT," George Orwell once wrote, "by which one can defend a poem. It defends itself by surviving, or it is indefensible."* So we judge achievements by their consequences. And what were the consequences of Hitler?

His war (and World War II was *his* war) ended with the greatest catastrophe for the German and also for the Central and Eastern European peoples—for the latter, because the Russian occupation and the subsequent Communist rule in that part of Europe was the consequence of that war. A consequence of the war was the division of Germany, which lasted for more than forty years, with mass expulsions from the east and protracted sufferings for the German people in the so-called "German Democratic Republic." A more enduring consequence was the drastic reduction of Germany in the east: the entire loss of East Prussia, together with other substantial portions of the former Prussia, Silesia, Saxony to Poland (and, in the case of the Königsberg enclave, to Russia). Even more enduring: the almost complete elimination of the presence of ethnic Germans from countries in Eastern Europe where some of their ancestors had lived for eight hundred years.

The year 1945 marked, too, the end of the predominance—political, cultural, intellectual—of Europe in the world, the end of the European age, and the end of the European state system.† There was something else, too: the end of the predominance of German intellectual influence in the world. For what had happened,

---

*Lukacs, HC, p. 93: "Its survival depends on the coagulating consensus of civilized tradition, and on authentic responses to quality; but that is a long-range consensus, formed by the historical thinking of generations and confirmed by existential experience. For it is in the long run that, somehow, truth may survive—through the decay of untruth."

†Haffner gives a telling summary of this (HF/AN, pp. 100–01): "Today's world, whether we like it or not, is the work of Hitler. Without Hitler there would have been no partition of Germany and Europe; without Hitler there would be no Americans and Russians in Berlin; without Hitler there would be no Israel; without Hitler there would be no decolonisation, at least not such a rapid one; there would be no Asian, Arab, or Black African emancipation, and no diminution of European pre-eminence. Or, more accurately, there would be none of all this without Hitler's mistakes. He certainly did not want any of it."

for about seventy years after 1870, was not only that the practices
and standards of German education and learning had influenced and
were adopted in many places of Europe and of the world, including
nations that were opponents of Germany in the two world wars.
Something that had begun after the French Revolution: a romantic
(and often sentimental and categorical) idealism, reacting against the
materialism (and often against the rationalism) of the Enlightenment. This most important and potentially fruitful intellectual
achievement—a great chapter in the history of the European
mind—was mostly represented and exemplified by Germans; and
then it was carried by some of them to extremes, to a deterministic
idealism* that proved to be more inhumane than the deterministic
materialism that had preceded and (lamentably) survived it—at least
for a while. And an incarnation of an unstinting belief in a determinist idealism was Adolf Hitler.†

The English historian of religion Owen Chadwick wrote: "The
Reformation would have happened without Luther. But without
Luther it would not have happened in the way it happened."‡ Four
centuries later the same condition—mutatis mutandis—applies to
nationalist socialism and Hitler. He was the greatest revolutionary
of the twentieth century. That is not an approbatory adjective.

"One has to go back a long way in history—perhaps to Alexander the Great—to
find a man who, in a below-average short span of life, transformed the world so
fundamentally and lastingly as Hitler. But what one would not find in the whole of
world history is a man who, with an unparalleled and gigantic effort, achieved, as
Hitler did, the exact opposite of what he had hoped to achieve."

*This is but a brief statement of what is summarized at somewhat greater length
in Lukacs, LEW, especially pp. 6–7 and pp. 519–27.

†Two random examples of an, alas, wholehearted belief in this deterministic
idealism by two of his generals. Jodl on 7 November 1943: "We will win because
we must win, for otherwise world history will have lost its meaning." Field Marshal
Model *on 29 March 1945:* "In our struggle for the ideals [*Ideenwelt*] of National
Socialism . . . it is a mathematical certainty [!] that we will win, as long as our belief
and will remains unbroken." Cited by Manfred Messerschmitt, "Die Wehrmacht in
der Endphase. Realität und Perzeption," *Aus Politik und Zeitgeschichte,* 4 August
1989, pp. 37–38.

‡Owen Chadwick, *The Secularization of the European Mind in the Nineteenth Century,* Cambridge, 1991, p. 73.

"Great" may be applied to criminals or terrorists, too. (Also, one need not be a reactionary to sense, especially at the end of the twentieth century, that to designate someone as a Great Conservative may be even more approbatory—at least in the Western world—than the epithet of a Great Revolutionary.) In any event, what followed Hitler was our still-present era of no great wars and no great revolutions—something that he had not foreseen, though Tocqueville had.

What he had seen—and, more or less, accurately—was the formidable attraction of populist nationalism in the age of the masses. That nationalism proved to be the principal political reality in the twentieth century. He was its most extreme representative. He sensed that sometime after 1870 nationalism and socialism came to supersede the older nineteenth-century categories of conservatism and liberalism, indeed perhaps even of Right and Left; and that, of the two, nationalism was more influential than socialism. The categories of socialism and capitalism themselves began to be outdated, because strength was more powerful than wealth, because nationality was more powerful than class, because nationalism was more powerful than internationalism. When there was national unity, the formerly rigid categories of socialist and capitalist, public and private ownership began to leak; what mattered was not ownership than management; and ownership and management and labor would be ultimately obedient to the dictates of nationalism.

Hitler was not the founder of National Socialism, not even in Germany. Among the principal figures of the century, Mussolini was the first national socialist who recognized, around 1911, that he was an Italian first and a Socialist second—this eight years before his creation of "Fascism." We have seen differences, not only in the practices but in the ideas, of Hitler's National Socialism and Mussolini's Fascism. But that becomes inconsequential when we look at the reciprocal influences of the main dictators in the 1930s and 1940s: Mussolini, Stalin, and Hitler. That comparison of reciprocal influences—more precisely, of their development—ought to tell us something. Mussolini was not (and did not become) a Communist; Stalin was not (and did not become) a Fascist; but both of them became influenced and impressed by Hitler's ideas and achievements to an extent that makes it both proper and precise to say that they became more and more nationalist socialists as time went on. That development (including their increasing inclination to anti-Semitism) ended with their deaths. So much for the war and the short run. But we must recognize that in the long run, too, in one sense Hitler's vision survived him. During the twentieth century the compound of nationalism with socialism has become the nearly universal practice for all states in the world. International socialism is a mirage. At the same time every state in the world has become a welfare state of sorts. Whether they call themselves socialist or not does not matter much. Hitler knew that. The economic structure of Germany that he had in mind had few of the characteristics of either Marxian or state socialism, but it could not be called capitalist, either. Fifty years later it cannot be denied that nationalism remains the most potent force in the world. We are all national socialists now. Of course, the proportions of the compound of nationalism and socialism vary from country to country; but the compound is there, and even where social democracy prevails it is the national feeling of people that matters. What was defeated in 1945, together with Hitler, was German National Socialism: a cruel and extreme version of nationalist socialism. Elsewhere nationalism and socialism were brought together, reconciled and then compounded, without remotely comparable violence, hatred, or war. But Hitler's nationalism was profoundly different from traditional patriotism, just as his socialism had few of the marks of the traditional philanthropy of the earlier Socialists.*

To this the objection may be raised: After all, has not the appeal of Communism long survived that of Hitler's National Socialism? Despite all the superficial evidence—examples: the surviving appeal of "Communist" parties in Russia and Eastern Europe, Chinese "Communism," Castro in Cuba—the answer is no, for three reasons at least. The first is that the surge of Communism that enveloped

---

*For the last time (see also above, chapter 4), he was a populist nationalist, not a traditional patriot. He knew better than most people that the true opposite of nationalism, with its cult of the people, is not so much a modern internationalism as a traditional patriotism, with its love for the land and for its history.

much of Eastern Europe after 1945 was not the result of popular revolutions but simply due to the presence of Russian armed forces in that part of Europe. The second is that the sporadic rise of Communist regimes in the oddest places of the so-called Third World— Cuba, Ethiopia, Angola, among others—was the obvious result of anticolonialism (and in Castro's case, of anti-Americanism) rather than of the appeal of Communism as such or the example of the Soviet Union. The third reason, connected with the second, is that the present—and probably transitory—reappearance of Communist or pro-Stalinist parties, especially in Russia, is not only inseparable from but fundamentally bound to a resurgent and populist nationalism. If International Socialism is a mirage, International Communism does not even qualify as an optical illusion.

As Karl-Dietrich Bracher put it: "The kernel of the phenomenon of Hitler was a fundamental underestimation of [the attraction of] National Socialism"—that is, not only of Hitler but of the idea he seemed to represent.* And in this respect it behooves us to consider the corresponding, and perhaps ominous, statement by another German historian, Hagen Schulze, buried in the debates of the Historians' Controversy, about that important experience "in our history: that the constitutionalists of the first German republic had nothing effective to counter the enormous emotional appeal of the nationalists. Certainly the experience of the Third Reich has considerably dampened the German inclination to nationalistic extremes," but it is questionable "whether this kind of dampening will last more than one or two generations, despite all of the political pedagogy about the efficacy of which one should have no illusions."† Neither

---

*SCH, p. 107. Consider, too, Perón's (a national socialist prototype) successful assumption of power in Argentina in October 1945, a few months after Hitler's death. Apart from its significance, the importance of that must not be overestimated, in view of the Latin American tendency to emulate other revolutions after a time span of many years: Bolívar and San Martín twenty or thirty years after Washington, Castro fifteen years after 1945, and so on.

†HS, p. 149. Consider also the tendency of the press and of commentators all over the Western world: their extreme sensitivity to every manifestation suggesting the appearance of so-called Right-wing political phenomena anywhere. That sensitivity is not comparable to anxieties about a resurgence of the extreme Left. This is not simply attributable to "political correctness" (a stupid term): It reflects an

should we have illusions about the permanent constitutional validity of laws according to which in Germany the public display of the swastika and of pictures of Hitler remains forbidden forever. What we must hope for and trust is that when the time for the removal of such proscriptions comes, such a legal decision will reflect a climate in which the symbols of Hitler's era* will attract nothing more than historical curiosity.

THAT TIME IS NOT YET; and now when the German state has become united, when the entire postwar period marked by fifty years of the so-called cold war has unraveled, when the entire century is ending, let us conclude with an attempt to identify—identify, rather than define—Hitler's place in the history of it.

The twentieth century—historically speaking—was a short century. Whereas the historical eighteenth century lasted 126 years, (from 1688 to 1815), marked by the world wars principally between England and France; and the nineteenth century lasted ninety-nine

---

anxiety about the mass appeal of extreme nationalism in the age of mass democracy. But here a historical, or, rather, a political comparison may be in order. It is generally accepted that Hitler's breakthrough came in September 1930, with the sudden 18 percent of the vote the National Socialists won in that year's German elections. In our day we may find that in many countries of the Western world so-called Right-wing movements (Le Pen in France, the neo-Fascists in Italy, Haider in Austria, perhaps Buchanan, too, in the United States) may count on a 12 to 20 percent support among the electorate . . . but not in Germany. There, in 1930, the National Socialists gained respectability because of their nationalism, the decisive element in Hitler's coming to power. A concerted opposition to that did not exist. This is not so today. History does not repeat itself. Still we must not eschew the possibility that in the future, as in the past, "hard" minorities may achieve important inroads into "soft majorities."

*Symbols matter; or at least they tell us something. The flag of the party and then of the Third Reich, the swastika in a red field, was Hitler's own, brilliant design. Yet he would have done better—probably in both the short and the long run—if he had kept the black-white-red flag of the imperial Reich. (Next to the swastika flag it survived in Germany until about 1935; and 18 January, the birthday of the Second Reich, remained a day of public celebration during the Third.) But now the swastika flag, like the Third Reich, is only an episode, and the republican-democratic black-red-gold flag has outlasted even the forty-seven years of the black-white-red one.

years (from 1815 to 1914), marked by the absence of world wars, the twentieth century lasted seventy-five years (from 1914 to 1989), marked by the two world wars and by their consequence—the so-called cold war between America and Russia. It ended in 1989, with the withdrawal of Russia from Eastern Europe and the reunification of Germany. The crucial period of this—transitional—century (marking the passage from the so-called Modern Age into something else) was its early one-third (1920 to 1945) in which, of course, the career of Hitler belongs.* During this period—again contrary to the popular and mistaken impression about the importance of the Russian Revolution in 1917—the history of the world (and not only of Germany or of Europe) was marked by the existence and the competition of a triangle of forces. There was parliamentary democracy, incarnated principally by the English-speaking nations, by the states of Western Europe, and Scandinavia. There was Communism, represented only by Soviet Russia, incapable of assuming power elsewhere. And there was National Socialism (and also other, to some extent similar but by no means identical, nationalist movements) in Germany, after 1933 incarnated by Hitler and the Third Reich, which proved to be so powerful that it took the unnatural and temporary alliance of Liberal Democracy and Russian Communism, of the English-speaking and the Russian empires, to defeat and conquer it. Neither side could do it alone.

That by itself identifies Hitler's place within the history of the twentieth century. But there was even more to it. This triangle, represented by liberal-conservative-democratic people, and by Communists and radical nationalists, repeated itself in every country in Europe, and in almost every country of the world—including the United States, South America, China, and Japan. (In 1945, the radical nationalists were silenced or subdued—temporarily. Later their successors reappeared again.) Not all of the radical nationalists were

---

*Conversely, the crucial phase of the nineteenth century (1815 to 1914) was *not* its first one-third (1815 to 1848), which was (as Napoleon had foreseen) a continuation of the appeal of the French and other European revolutions. After 1849, the period of repeated revolutions was succeeded by a period of wars (that Bismarck had correctly foreseen), which was much more decisive; in spite of the recognition of Marx, the struggle of nations succeeded the struggle of classes. *That* period ended in 1945.

followers or admirers of Hitler, though many of them were.*
Schramm wrote that we cannot ignore the fact that Hitler represents a key phenomenon in the history of Germany in the twentieth
century, but not only in the history of Germany.†

The German term "Ortsbestimmung" is defined as "position-
finding" in a dictionary sense; but it is a word often used by German
historians, meaning the definition of a place in history, and suggesting that while historical judgments of an event or person may
vary, the *place* of the events or persons within the sequence of history is—eventually—ascertainable. In this respect Schreiber's relatively recent conclusion is still valid: "The place of the National
Socialist period in history [*die historische Ortsbestimmung*] still re-

---

*Deuerlein in D, p. 143, correctly put it: "Meanwhile he had become a global
political phenomenon—an object not only of hate but of hope (for many)." Fest, F,
p. 148: Hitler's "superiority over many of his opponents and competitors had much
to do with his grasp of the essence of a world crisis of which he himself was the
symptom." On F, p. 569, Fest cites the Austrian writer Robert Musil in 1933, who
also admitted that his resistance is bereft of alternatives: he cannot think that the
old or an even older order might return and replace this new kind of a revolutionary order. "What explains this feeling is that National Socialism has its destiny
and its hour, that it is not a whirl [*Wirbel*] but a phase of history." A general statement by Jäckel in JH, p. 43: "[Hitler] undoubtedly developed a program of his own,
individually and alone, but his program must have coincided with the deeper tendencies and ambitions of his country and of his time. We may not be able to explain
this, and yet we have to recognize it. Was he an author or an executor, a producer
or a product? Was he so successful for a long time as an author because he was exe-
cuting deeper tendencies? Or had he simply a better understanding than most of
his contemporaries of the requirements and the possibilities of his time? These are
fundamental questions about not only the role of the individual in history but also
about historical understanding in general." (These generalizations of Jäckel's are
too categorical and somewhat pedestrian in their expressions; moreover, they are
not only applicable to Hitler.)

†Again Deuerlein, in a trenchant conclusion of his small book (D, p. 170): There
is plenty of proof that "the historical appearance of Hitler was not only a problem
of his person alone, but in a much wider sense that of his environment, of the
German and also the extra-German world—a fact that explains why the preoccupation with Hitler has not come to an end after his death, and at the same time
directing our attention to its obstacles and difficulties." Bullock, BU, p. 808: "Hitler,
indeed, was a European, no less than a German phenomenon. The conditions and
the state of mind which he exploited . . . were not confined to his own country,
although they were more strongly marked in Germany than anywhere else. Hitler's
idiom was German, but the thoughts and emotions to which he gave expression
have a more universal currency."

mains a desideratum of further research."* But is the problem still that of "research"? Perhaps—even though there is reason to believe that no more important, or even significant, documents by or about Hitler will come to light. But then history does not only consist of documents.

ALLOW ME NOW, at the risk of presumption, to sum up three long-range considerations: (a) about a necessary Christian view of Adolf Hitler; (b) about his place in the culture-civilization antithesis; and (c) about his place at the end of the so-called Modern Age.

On 2 June 1945, hardly a month after Hitler's suicide, Pope Pius XII spoke before the College of Cardinals about "the satanic apparition [Gespenst: ghost, apparition] of National Socialism." With all respect due to this much, and sometimes unjustly, criticized pope, I am inclined to agree with Friedrich Heer: "Again this is being metaphysical, removing something from history and from the responsibility for history, acquitting Catholics of their responsibilities. For a 'satanic apparition' no one is responsible—at best, an exorcist. . . . The Pope overlooks entirely that this 'satanic apparition' was a very concrete human incarnation who, before all in the Munich so loved by the Pope but also elsewhere, was promoted and helped into power by very responsible and notable men. . . ."† In the first chapter of this book I wrote that Hitler represented many half-truths; and that a half-truth is not only more dangerous but worse than a lie, because human acts and expressions are not frozen into mathematical categories: hence a half-truth is not a 50 percent truth but something else. To this let me add La Rochefoucauld's great maxim: "There are evil men in this world who would be less dangerous if they had not

---

*SCHRB, p. 332. A long but essentially uninspiring attempt (in reality not much more than a bibliographical disquisition) was made by Klaus Hildebrand in HZ, pp. 583–632, "Hitlers Ort in der Geschichte des preussisch-deutschen National-staates." In 1988 the neoconservative Michael Stürmer wrote that Germany "today is a land without history." In some ways the opposite is true. Maser in his conclusion of M/A was proved wrong (p. 439): "Only when West and East Germany are unified will Adolf Hitler, the all-German trauma, be finally superseded." It did not happen thus.

†HR, pp. 535–36.

something good about them."* Let me repeat: Does this mean that Hitler was "only" "50 percent bad"? No. It was not only, as I wrote in chapter 1, that he had great talents given to him by God which he used for evil purposes, whence his responsibility; it is also, as I suggested in chapter 6, that his evil characteristics were spiritual. In this day and age it is unfashionable to cite great Fathers of the Church; but it was St. Thomas who wrote about a half-truth being worse than a lie; and allow me now to bring up St. Augustine, who wrote that "whatsoever things are, are good," while evil is spiritual, because it is part of the human condition. What this means is not only that the sins of the spirit are worse than those of the flesh but that the two are inseparable; that there are no sins of the flesh without their—preceding as well as simultaneous—sins of the spirit.†

---

*This is much more profound than Graham Greene: "The greatest saints have been men with more than a normal capacity for evil, and the most vicious men have sometimes narrowly evaded sanctity." (Cited in Toland's Foreword, TO, p. xiii, where he wriggles around the question of Hitler's "greatness.")

†In this respect we ought to, again, reject the "demonization" of Hitler, or the temptation to attribute to him the qualities of being "diabolical" or "satanic." To the contrary, we can see elements in his career that bear an uncanny reminder of what St. John of the Apocalypse predicted as the Antichrist. The Antichrist will not be horrid and devilish, incarnating some kind of frightful monster—hence recognizable immediately. He will not seem to be anti-Christian. He will be smiling, generous, popular, an idol, adored by masses of people because of the sunny prosperity he seems to have brought, a false father (or husband) to his people. Save for a small minority, Christians will believe in him and follow him. Like the Jews at the time of the First Coming, Christians at the time of the Antichrist—that is, before the Second Coming—will divide. Before the end of the world the superficial Christians will follow the Antichrist, and only a small minority will recognize his awful portents. Well, Hitler did not bring about the end of the world, but there was a time—not yet the time of the mass murders but the time of the Third Reich in the 1930s—when some of St. John's prophecies about the Antichrist accorded with this appearance and his appeal. And it may not be unreasonable to imagine that in the coming age of the masses he was but the first of Antichrist-like popular figures.

In 1933 Joseph Roth wrote: "The Third Reich is now a country of Hell." No: but it did have some of the features of a nation led by an Antichrist. (Already in 1923 some of Hitler's followers had compared his life to that of Christ: thirty years of obscurity and then suddenly three years of a shining revelation.) Carl Jung: "Hitler's power is not political; it is magic." Also Lukacs (LEW, p. 524, note 194, and HC, p. 298). Klaus Mehnert in 1951: "The German people's journey from Liebknecht to Hitler and the Russian people's journey from Lenin to Stalin. . . . In both cases . . . the journey was one from dialectic to magic." An exaggeration of a generalization; but not without some substance.

Another consideration—because, but only partly because of Hitler—may be due to the originally German but by now worldwide, accepted notion of the superior nature of Culture over Civilization. Civilization is essentially material and bourgeois; culture is spiritual and creative. Civilization, at best, is marked by a security and a solid social order; at worst, it is hypocritical and philistine. The origins of this idea go back to the nineteenth century, but it was something that appealed to Germans and then to a class of people, intellectuals, worldwide, and then it was loudly asserted and categorically hammered down by Oswald Spengler. For intellectuals, culture follows or, rather, rises beyond civilization: from Babbitt's Zenith, U.S.A., to places like Greenwich Village, or from Belgravia to Bloomsbury. For Spengler the direction is the reverse, from a youthful culture to an ossified civilization.* It was something Hitler believed in. Germans and Aryans, to him and his followers, were more than the supreme custodians of culture. "True art is and remains eternal," he said on one occasion. "It does not follow the law of fashion; its effect is that of a revelation arising from the depths of the essential character of a people."† Besides his, here again expressed, belief in populism (rather than in refinement) we cannot deny that Hitler was both a proponent and promoter of art and of "Kultur"; but was he a champion of civilization? Not at all. As a matter of fact, he was its enemy. This is not the place to discuss the origins and development of the two terms, except to note that the Greeks had no word for culture, whereas they and the Romans were the founders of our still extant urbane notions of a civilization; and—more important—that "civilization," as *we* know it, is a concept and a product of the last four hundred years. In English, "civilization" first appeared in 1601 and was defined as the antithesis of "barbarism."

---

*During World War I, many Germans held the belief that German "Kultur" was infinitely superior to the English "Zivilisation." Of course there are national and linguistic problems here. Consider "Sebastian" in *The Edwardians*, at their elegant house parties in 1906: ". . . sometimes so vehemently did he deprecate them, sometimes he thought that they had mastered the problem of civilisation more truly than the Greeks or Romans." This would be unintelligible to many Germans, while the substitution of the word "culture" for "civilisation" in such a sentence would be senseless in English.

†Cited in Peter Adam, *Art of the Third Reich*, NY, 1992, p. 129.

I hope that my readers will allow this brief summary disquisition, if for no other reason than the existence of a recognizable condition: at the time of this writing, fifty or more years after Hitler took his own life, we in the Western world are threatened not by an endangerment of "culture" but by grave dangers to civilization.* Let me repeat: The kind of civilization that we still know was the product of the so-called Modern Age. The term "Modern" is both unhistorical and imprecise, suggesting that this "modern" age would last forever.† It would be more accurate to name the last five hundred years the Bourgeois Age, characterized as it was by the coexistence of aristocracies and bourgeois, and with the gradual and uneasy rise of the latter. That Hitler was the enemy of almost everything that was "bourgeois" needs no further explanation.‡ He belongs to the end of an age, and he was defeated, and—for a while—bourgeois civilization has been restored, at least in Western Europe and West Germany. But if Western civilization melts away, threatening to collapse, two dangers lie in the future. During a rising flood of barbarism his reputation may rise in the eyes of orderly people, who may regard him as a kind of Diocletian, a tough last architect of an imperial order. At the same time he might be revered by at least some of the New Barbarians. But this book is the work of a historian, not of a prophet.

---

*Speer in prison already in 1947: Hitler's war " 'has proved the sensitivity of the system of modern civilization evolved in the course of centuries. Now we know that we do not live in an earthquake-proof structure. . . . The danger is that the automatism of progress will depersonalize man further and withdraw more and more of his self-responsibility.' "Dazzled by the possibilities of technology, I devoted crucial years of my life to serving it. But in the end my feelings about it are highly skeptical." This is the opposite of Spenglerianism.

†The Middle Ages is a misnomer, too, because the term suggests a position in the "middle," between Ancient and Modern. But there is a difference, due to our historical consciousness: People during and at the end of the Middle Ages did *not* know that they lived in the Middle Ages, whereas we know that we have been living in the Modern Age, and that we are near the end of it.

‡We must recognize, too, that in an essential way he belonged to his age, for in his own way, he believed in Progress—unable and unwilling to recognize that the grave task before civilization now is a necessary rethinking of the entire meaning of Progress (a term that Tocqueville abhorred, but Hitler did not).

BIBLIOGRAPHICAL NOTE
AND
ABBREVIATIONS

No complete bibliography of Hitler is possible. The best guides
are SCHRB and the seriatim bibliographies of VFZ. What follows
is a list of works cited in the text of this book with, at the left, the ab-
breviations by which they are identified after the first mention in
each case. The most frequent places of publication are abbreviated
in the footnotes as follows: B—Berlin, D—Düsseldorf,
M—Munich, L—London, NY—New York, O—Oxford,
P—Paris, S—Stuttgart, Z—Zurich.

ADAP	Akten zur deutschen auswärtigen Politik.
AII/B	*The Testament of Adolf Hitler*. The Hitler-Bormann documents. L, 1961.
BU	Alan Bullock, *Hitler: A Study in Tyranny*. L, 1952,: rev. ed., 1962.
C	William Carr, *Hitler: A Study of Personality and Politics*. L, 1978.
D	Ernst Deuerlein, *Hitler: Eine politische Biographie*. M, 1969.
DL	John Lukacs, *The Duel, 10 May–31 July 1940: The Eighty-Day Struggle Between Churchill and Hitler*. NY, 1991.
F	Joachim Fest, *Adolf Hitler: Eine Biographie*. B, 1973; new ed. with a new introduction, 1995.
FAZ	*Frankfurter Allgemeine Zeitung*.
FL	Gerhard Fleming, *Hitler and the Final Solution*. Berkeley, Calif., 1982.
FR	Hans Frank, *Im Angesicht des Galgens*. M, 1953.
GD	German Documents of Foreign Policy.
GI	Hans Bernd Gisevius, *Adolf Hitler: Versuch einer Deutung*. M, 1963

GQ   Walter Görlitz and Herbert A. Quint (both pseudonyms),
            Adolf Hitler: Eine Biographie. s, 1952.

GR   Hermann Giesler, *Ein anderer Hitler.* Leoni am Starnberger
            See, 1977.

GWU   *Geschichte in Wissenschaft und Unterricht.*

HB   Helmut Heiber, *Adolf Hitler: Eine Biographie.* B, 1960.

HC   John Lukacs, *Historical Consciousness.* NY, 1968; extended ed.,
            1994.

HD   Konrad Heiden, *Adolf Hitler.* Z, 1935.

HF/AI   Sebastian Haffner, *The Ailing Empire: Germany from Bismarck
            to Hitler.* NY, 1991.

HF/AN   Sebastian Haffner, *The Meaning of Hitler.* NY, 1979.

HM   Heinrich Heim (Werner Jochmann, ed.), *Hitler: Monologe im
            Führerhauptquartier.* Hamburg, 1980.

HR   Friedrich Heer, *Der Glaube des Adolf Hitler: Anatomie einer
            politischen Religiosität.* M, 1968.

HS   *Historikerstreit* (Piper, ed.). M, 1987.

HST   Andreas Hillgruber, *Hitler's Strategie: Politik und
            Kriegsführung 1940–1941.* Frankfurt, 1965.

HS/W   Hans-Ulrich Wehler, *Entsorgung der deutschen Vergangenheit?
            Ein polemischer Essay zum "Historikerstreit."* M, 1988.

H2B   *Hitler's Secret Book.* NY, 1961.

HZ   *Historische Zeitschrift.*

IFZ   Institut für Zeitgeschichte.

I/H   David Irving, *Hitler's War.* NY, 1977.

IMT   International Military Tribunal (documents).

I/W   David Irving, *The War Path: Hitler's Germany 1933–1939.*
            L, 1978.

JH   Eberhard Jäckel, *Hitler in History.* Hanover, New Hampshire,
            1984.

JHH   Eberhard Jäckel, *Hitlers Herrschaft.* S, 1988.

JHW   Eberhard Jäckel, *Hitler's Weltanschauung: Entwurf einer
            Herrschaft.* Tübingen, 1969, new and extended ed.,
            s, 1981.

JMH   *Journal of Modern History.*

JO   A. Joachimsthaler, *Adolf Hitler 1908–1920. Korrektur einer
            Biographie.* M, 1989.

K   Leon Krier, *Albert Speer: Architecture 1933–1942.* Brussels,
            1985.

KER   Ian Kershaw, *Hitler: Profile in Power.* NY, 1991.

KER/HM   Ian Kershaw, *The Hitler Myth: Image and Reality in the Third Reich*. O, 1987.
KER/PO/PD Ian Kershaw, *Popular Opinion and Political Dissent in the Third Reich, Bavaria 1933–1945*. O, 1983.
KTB/OKW   Kriegstagebuch, Oberkommando der Wehrmacht.
KTP/SKL   Kriegstagebuch, Seekriegsleitung.
LEW   John Lukacs, *The Last European War, 1939–1941*. NY, 1976.
M/A   Werner Maser, *Adolf Hitler: Legende, Mythos, Wirklichkeit*. M, 1971.
M/F   Werner Maser, *Die Frühgeschichte der NSDAP: Hitlers Weg bis 1924*. Frankfurt, 1965.
M/HB   Werner Maser, ed., *Hitler: Briefe und Notizen*. D, 1973.
MK   *Mein Kampf*.
NPL   *Neue Politische Literatur*.
OED   *Oxford English Dictionary*.
PH   Ernst Günter Schenck, *Patient Hitler: Eine medizinische Biographie*. D, 1989.
SCH   Percy Ernst Schramm, *Hitler: The Man and Military Leader* (Donald Detwiler, ed.). Chicago, 1971.
SCHO   Günther Scholdt, *Autoren über Hitler*. Bonn, 1993.
SCHRB   Gerhard Schreiber, *Hitler: Interpretationen 1923–1983* (2nd, extended ed., Darmstadt, 1988).
SP   Albert Speer, *Erinnerungen*. B, 1969.
ST   Marlis Steinert, *Hitler*. P, 1991.
ST/HK/D   Marlis Steinert, *Hitlers Krieg und die Deutschen: Stimmung und Haltung der deutschen Bevölkerung im II. Weltkrieg*. D, 1970.
TO   John Toland, *Adolf Hitler*. NY, 1977.
VFZ   *Vierteljahrshefte für Zeitgeschichte*.
ZIT/A   Rainer Zitelmann, *Adolf Hitler. Selbstverständnis eines Revolutionärs*. S, 1987, 1991.
ZIT/B   Rainer Zitelmann, *Adolf Hitler: Eine politische Biographie*. Göttingen, 1989.
ZIT/PR   Michael Prinz and Rainer Zitelmann, eds., *Nationalsozialismus und Modernisierung* (extended ed.). Darmstadt, 1994.

INDEX

All page numbers include references
to footnotes on the given page
as well as to the text.

HITLER AND STALIN
Parallel Lives
by Alan Bullock

A dual biography of the two most destructive figures of our century, *Hitler and Stalin* examines its subjects' origins and personalities, traces the arc of their careers, analyzes the methods by which they seized and clung to power, and assesses the scars they left on their world with a clarity and mastery of detail that are nothing less than breathtaking.

Biography/History/0-679-72994-1

IN EUROPE'S NAME
Germany and the Divided Continent
by Timothy Garton Ash

For forty-five years Europe was divided, and at the center of that divided continent lay a divided Germany. In this brilliantly nuanced book, one of our most respected authorities on Central Europe tells the story of German reunification. Drawing on sources that range from files of East Germany's secret police to the personal papers of West German leaders—and on interviews with such figures as Helmut Kohl, Eduard Shevardnadze, and the imprisoned Erich Honecker—Garton Ash has produced a panoramic, dramatic, and definitive account of events.

Current Affairs/History/0-679-75557-8

VINTAGE BOOKS
Available at your local bookstore, or call toll-free to order:
1-800-793-2665 (credit cards only).